The
Barbary Corsairs

'That which fortune has done for me in the past that will it continue to do for me in the future. Age has not enfeebled me, continual exercise has but rendered me stronger; I can therefore promise you, my Sultan, the most ready service both by land and sea. The desire which has been mine to persecute the Christians caused me to conceive the idea of serving in your army of the sea'.

– Kheir ed-Din Barbarossa

The
Barbary Corsairs

Pirates, Plunder, and Warfare in the Mediterranean,
1480-1580

By Jacques Heers

Translated by Jonathan North

Skyhorse Publishing

This edition published in 2018 by Skyhorse Publishing

Copyright © 2001 Perrin

Translation © 2003 Jonathan North

First published in 2003 by Greenhill Books, Lionel Leventhal Limited

The Barbary Corsairs is an English-language translation of Jacques Heers'
Les Barbaresques

Skyhorse Publishing books may be purchased in bulk at special discounts for
sales promotion, corporate gifts, fund-raising, or educational purposes. Special
editions can also be created to specifications. For details, contact the Special Sales
Department, Skyhorse Publishing, 307 West 36th Street, 11th Floor, New York,
NY 10018 or info@skyhorsepublishing.com.

Skyhorse® and Skyhorse Publishing® are registered trademarks of Skyhorse
Publishing, Inc.®, a Delaware corporation.

Visit our website at www.skyhorsepublishing.com.

10 9 8 7 6 5 4 3 2 1

Library of Congress Cataloging-in-Publication Data is available on file.

Cover design by Rain Saukas
Cover image: Horusce and Hareaden Barbarossa by Ignatius Lux

ISBN: 978-1-5107-3164-6
Ebook ISBN: 978-1-5107-3168-4

Printed in the United States of America

Contents

CONTENTS

List of Illustrations

Plates (pages 129–144)

Maps

Chronology

1302	The Catalan Company of Iberian mercenaries is founded.
1303	Rhodes is seized by the Order of the Knights of St John (the Hospitallers).
1311	The Catalans control Athens (until 1388).
1339	Umur Pasha menaces Athens.
1344	Smyrna besieged by the Crusaders.
1366	The Turks establish a capital at Adrianople.
1389	The Turks are victorious against the Serbs at the battle of Kosovo.
1396	The Crusaders are defeated at Nicopolis in Bulgaria.
1398	Crete arms and equips its first galley to counter the Turks.
1406	Venice begins a programme of shipbuilding for war against the Turks.
1423	The Catalans sack Marseilles.
1426	The Turks invade Cyprus.
1440	The Sultan's armies are defeated before Belgrade.
1453	Constantinople falls to the Turks on 29 May.
1462	The Turks seize Lesbos.
1469	Ferdinand of Aragon marries Isabella of Castile.
1475	Kaffa, a Genoese possession in the Crimea, falls to the Turks.
1480	The first siege of Rhodes by the Turks fails.
1489	Cyprus is ceded to Venice by the widow of the last king.
1492	Granada falls to the Spanish on 6 January.
1502	The Barbarossa brothers land on Djerba.

| 1504 | The Barbarossas seize two Papal galleys. |

1504   The Barbarossas seize two Papal galleys.
1509   The Spanish capture Oran on 17 May.
1510   Tripoli falls to Spain but Djerba holds out.
1515   Francis I becomes king of France.
1516   The Turks defeat the Egyptians north of Aleppo. Aroudj takes Algiers. Ferdinand of Aragon dies, Charles becomes king of Spain.
1517   The Turks enter Cairo. Aroudj takes Tlemcen.
1518   Aroudj Barbarossa dies.
1519   Charles is elected Holy Roman Emperor, becoming Charles V.
1520   Selim dies, Suleiman the Magnificent becomes Sultan.
1521   The French army supports a revolt in Castile. Kheir ed-Din takes Constantine.
1523   Rhodes capitulates to the Turks on 1 January.
1525   Francis I is defeated and captured at Pavia. France sends its first ambassador to Constantinople.
1526   The Treaty of Madrid is signed and Francis is set free. The Turks crush the Hungarians at Mohacs.
1528   Andrea Doria leaves the service of Francis I and becomes Charles V's admiral.
1529   The Peñon fort at Algiers is captured by the Turks on 21 May. The Turks are defeated before Vienna.
1530   Suleiman and Charles sign a peace treaty.
1531   Doria attacks Cherchell and the Spanish take Honein.
1534   Barbarossa attacks Fondi in Italy.
1535   The Spanish take La Goulette on 14 July. Moulay Hassan, king of Tunis, becomes a vassal of the emperor.
1536   France and Turkey form an alliance.
1537   The Venetian fleet is defeated at Preveza.
1538   Charles V, the Pope and the Venetians join the League of Nice.
1539   The Peace of Cateau-Cambrésis is signed.
1540   Francis and Charles meet in Paris. Moulay Hassan and Doria seize Sousse and Monastir.
1541   Charles V's expedition against Algiers is defeated.
1543   In July the Turkish fleet enters Marseilles and in August Barbarossa and his French allies lay siege to Nice. In October the Turks arrive in Toulon and winter there.

1544	The French fleet accompanies the Turks to Constantinople. In September Charles and Francis sign a peace at Crépy.
1545	The Council of Trent opens.
1546	Hassan, Barbarossa's adopted son, becomes Pasha of Algiers.
1547	Francis I dies, Henry II is crowned king of France.
1551	Dragut fights Doria off Djerba.
1555	The Janissaries revolt in Algiers.
1556	Charles V abdicates as emperor on 12 September.
1558	Charles dies on 21 September.
1559	Henry II dies and Francis II is proclaimed king.
1560	Francis II dies and Charles IX is crowned.
1565	Malta is besieged by the Turks from 19 May to 11 September.
1570	The Turks invade Cyprus and lay siege to Famagusta.
1571	Famagusta surrenders on 4 August. The battle of Lepanto is fought on 7 October.
1573	Don Juan, victor of Lepanto, takes Tunis.
1574	Charles IX dies, Henry III becomes king of France. Euldj'Ali takes Tunis and La Goulette.
1575	Miguel Cervantes and his brother Rodrigo are captured by corsairs off the Camargue coast.
1577	Hassan, a renegade from Venice, becomes Pasha of Algiers.
1581	Peace is declared between the king of Spain and the Turkish Sultan.

Sultans and Kings

Ottoman Sultans

1413–1421	Mehmet I
1421–1451	Murad II
1451–1481	Mehmet II
1481–1512	Bayazid II
1512–1520	Selim I (the Cruel)
1520–1566	Suleiman I (the Magnificent)
1566–1574	Selim II (the Drunkard)

The Corsair Kings of Algiers, according to a list in Haedo's *History*

1516–1518	Aroudj Barbarossa
1518–1533	Kheir ed-Din Barbarossa
1533–1543	Hassan, a eunuch from Sardinia
1543–1544	Hadi Pasha, a Janissary
1546–1551	Hassan Pasha, son of Kheir ed-Din
1551–1552	Caid Saffa, a Turk
1552–1556	Salah Pasha, a corsair from Alexandria
1556	Hassan Corso, a Corsican renegade
1556	Tekelerli (ruled for three months)
1556	Youssuf, a Calabrian renegade (ruled for six days)
1557	Yahya Pasha, a Janissary
1557–1561	Hassan Pasha's second reign

THE BARBARY CORSAIRS

1561–1562	Hassan the Bosnian
1562	Ahmed Pasha, a favourite of the Sultan
1562	Yahia
1562–1567	Hassan Pasha's third reign
1567–1568	Mohammed Pasha, son of Salah Raïs
1568–1571	Ochali Pasha (Euldj'Ali)
1572–1574	Arab Ahmed Pasha, from Alexandria
1574–1577	Rabadan Pasha
1577–1580	Hassan Pasha, a Venetian slave employed by Euldj'Ali
1580–1581	Djafer Pasha, an Hungarian eunuch
1582–1583	Hassan Pasha the Venetian's second reign

'The old people were taken out, robbed of their clothes and cut open whilst still alive. All this was done out of spite and when we asked the corsairs why they treated these people with such cruelty they replied that among them such a cruelty was deemed a virtue.' – Jerome Maurand, watching corsairs raiding Lipari

Introduction

'The Turks, but above all the corsairs of Algiers, Tunis, Tripoli, and other places in Barbary, make war for gain rather than glory' – Chastelet des Boys

The use of the word Barbary to describe the pirates of North Africa, or to describe the kingdoms of Algiers and Tunisia, has worked its way into the modern vocabulary. Right up until the sixteenth century Christian merchants, adventurers, or pilgrims would have spoken and written about Moors, Saracens, or, more rarely, Africans. The term Barbary was coined in Italy around 1500, when it was applied generally to 'barbarian' peoples. As a word it wasn't an instant success, but it later enjoyed something of a Renaissance, being used by various authors, cited in dictionaries, and, ultimately, working its way into common usage as a descriptive term for the people and territories of North Africa. From then on sailors, merchants, civil servants, novelists, and dramatists referred almost exclusively to the Barbary corsairs from the Barbary states.[1]

But, whether intentionally or not, it was a term which was something of a misnomer. The kingdoms, or more precisely the governments, of North Africa and their corsairs had long since shed their barbarous origins. From around 1500 they were intrinsically connected to the Ottoman empire and its struggle against Rome and Christian Europe. The leading captains of the corsairs, notably the legendary Barbarossa brothers, weren't even African Moors at all but were either Turks or renegade Christians in Turkish service. Their soldiers consisted of Janissaries, who were converted slaves drawn from the eastern Mediterranean, particularly from the Balkans; whilst their crews – mostly galley slaves – were Christian captives caught at sea or abducted from the coasts of Italy and Spain.

These corsairs lived in a world in which Christians and Muslims were bitter enemies, each seizing plunder, killing and carrying off slaves from the other. Piracy was a key part of this conflict – a conflict which, although inspired by the ideals of holy war, subjected families or entire communities to abject terror and misery.

Piracy in the Western Mediterranean

The warriors of Islam became masters of North Africa between 670 and 710 AD, then surged into the Iberian peninsula, the Balearics, Sicily, and even parts of mainland Italy. In truth they did not found a powerful empire in North Africa, one which was formidable both on land and at sea, but instead created a collection of states, independent of the Caliphate of Baghdad, which were forever quarrelling among themselves. This inherent weakness manifested itself in certain periods as anarchy, and meant that considerable freedom of action was granted to nomadic tribesmen on land and to corsairs at sea.

Some time during the ninth century Islamic pirates – either Berbers or converted Slavs – established themselves between Almeria and Denia on the coast of eastern Spain. Meanwhile bands of brigands, whom the Christians quickly termed Saracens, cruised out from North Africa and attacked the islands and coastline of Italy, raiding into the Adriatic and seizing Bari. In 846 they attacked Rome, sacking St Peter's and St Paul's-Outside-the-Walls. Then they sought shelter in fortified camps along the Liri in Campanie, at Fraxinetum in the Maures, and in the bay of Saint Tropez. Hardy and energetic, these raiders penetrated as far as the Alps.[2]

For the next two centuries such corsairs waged a bitter war on the cities of Christendom. The Africans took Genoa by storm in 933 and, three years later, once more appeared beneath its walls with a fleet of 200 sail. The Christians had to wait some time before exacting their revenge, but in 1087–8 a fleet furnished by Genoa, Pisa, Amalfi, Salerno, and Gaeta seized Mahdia, the most infamous haunt of the corsairs, in a campaign that was the first large-scale maritime crusade. An expedition against

Almeria on the Andalusian coast followed in 1146. In the struggle against Islam, Italian states such as Pisa and Genoa frequently gave their all.[3]

From then on the chief aim of the Christian rulers was to reduce the power of Islam in Africa and in Spain. The actual reconquest of the Spanish mainland would follow. It was only in 1229, some 150 years after the raid against Mahdia, that James I, King of Aragon and Count of Barcelona – known as 'the Conqueror' – would be able, with the support of Genoese and Pisan ships, to take Majorca. Between 1232 and 1245 a remorseless war was waged as the Christians launched expedition after expedition against southern Spain. Valencia fell in 1237.

At first the strength of the Barbary pirate-states had seemed undiminished. But in reality the Italians had asserted their influence over the western Mediterranean by their raids on Almeria, Mahdia, and Bougie. The kings and knights of Aragon had carved an empire for themselves opposite Africa. Other Christian monarchs followed suit. Crusades against Islam would not be confined to the Holy Land or to Egypt. Saint Louis' expedition against Tunis in 1270 was declared a crusade by Pope Clement IV, a native of Languedoc. Participation in this holy expedition was not restricted to Frenchmen – Castilians, Catalans, Flemings, and Frisians also took part. Alphonse de Poitiers brought a strong contingent from Languedoc, drawn mainly from the lands around Beaucaire and Carcassonne. A century later Gregory XI – the last pope to reside at Avignon – and Boniface IX sought to raise the standard of holy war again, and in 1389 the Christians seized Djerba and the Kerkenna Islands. Such short-term gains were quickly forgotten, but they do reveal a strong impulse to attack and eradicate the haunts of African pirates. Alphonso the Magnanimous of Aragon even furnished a fleet of 100 sail to cruise off Sicily and attack and capture any Saracen vessels, despite being embroiled in a war against the Angevins in Naples.

Further to the west the Portuguese and Castilians naturally assumed that the reconquest of their territory from the Muslims should be accompanied by raiding expeditions against Africa. They took advantage of increasing divisions within the Barbary states as Moorish potentates found themselves locked in a struggle with Arabic or Berber tribes of the interior. The Almohad empire, which at one point stretched from the Atlantic to Kairouan, had been founded here in the twelfth century by Berber chieftains from southern Morocco. However, it collapsed around 1230 and left anarchy in its wake. From this emerged three strong kingdoms, each mutually hostile. The Hafsids, drawn from a powerful Almohad family, proclaimed themselves caliphs of Tunis; the Beni Abd-el-Wäd established themselves at Tlemcen; and the Marinids – another Moroccan tribe, and traditional enemies of the Almohads – seized Fez in 1248. In the 1280s the Marinids even laid siege to Tlemcen, their mighty host camping beneath the clay-brick walls. But the city only fell in 1337.

These African states owed their power not to any religious movement or to the mobilisation of vast bands of people gathered for some holy war. Rather, they drew their strength from family hierarchies and connections. Bitter wars would be waged to establish the succession to a throne. Such states found it impossible to subdue the nomads who ravaged their lands and held their cities to ransom. Neither could they resist the armed might of the Portuguese, Spaniards, or Turks; such powers cleverly made use of internal divisions, supporting one faction, protecting another, whilst simultaneously confirming their suzerainty.

The Portuguese were quick to seize vital enclaves on the mainland of Africa, and a fleet commanded by King João I and his sons captured Ceuta in 1415. Although their progress was temporarily halted at the catastrophic battle of Tangiers in 1437, where Prince Ferdinand was taken prisoner by the Moors (he died in 1443), they did manage to seize that city in 1471. They also eliminated a pirate base on the present site of Casablanca and forced the chieftains of Safi and Azemmour to pay tribute.

The Castilians, victorious over the Moors at the battle of Las Navas de Tolosa in 1212, took Seville in 1246 and soon established an arsenal and an impressive port from which they could launch expeditions against Africa. Before even subduing the Moorish kingdom of Granada, King Alfonso XI of Castile allied himself with his father-in-law, Alfons IV of Portugal, and seized Tarifa from the Marinids. Then, in 1340, at the battle of the Four Kings (the rulers of Castile and Portugal being present on one side and those of Granada and Fez on the other), the Christians seized such a vast haul of treasure that the price of gold collapsed throughout Spain. Three years later the Castilians and Portuguese once again united, and, mobilising a vast international army which included Frenchmen (Gaston de Foix and Philippe d'Evreux), Englishmen (Henry of Lancaster), and Germans, supported by Catalan and Genoese squadrons, laid siege to Algeciras. The city's fall was accompanied by rejoicing the like of which had only previously been seen at the capture of Jerusalem. Control of the straits fell to the Christians.

Meanwhile, in the Iberian peninsula, the *Reconquista* gathered pace.[4] It had been hindered, and occasionally altogether prevented, by dynastic squabbling such as the 1362–9 civil war between the factions of Peter the Cruel and Henry of Trastamare. Castilian attempts to conquer Portugal delayed the process too, although Portugal affirmed its independence in 1385 at the battle of Aljubarrota. The war against Granada only began in earnest in 1460. Ironically, success for the Christians was partially brought about by support from dispossessed Muslim princes hostile to the Granadan king. The marriage of Ferdinand of Aragon and Isabella of Castile in 1469 united and strengthened these two Christian powers; Malaga fell in 1487 whilst Almeria – refuge of pirates – succumbed in 1489. The Catholic monarchs marched victoriously into Granada itself on 6 January 1492.

Throughout the twenty-year struggle for control of Granada, Barbary pirates and potentates – particularly those of Tlemcen and Morocco – supplied their Muslim allies by sea. They brought weapons, horses, munitions, and wheat, and aided and abetted fugitives and refugees. They were rewarded with ceramic ware, fruit, and Christian slaves as payment for their services. The slaves were shipped across in no small number. We know that hundreds of Christian captives were already hard at work in Malaga, Granada, and Ronda; as the years wore on, and the hostilities intensified, more and more were seized.

Actual expeditions were also launched from Africa. Christian lands were pillaged, villages were burnt, and captives were carried off. Arms and munitions were supplied to those who chaffed beneath the Spanish yoke. Moorish revolts in the mountains around Granada raised grave fears and brought ruthless countermeasures quickly in their wake.[5]

In the spring of 1505 corsairs from Mers-el-Kebir launched a series of devastating raids against the Iberian coast, particularly at Malaga, Elche, and Alicante. On 9 September that same year Diego Fernandez de Cardona counterattacked, seizing the corsairs' base on 23 October and quickly erecting a fortress. Pedro Navarro attacked the Peñon de Velez in 1508 and, after a bitter four-year struggle, took Oran on 17 May 1509. He took 8,000 prisoners and killed more than 4,000 enemy defenders. The Spanish then marched into Bougie, meeting practically no resistance. Tripoli, to the east, defended itself with vigour, however: 'The populace fought with a courage born of despair for each and every street, each and every house; more than 5,000 lost their lives.' Attempts to seize Djerba were frustrated by a defeat in 1510.[6] Even so, numerous coastal towns and cities, including Dellys, Cherchell, and Mostaganem, sought to place themselves under the protection of Spain and paid the appropriate tribute. Even Algiers allowed the Spanish to occupy the islands controlling access to the port. The Iberians lost no time in constructing a strong fortress – the Peñon – which was capable of resisting even the most tenacious attacks.[7]

Piracy in the Levant

The Levant also offered ample opportunity for shelter. The coasts of Albania and Epirus, the gulfs of Messenia and Nauplia, the sea of Marmara, Cyprus, and the myriad isles of the Aegean provided secluded hideaways where pirates wanted for nothing, and had nothing to fear. There they could repair their vessels, sell their booty, make agreements, and negotiate terms.

As far as the Venetian Marino Sanudo Torcello (1270–1343) – an historian who had made five voyages through the Levant and offered up maps of the Holy Land to Pope John XXII – could tell, the island of Negroponte (Euboea) served as an ideal refuge for pirates. Despite being a Venetian possession, they flocked to the island from Spain, Catalonia, Provence, Genoa, Pisa, Sicily, Venice, Dalmatia, and Lombardy.[8] True, a few of them were merely there to escape their creditors, something relatively common, even in the east, at that time. After being ruined by unhappy speculation, Landolfo Rudolfo d'Amalfi – one of the heroes of a story in Boccaccio's *Decameron* – managed to put together a fleet and, within a frighteningly short space of time, gained notoriety in the Greek archipelago and amassed a huge fortune. All good things must come to an end however, and his capture by a Genoese fleet put an end to his exploits.[9] Thieves such as this, many of them of unknown origins, came and went, barely making their mark on the contemporary scene.

There were, however, others of more celebrated renown. Captains of adventure, conquerors chasing their fortunes, risking their lives in dangerous expeditions. They were spread from the mouth of the Danube or the Dniester in the Black Sea to remote valleys in the Caucasus. Others, supported by loyal clans, formed dynasties of their own. Venetians in the Cyclades and Genoese in the northern Aegean reigned like monarchs over

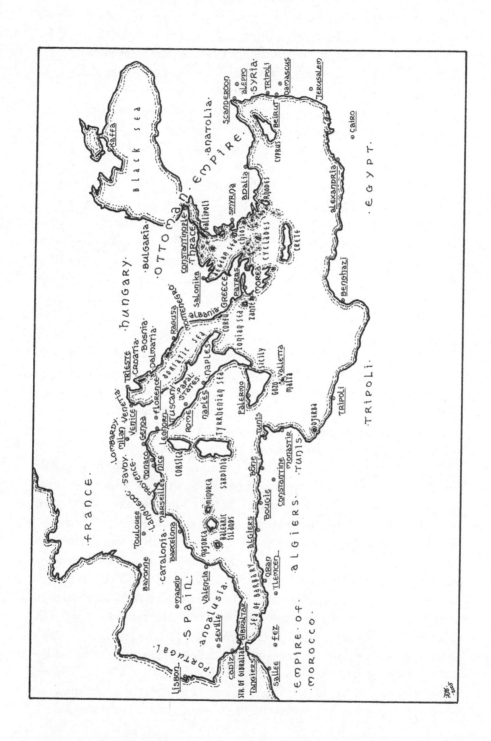

islands and ports. They imposed laws and subjugated the mainly Greek populace, and lived, for the most part, on the spoils of their raids. The Gattilusi, for instance, alternatively mercenaries and pirates, were originally from Genoa. They seized several islands and established bases on the Turkish coast. Their chief pride lay in two superb natural harbours – the gulfs of Kalloni and Vera. In 1453 they were chased out of their Turkish possessions but, otherwise unaffected by this setback, continued to despatch their ships on numerous raids. Giuliano Gattilusio burst into Chios harbour and made off with the entire cargo of a Cypriot fleet. His father, Battista, captured by Antonio Doria, was fined 6,000 ducats by a Genoese court. He had to pay a further 4,000 for having taken a ship sailing between Genoa and Tunis. Robert Sturmy of Bristol – possibly the first Englishman to attempt to ship spices directly to Britain – was attacked by Battista on the return leg of his journey. He lost everything – his three ships, his goods, and his life.[10]

In addition numerous political exiles, many of whom had been expelled from Italy, sought to maintain their status (or, more likely, to survive) by turning to piracy and brigandage. Around 1325 scores of Ghibelline galleys from Genoa attacked convoys, raided, and robbed. They wintered in the Black Sea where, caught in a trap at Sinope, they were massacred. Another Genoese rebel, Ambrogio Spinola, was perhaps slightly less adventurous but firmly established himself on the Ionian coast between Corfu and the Venetian possession of Modon.

Catalan knights, left unemployed by the peace signed by Frederick of Aragon and Charles of Anjou in 1302, rallied to the standard of Roger de Flor. This former Templar was a mercenary and sailor boasting a tremendous reputation as a leader of men. The Catalan Company first waged war on behalf of the Byzantines, fighting the Turks in Anatolia. Victorious, they installed themselves at Gallipoli before falling out with their paymasters and inflicting a crushing defeat on a Byzantine army sent to pursue them. They occupied Athens in 1311 and reigned there until 1388, launching daring raids into the eastern Mediterranean to bring back slaves of all kinds who were sold in Athens and Thebes.[11] The Catalans hired themselves out to those with deep pockets; if pay wasn't forthcoming they took retribution. In 1426 King Janus of Cyprus called upon them to repel an invasion of Egyptian 'Saracens' who had landed there in considerable force. The Catalans defeated them without too much difficulty, then began a veritable reign of terror on the island.

Masters of dozens of ports, arsenals, and markets, the Catalans attacked wherever and whenever they pleased. Few merchants who wanted to ensure the safety of their goods and boats could venture into the Aegean without placing themselves under the Company's protection.

Venice and Genoa continued the war they fought in the west in the Levant. The Venetians provided the fleet which transported the crusaders – mostly Burgundians and Flemings – to Constantinople in 1204. They had one of their priests imposed upon the city as Latin patriarch and their candidate Baudouin, Count of Flanders, defeated the Genoese-backed Count of Montferrat to become emperor of the east. However, the Greeks established their own emperor at Nicaea, one who soon began to threaten the westerners. On 25 July 1261 this emperor, Michael VIII, having crushed Charles of Anjou, king of Sicily, in 1259, entered Constantinople. The Genoese had generously backed the emperor and now found themselves restored to favour and amply rewarded. They were given important trading privileges in imperial ports, especially those in the Black Sea. They took over the Venetian palace in Constantinople, evicting its occupants, and also founded Pera on the other side of the Golden Horn. This Genoese town was granted a kind of autonomy and was soon inhabited by craftsmen, merchants, and sailors.

The war of 1294–9 saw the Genoese victors over the Venetians near Curzola in the Adriatic. This conflict spawned a similar struggle in the Levant, where the Catalans and Greeks sided with one power or the other. Numerous further conflicts resulted, such as the war of Tenedos (1377–81). Captains of merchant ships were also drawn into these struggles, but never hesitated to take advantage. In November 1403 two huge Genoese ships stopped and pillaged Venetian vessels returning from the Black Sea. In 1432 it was the Genoese turn to suffer – its ships were ordered not to approach straits where Venetian convoys were expected.

Crimes committed on the open sea or on the coasts of the Levant were difficult to prevent and almost impossible to punish. Some Venetian sailors aboard the *Galea di Romania* raided a little Dalmatian city and killed a number of inhabitants. They received extremely light sentences. The owner of a Venetian ship and two of his sailors were accused of taking aboard a number of Tartars – apparently subjects of the Genoese – as passengers for Kaffa in the Crimea and of selling them as slaves somewhere along the way. The three Venetians received terms of a few months imprisonment and a fine of 50 livres.[12]

Everybody had everything to fear. In 1444 a Burgundian fleet was sent into the Levant to support crusaders fighting their way through the Balkans. One of its officers, Giacomo di Biglia, drew up an agreement with Giovanni Fertuna, a Genoese pirate and rebel. They sailed right into the Black Sea, trespassing as far as the Genoese stronghold of Kaffa, and Trebizond. Detained, Biglia should have been, by rights, executed. But the Genoese sold his ship and its cargo and the captain and his crew were liberated as soon as the Burgundians had left the Black Sea. Philip the Good of Burgundy finally managed to obtain compensation for this act, winning 7,000 ducats after a lengthy exchange of letters.[13]

State Sponsored Piracy

The maritime powers of Italy lost considerable numbers of men and ships. Maintaining warships to protect merchantmen and patrol the sea-lanes demanded considerable energies on the part of captains and states. Freight was forced to suffer delays, cancellations, additional expenses, and increased insurance premiums, all of which had an effect. To the great displeasure of merchants, who could see their profits haemorrhaging, ship owners kept their vessels anchored safely in port until they were completely sure there were no risks to run. Sometimes contracts were broken and merchants would have to unload their goods and store and take care of them. Notaries were kept busy attempting to sort out the resultant complaints. Communal magistrates sat for days on end attempting to decide whose responsibility the consequent losses were, and who should pay. In Italy and Provence news of delay was frequent; markets speculated and merchants waited. There was a whole culture of attempting to interpret rumours. In November 1394 a worried merchant of Avignon wrote to some business associates in Tuscany that 'a letter received in Montpellier informs us that certain Spanish pilgrims have arrived in that place having come from the Sepulchre of Jerusalem. They said that they boarded a merchantman belonging to Guillaume Pons of Narbonne at Rhodes and journeyed as far as Famagusta without mishap. There however the pilgrims heard that there were corsairs about and some merchants were deciding to spend the winter there. The pilgrims went aboard a different vessel. It seems to us important that the merchantman did not wish to venture out of Famagusta. Pray, tell us if you have heard anything of this.'[14]

Rumours flew this way and that as to which ships had set out and which had taken shelter. Were these subterfuges to raise the price of spices?

Those merchants who did take care, and who paid their customs dues and bided their time, had to compete with others less worthy; those who would reach an understanding with a corsair captain or who would smuggle goods ashore and avoid duty.

In Egypt, dominated by the descendants of Saladin and later by the Mamluks, sending ships out to raid and rob wasn't a well-established tradition – indeed, there was little seaborne fighting between Christian and Muslim. However, the advent of a new Ottoman Turkish empire in Anatolia changed things dramatically and marked the beginning of a new phase in the age-old struggle: one of outright conquest. This Turkish expansion was slow and patient, but it ushered in colonisation, a new order, the imposition of the Muslim religion, and a new way of subjecting a conquered people to total domination. The Turks could not countenance a sea ruled by 'Ferengi' or Franks (Europeans). Gradually they built up their fleets and, under the leadership of celebrated pirates or Barbary emirs, contested western control of the sea-lanes.

Constantinople fell in 1453. Countless Genoese and Venetian strongholds followed, as did Rhodes and even Mamluk Egypt. The Turkish drive along the North African coast was a Holy War and seemed like the expansion of an empire that knew no limits. In 1516 the Barbarossa brothers, sons of a Christian taken prisoner by the Turks in Albania and converted to Islam, seized several cities along the African shore. This was but the beginning of the harsh and brutal conquest of the Moorish kingdoms by the Turkish Janissaries and the corsairs. Overnight this transformed piracy in the region. From being the pastime of a handful of brigands it became a full-blown state enterprise, encouraged by a sultan and supported by his troops, his arsenals, and his money. Everything was decided in the courts and palaces of Constantinople. Turkish men and ships were seen everywhere across the Mediterranean, even entering Toulon as allies of the king of France. Each month they landed expeditions on the coasts of Christendom, particularly in the kingdom of Naples, Calabria, and Sicily. These raids weren't intended to enrich anyone, or to hazard personal fortunes, but were operations of war conducted by entire fleets as part of a comprehensive strategy, for the

Ottomans were contemplating conquering the Mediterranean and even invading Italy. The Barbary corsairs were no longer mere pirates, but were squadron commanders or admirals in a total war against Christendom, one waged by land and by sea.

Islam's offensive against the king of Spain, against the Pope, the Knights of Malta, and the Venetians lasted for three-quarters of a century, only abating around 1571 after the victory of the Holy League at Lepanto. From then on there was a wary truce, followed in 1581 by a more general peace which, however, went unsigned. Indeed, 1581 is an important year in the history of the corsairs. Their war at sea was set to continue for some time – they attacked Crete in 1644, and went on to be defeated by the Venetian admiral Morosini in 1694 off the coast of Greece – but they never again went on the offensive to the same extent as they had before; the Sultan, willing to attack by land, was no longer in favour of launching massive naval operations against Spain or Italy. For the Barbary corsairs this marked the end of an era. They stepped out of the war, turning their backs on it and concentrating instead on simple raiding and robbing without thought to grand designs or imperialistic schemes. Their presence in the Mediterranean would continue to be felt for some time[15] and they would seize and sell slaves as never before, but after 1581 the menace of an invasion by corsairs simply disappeared.

Focusing on the period between 1510 and 1580, which was dominated by the Barbarossas, allows us to examine the age of the corsairs' most brilliant success; a period when they not only held in check the maritime powers of Christendom but also menaced the coast of Italy and, thanks to their alliance with France, played an important part in influencing the balance of power in European politics. Such fortune, for that is what it was, resulted from the Mediterranean's rich maritime history, in which pirates, robber chiefs, Knights of Rhodes, emirs, and sultans all jostled for power. And it is to this history that we must turn first.

Chapter I

Before the Barbarossa Brothers

Italian, Spanish and French sailors, merchants and pilgrims were wracked by images of disastrous fortune on the high seas – gale-force winds, ships tossed about in a storm or driven far from land, or bodies hurled overboard. Few would set foot aboard a ship without having heard Mass or without commending their souls to God. Those who had survived shipwreck regaled their listeners with tales of boats being driven ashore and their crews set upon by gangs of cruel men; fortunate was he who was taken for ransom. In the spring of 1432, Jacques Coeur boarded the *Sainte-Marie-Saint-Paul*, a galley armed and owned by one Jean Vidal of Narbonne. The ship was to sail to Beirut and then on to Alexandria.

Returning from this voyage, the vessel put into a little port near Calvi on Corsica. There, the crew and passengers were seized by the inhabitants, had their possessions snatched, and were stripped down to their shirts. Then, half-naked, they were thrown into dark caves or dank cellars. Vidal was held in these conditions for fourteen months, the time it took to raise 800 golden ducats ransom on his behalf. Those guilty of this act were not pursued or punished. Several years later, after endless enquiries and discussions over damages incurred, the victims were awarded modest compensation.[1]

On 7 May 1470 Anselme Adorno, a Genoese nobleman, accompanied by his son and five companions, boarded a huge ship in order to sail to the Holy Land. The 700-ton ship 'was well provided with cannon, crossbows and javelins and had a complement of 110 armed men to repel pirates or Turks'. Like so many Genoese vessels, deemed impregnable, it was so large and so high in the water that it could have literally crushed any vessel which attempted to bar its way. However, the voyage was not without its dangers. The ship was too large to enter the port of Alghero on Sardinia, and the pilgrims had to be put ashore by means of its long-boats. However, upon their return they were pursued by pirates, and these sought to come between them and the ship. The Genoese captain opened up on the pirates and despatched two barques, each crewed by twenty-four men, to the pilgrims' rescue. 'In the tumult of gun-fire and the blaring of trumpets' the pilgrims only just managed to regain their ship. But the pirates were everywhere – both in Africa and the Levant – dogging the ship's every move.[2]

Encounters on the open sea usually led to damage or disaster. The notaries of Genoa and Pisa, seated on their benches in the city's public places, or in the merchants' shops or by the quays, spent much of their time noting down losses or listening to the testimonies of traders or sailors who had experienced mishaps at sea. An appeal for compensation would usually be looked upon with favour if it came from someone accustomed to negotiation. Gradually, however, appeals evolved into a rather more simple process. The applicant would describe the goods he had lost, giving their nature, weight, and estimated value. The circumstances around the loss would then be listed – the date, place, and, if possible, the name of the felon. In the absence of a name the origin of the pirate was noted, the pirates of Fréjus, Toulon, Cassis, and Marseilles being those most frequently blamed.[3]

Some of these felons inhabited ramshackle camps constructed out of wood, canvas, and rope. Putting to sea in fair weather, they would shelter by some cape and await easy pickings. Their chief would land his booty at dusk and make arrangements to transport it to market on a mule train. It would then be disposed of, anonymously and safely. This was small-time thievery, preying on the weak.

However, there were captains who, cruising along all the major shipping lanes, became veritable lords of the sea. Whilst the small-fry pirates would disappear back to their villages after a successful expedition, these *seigneurs* remained outside the law as rebels, exiles, or the proscribed. Many of them came from Italy. It is somewhat unfortunate that our impression of medieval Italy is one of city states peacefully trading and going about their business. Far from it; each of these cities was frequently torn apart by bloody factional feuds in which power was at stake.

These struggles would only terminate with the insolent triumph of one side and the annihilation of the other. Houses and palaces would be plundered, burnt, and razed to the ground; noblemen would be assassinated then dragged through the streets; others would be banished for life, and barred from taking any possessions with them. Such exiles would be forced, almost literally, to take up the profession of arms in order to survive. Some became freelance mercenaries, others *condottieri* in the service of princes. Still more became pirates, boosting the numbers already preying on Mediterranean trade.[4]

Corsairs would go to ground in their haunts, which were veritable fortresses manned by their followers and vassals. In 1387 Marie, widow of Louis, Duke of Anjou and Count of Provence, granted Balthazar Spinola, a Genoese nobleman, the seignory of Bregancon. He made the port into a base and refuge for pirates and these quickly began to stop ships and bite into Provencal trade. Merchants sought to protect themselves and their associates whilst the authorities in Marseilles sought to find ways to eradicate this nest of brigands. Marie appealed to all maritime powers to arm their vessels in order to protect them from these robbers, but such efforts were in vain. Negotiations began. Spinola and the Council of Marseilles went into talks which lasted for weeks. Eventually the pirates quit Bregancon and returned to Genoa, to begin anew their quest for wealth. They had dabbled in politics and, for ten years, had defied all the Mediterranean powers and their fleets.[5]

On 18 June 1393 two Tuscans were aboard a barque belonging to Esteve Michel which was attacked off Bonifacio 'in the second third of the day'[6] by a galley and galliot crewed by Genoese subjects. The pirates stole their clothes, their books, and the ship's rigging. That same year, Esteve's brother Pierre set out from Arles and was seized and taken aboard a gondola. From there he was transferred to a different ship 'which was known hereabouts and some say it is Genoese'. His abductors bound him to a stove, stripped him of his clothes, and subjected him to long tortures in order to force him to reveal the whereabouts of any valuables. Another brother, Bartolomeo, was also captured by pirates (presumed, again, to be Genoese). All three journeyed to Tarascon to supplicate Marie for letters of marque which might force Genoa and Savona to pay indemnities. They had suffered losses 'on three separate occasions' and they were rewarded by promises that some kind of payment would be forthcoming. But promises were all they received.[7]

Genoa, in the *Quattrocento*, witnessed the death in office of just one of its doges; all the others were deposed and chased out of the city. Paolo Fregoso, simultaneously archbishop and doge, fled the city in 1464 after a rebellion. He became an exile and spent the rest of his life a pirate. Indeed, this tyrant was, without doubt, the most infamous of all the Genoese exiles. He seized a number of fine ships whilst they were at anchor and, for many a month, attacked any ship he encountered, particularly if they happened to be Genoese. He based his enterprise on Corsica, establishing his headquarters at Bonifacio, and could field more than 500 men. Merchants lost thousands of ducats to his brigandage. Finally his enemies assembled a fleet, supported by armed galleys, and in a battle off the Corsican coast he lost most of his ships, though he himself escaped ashore. Taking up arms once again he continued to cause trouble for some years, living, albeit modestly, off his pillage.[8]

In 1423 a heavily-armed squadron of Aragonese ships broke into Marseilles harbour. Men boarded ships anchored in the port, set fire to homes and warehouses, carried off an immense quantity of loot and sailed off, leaving destruction in their wake. Marseilles was only just beginning to recover when, eight years later, a second assault took place. Again, it was the subjects of the king of Aragon who were responsible and the notaries scribbled down 'those Catalan dogs' in their records.

In the summer of 1451, Audinet, captain of a galliot from Marseilles or Port-de-Bouc, attacked Rosas in Catalonia in broad daylight. Three years later he descended upon boats fishing off the Catalan coast and made off with them, in full view of the inhabitants. The next year, having formed an alliance with a certain Grimaldi of Genoa, he audaciously broke into Barcelona's harbour and took a caravel just arrived from Majorca. Further south he landed his men below the walls of the town of Salou, broke in, and sacked it.[9]

Between 1450 and 1470 the Florentines were attempting to import grain, salt, and wine and to export cloth, but trade did not always go smoothly. The city scribes hardly ceased recording crimes and requests for reparation. On 8 July 1454 Florentine officials sent a letter off to the doge of Genoa: a citizen of Florence, travelling on a barque out of Livorno, had been robbed of his goods, books, clothes, and money by a galley belonging to Grimaldi of Monaco.[10] On 11 September 1455 a letter to the consuls of Nice complained that grain, belonging to the Neroni Company of Florence, had been seized by Melchione de Grimaldi somewhere between Sardinia and Corsica.[11] Two years later, in 1457, complaints poured in about a pirate of Genoese extraction who had styled himself Scarinxo. A Pisan ship carrying 6,000 golden ducats worth of cheese, butter, and grain was seized by this brigand whilst on its way to Palermo. He sold the merchandise at Savona and Genoa.[12] On 18 November 1461 a letter was sent to Filippo Tornabuoni, captain of galleys:

> It has come to our knowledge that a number of corsairs, among them Scarinxo, have been preying on our merchants between Genoa and Naples and causing them grievous loss. They have taken twelve ships or more. We have despatched a messenger to Modon to raise levies of armed men. You, Tornabuoni, captain, should take heed not to be surprised and should await at Messina two further galleys which we are sending you by way of reinforcement.[13]

Three days later a long letter was sent off to the doge of Genoa:

> Scarinxo is one of yours, you cannot deny it; he is becoming bolder and bolder and has been selling the Florentine cloth he seized in Africa. You are certainly aware of this as we have written to you a number of times. You must banish him from your coasts, ports, and markets and send out dire warnings of punishments for any found aiding him.[14]

But what could the doge and his council really do to prevent such crime? Indeed, what could anyone do?

For many years this robbery at sea, some of which received state support, had a grave effect on the region's commerce and food supplies. Chancelleries echoed to the noise of complaint, petitions overwhelmed bureaucracies. Of those who had suffered misfortune, few were spared a long and painful judicial process and many faced complete ruin.

Christians and Muslims

Few would allow that Henri Pirenne's thesis of the 1830s, that Muslim conquests ruined Mediterranean commerce, has stood the test of time. Indeed, evidence seems to suggest the opposite. Italian, Provencal, and

Spanish ships had always anchored in Egyptian, Syrian, or Byzantine ports and taken on board cargoes of fruit, drugs, and silks. A rather less exotic trade also flourished – grain, salt, wine, wool, and leather formed the basis of long-lasting, enriching trade; indeed it was this commerce, rather than the fabulous and much lauded trade in spices, which made the fortunes of the great trading nations. Venice exported salt, Genoa both salt and grain, whilst Barcelona sold wood, wool and, later, cloth. Did ships merely pass over the Tyrrhenian Sea in their haste to fill their holds with magnificent cargoes of spices?

This image of Mediterranean commerce as being one in which trade was in rare products, acquired at a high price, needs looking at again. We have been beguiled by our taste for the unusual and our fascination with the exotic. The Mediterranean was criss-crossed with hundreds of trading routes; these were diverse, constantly modified by the success or failure of this or that enterprise, or by politics, diplomacy, and war. The system was so dense and so complex that it defies description. The Italians of Genoa and Pisa, the people of Provence and the Catalans fetched leather, wool, and gold from the ports of North Africa. The gold had been brought up from the Sudan – or, more precisely, from the valley of the Senegal river – in the caravans of Arab traders. Catalans and Italians exchanged leather, shells, and pearls for it at Oran or Tunis. Christian merchants also offered high quality woollen cloth from Tuscany and England – much of it dyed blue – to the inhabitants of North Africa's cities, as well as to the nomadic tribesmen of the interior. This was high-class commerce and one in which traders were aware of the needs, demands, and tastes of their clients. Those salesmen who sought to bend the rules were quickly brought to book; this was no 'colonial' traffic, but, rather, was commerce between equals. True, the merchants were well aware that there were risks and that friction with local customs officials was more likely than elsewhere; but the opportunities for profit outweighed such concerns.

The incessant coming and going of the Christian ships – vessels of all kinds and of diverse tonnage – was not restricted to any particular season, nor was it subject to protection by any particular state. Trade was left to the initiative of individuals, or to that of companies, and it was predominantly concentrated in private hands. To have representatives stationed on the ground was a favoured technique. Even the petty merchants of Genoa, Pisa, and Barcelona could attempt to become involved in the trade, either personally or by trusting a contact to bring back gold or to purchase wool and grain at advantageous prices. A few companies even ventured into the African interior to get a better deal or to oversee trading. In 1460 Quilico Imperiale, a Genoese, established one trading post at Stora, on the African coast, and another at Constantine.[15] At around the same time a number of grain merchants, many of them well-established firms such as Emmanuele Grimaldi and Benedetto di Negro, also set up shop in the little port of Stora.[16]

A Genoese company obtained rights to fish for Tuna off Sousse.[17] Another, this time of considerable size and importance, enjoyed rights to fish for coral between Bône and Mers el-Kharez.[18] These rights created a revenue of 20,000 golden pieces a year to the king of Tunis. The coral was distributed unprocessed or as buttons or beads throughout the Levant – Beirut was a strong market – and Arab merchants even sent it on to China. The Genoese established a veritable trading colony, protected from pirates by fortress walls, in which there was a church and accommodation for merchants, workers, and artisans.[19] Companies such as these developed quickly, and through their contacts with royal officials obtained safe-conducts, privileges, and even monopolies. Soon they reached a stage which enabled them to meddle in politics.

Frequently it all began with business associates, friends, or brothers gaining familiarity with a market by acting as agents or representatives in Italian or Spanish ports. Next they would call in financiers to support their new enterprise. Their capital would then be divided into twenty-four parts or shares and these would be traded openly on the Genoese market. In this manner many private individuals gained a direct link with African affairs. One company traded in silks and fruit, especially raisins, cultivated in the Muslim kingdom of Granada.[20]

Genoese or Catalan ships, or those from Provence, frequently put in at ports such as Honein, Tlemcen, or Tripoli. The Genoese kept to a well-organised and subtle system thanks to the unique flexibility of their finances. Each and every year their ships sailed directly to the east from England or Flanders, avoiding Genoa itself and thereby evading duties or taxes. From Cadiz or Malaga the ships would proceed to the Levant or the North African coast. They would anchor at places designated by the merchants of Southampton or Bruges and commence trading *ad costeriam* – doing the coast, in modern parlance. Merchants, scribes, and magnates would renew contracts, trade, and account. Shipowners would seek out new contracts, update their prices, and test the water. Potential customers for the merchandise would be sought out, especially those who could pay in gold. English cloth, which was worth a fortune, would be sold piece by piece and any transaction recorded in astonishing detail.[21]

It should not be assumed that Muslim traders were excluded from the beneficial trade between the Muslim and Christian worlds. Nor were they restricted to small-scale operations – trading agricultural products or craftwork from town to town, or from souk to souk. Muslim merchants were just as adept at reaping the benefits of overseas trade. A well-known trading route was that between Malaga and Tunis or Alexandria. In the 1420s the king of Aragon employed a spy, based at Tunis, to record the departure of every vessel, and to note down the nature of their cargo.[22] In June 1453 two Catalan captains were ordered to 'cruise off the African coast in an attempt to surprise the convoy of ships belonging to Muslim merchants which cruises between Alexandria and Tunis at this time of year.'[23] Muslim merchants worked round any bans on trading in the countries of the infidel, either hiring Christian ships or even travelling as passengers upon them. They exported silk from Granada, linen from Egypt, cotton from Egypt and Syria, ostrich feathers, slaves, and gold. Muslim merchants from Valencia frequently obtained conducts promising safe-passage – valid for a year or more between Granada and Africa – from the king of Aragon. Small-time traders took cloth, leather, and ceramics to sell, but larger enterprises, such as those run by the Ripoll, Bellvis, and Xupis families, also flourished.[24]

It wasn't unknown for Italian ships, especially Genoese, to take on board Moorish merchants and their cargoes of merchandise or slaves. In 1457 Vinciguerra de Vivaldi, owner of a large vessel, was hired by the king of Tunis to take a shipment of barley, wheat, wool, leather, and rose water to Tripoli. A Moorish merchant and three of his slaves – one male and two females – were to accompany him. At Tripoli Vivaldi was to receive 600 doubloons for his trouble. Some 400 of these would remain after he paid his crew. Two years later Leonardo de Maris, owner of a 600-tonne ship, signed a contract with seventeen Muslims (nine from Tripoli, five from Tunis, and three from Granada) to transport a cargo of linen from Chios to Tunis. They would pay three ducats a sack if the shipment made it to Tunis, but only two if the ship had to put in at Sousse due to bad weather, and just one-and-a-half if the voyage was curtailed at Tripoli. Leonardo provided the merchants with three well-appointed rooms on his ship and supplied water and wood for heating. Their passage, as well as that of their servants and representatives, was free. At least 300 sacks were taken on board, making some 1,000 ducats for Leonardo. From Chios the ship followed the Anatolian coast, pausing some seven weeks before finally setting sail for the west. The Moors were consequently on board for more than three months.[25]

On one Genoese ship heading for the Holy Land, Christian pilgrims came across 100 Moors as well as Jews. The three religious groups worshipped on board ship – the Christians on Sunday, the Jews on Saturday, and the Muslims on Friday.[26]

Trading against the Odds

Rather than chancing all on the field of battle, princes and magnates on both sides of the Mediterranean much preferred to negotiate. Pedro 'the Ceremonious' of Aragon (1336–87) attempted to maintain peace with the king of Tunis by paying that monarch a handsome tribute. Instructions given to Pere de Manresa, sent as ambassador to Granada in July 1376, contain eight explicit instructions. Six years later peace with Granada was solemnly declared 'by public announcement, as is the custom' by the grand council of the kingdom of Valencia.[27] Ambassadors were increasingly despatched from both sides of the Mediterranean. Michel Fabre, secretary to King René of Anjou, boarded the *Sainte-Marie-Sainte-Barbe* in 1473. Accompanied by a small retinue, and a great number of presents, Fabre embarked for Tunis and stayed there for four years. He established an excellent rapport with the court, and gained contact with the king's closest advisers. Initial negotiations concerned the delivery of certain kinds of beasts – Arab horses, giraffes, lions, and wild cats – but later progressed to implementing safe-conducts and mutual guarantees. In 1478 'agents of the Moors of Bône' resided at Aix-en-Provence.[28]

Naturally, such relationships could not be maintained without undergoing some form of risk or danger. Piracy, provocations, and reprisals all had an impact.

Catalans and Aragonese – especially the natives of Barcelona, Majorca, and Valencia – made piracy a continuation of war by other means. Royal proclamations, declaring an absolute ban on hostile actions against subjects of the kings of Granada or Valencia, provoked open or furtive opposition. The king attempted to overcome such opposition by pursuing those who dared to break the peace. He ordered that corsairs be arrested, and that the goods of the corsairs, and of their backers, be seized. Those governors who did not conform to the royal will would be treated to the full rigour of the law (*ira Regis*), and punished severely. Simultaneously, however, Iberian kings authorised action against known or suspected Barbary corsairs and took a cut of the profits. Of sixty-three prizes taken in just one campaign against the Moors of Granada and Africa, the king's fiscal officers retained thirteen – nine for the Crown and four for the commanding admiral. Evidently such letters of marque allowing action against 'Saracens' or permitting 'piracy against Saracens' were quite difficult to obtain. Those who were accorded such rights had to agree not to molest good and loyal subjects of the Maghreb princes, but only to single out pirates and their ships, arsenals, and haunts.

At Majorca, where the two worlds met and clashed, such privateering formed an important aspect of naval power. The pirates seemed to know when and how to strike or to lay low.[29] The sea offered a thousand and one possible refuges in isolated bays far from the coming and going of the galleys.

Some pirates mixed commerce with brigandage. Raiding and kidnapping the inhabitants of the African coast – far from any urban sprawl – was easy and risked nothing. The kings of Tlemcen and Tunis were constantly wracked by dynastic quarrels and tribal revolts provoked by usurpers or ambitious governors. The towns shut themselves up within their walls and held but weak authority over the Bedouin nomads – wrongly termed 'Arabs' by the Christians. The merchants of the larger cities were loath to travel by land; more frequently they would travel from Tunis to Cairo by sea in order to avoid the 'Arabs of Barca'. In 1465 the Bedouins practically laid siege to Fez; the inhabitants 'underwent privations and disorder reigned; so much that the merchants and caravans didn't dare venture forth'. A party of merchants from Tlemcen even went as far as attempting to deceive the bandits 'by disguising themselves as lepers, with their bodies covered with mud and dust. They arrived without difficulty, which was most just, as hitherto only birds had come safely through the Bedouins.'[30]

The Christians, especially the Catalans and Genoese, took advantage of this disorder, recognising that they would meet but light resistance.

Pirate captains would cruise along the coast, launching raids against fishing villages and against peasants in their fields. Bedouins also assisted them, selling them Moorish captives they had captured on the road.

Naturally, Muslim princes and governors would, if warned in time, attempt to oppose such incursions and would assemble troops to try and drive the pirates off or to capture them. In 1464 some Christian corsairs were attacked on a beach in the kingdom of Tlemcen by local inhabitants supported by hastily-assembled soldiers. Some managed to escape and sail away, but eleven were captured. Of these, six were executed at once whilst five 'who seemed to be wealthy' were ransomed.[31] Such a success was, however, rare and was sufficient neither to deter the brigands nor to reassure the inhabitants of their safety. Fear stalked the coast, inspiring dramatic stories and nurturing legends. A Genoese explorer noted in 1470 that two rocky headlands near Monastir closely resembled the shape of a galley. According to the Moors these Christian 'ships' had attempted to burst into the port to pillage and rob; but holy men had run down to the beach and commanded that the ships be instantly turned to stone – which they were.[32]

The kings of Tunis and Tlemcen had much to complain of regarding the sailors of Aragon. Their ships were being pillaged even when they were in harbour, loading up alongside the city quays. Two corsairs seized two *lenys* at Tunis and took four captives at Sousse. Others had descended on the harbour at Tenes, where they had burnt one boat and seized fifteen of the harbour guards. Bernet de Vilagent of Barcelona, owner of a galliot and sixteen boats, and Johan Funya of Majorca, owner of nine boats, even signed a contract before a notary obliging each to sail in African waters and attack the Barbary peoples.[33]

Granada suffered perhaps even more than the kings of Tunis and Tlemcen. In just one episode two pirates seized a ship from Malaga carrying wine, a ship from Almeida, and a grain transport belonging to the Muslims of Valencia. Fifteen slaves were subsequently sold at Ibiza. Such raids compromised the very survival of the kingdom of Granada, which was largely dependent on African grain to keep it going, having given over its arable land to vineyards and its orchards to the production of sugar cane. Whilst the kings of Aragon and Castile formally distanced themselves from such piracy, there were those in the royal councils who saw such activity as a form of blockade, which might pave the way for conquest.

Throughout this period there were some nobles in Aragon who turned a blind eye towards royal instructions. In 1421 a fleet sacked the Kerkenna Islands, bringing back a number of prisoners including sailors, carpenters, rope-makers, and caulkers.[34] Nicolas Pia, of San Feliu de Guixols, and Captain Jaime Carbó embarked on a pirate cruise along the Barbary Coast, but in two voyages did not capture a single vessel; even so, they returned with some booty and the record of the ensuing auction survives: weapons, clothes, leather, rattan, baskets of dates – ninety-five different lots were sold off to the merchants and shopkeepers of Barcelona.[35] Catalans also launched expeditions against the Barbary Coast from Palos, Huelva, and Puerto de Santa Maria. They raided the coast between Morocco (especially the areas around Mazagan, Ceuta, and Safi) and Tunis. The sale of their booty generated important commercial activity in their home towns, where the goods were sold off either openly or clandestinely. Some received ransom payments from Moors seeking to recover captured members of their families. Accounts for the city of Cadiz show that during the period between February and December 1485 eight Moorish ships were captured by vessels operating from its port, along with 200 prisoners, an enormous amount of grain, and quantities of flour, leather, fish, silk, and oil – in all, goods worth more than a million *maravedis*. Andalusian corsairs grew steadily more dangerous, fitting out caravels which could hold a complement of sixty armed men. 'The men would land on the beaches of Africa, or in their ports; they would seize captives and burn and pillage any unprotected place'.[36] The *Mémorial sur la guerre du Maroc* by Cardinal Cisneros, published in 1505, describes in detail the kind of preparations these grand expeditions necessitated. When discussing the recruitment of crews, Cisneros candidly observes that 'it is not necessary to pay them; there will be enough of them to mount five such expeditions'. Everything was well thought-out, including where to attack and the routes to be taken on the outward and return legs.[37]

In Africa and in Granada alike the villagers and fishermen gave as good as they got whenever they could. For the Christians, minor setbacks in these regions could lead to disaster. Letters from the kings of Aragon to the Muslim princes reveal, year after year, a litany of anguish arising from sailors cast up on the African shore by bad weather. In April 1471 a captain from Collioure in Languedoc and the six-man crew of his barque were seized after being swept ashore. That same year a large *nao* from Barcelona lost its mast and sails and began to sink. The crew attempted to reach

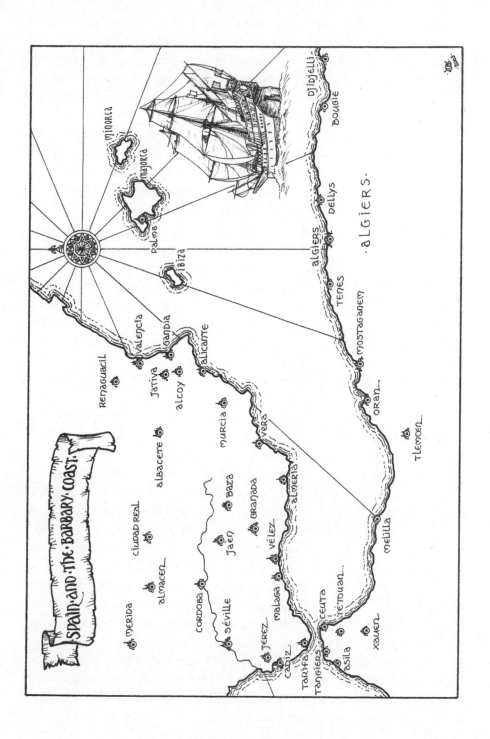

SPAIN·AND·THE·BARBARY·COAST·

MÉRIDA
CIUDAD REAL
ALMADÉN
ALBACETE
RENAGUACIL
CÓRDOBA
JAÉN
BAZA
JÁTIVA
ALCOY
VALENCIA
GANDÍA
SÉVILLE
GRANADA
MURCIA
ALICANTE
VÉLEZ
ALMERÍA
JEREZ
MÁLAGA
VERA
CÁDIZ
TARIFA
CEUTA
MELILLA
TANGIERS
ASILA
TETOUAN
XAUEN
ORAN
TLEMCEN
MOSTAGANEM
TÉNÈS
ALGIERS
DELLYS
BOUGIE
DJIDJELLI
·ALGIERS·
IBIZA
PALMA
MAJORCA
MINORCA

the coast of Spain in a fisherman's boat but were carried towards Africa by the current. There they were seized, shackled, and thrown into prison. Ten years later a *panfil* from Valencia, loaded with grain, pepper, silk, cow-hides, and forty-six falcons, was on the return leg of its journey from Africa when it ran aground on the Granadan coast in the middle of the night. Suddenly two warships appeared, sent from Almeria, as did a body of armed men, some mounted and some on foot. The sailors fled into the mountains, but a Jewish passenger was captured and another murdered. In the same region, a Christian boat put into the little port of Vera, desiring merely to trade. One of its sailors was killed and three more were seized and sold as slaves at the market in Granada.[38]

Hardly anyone paid much attention to treaties. The king of Tunis once ordered the governor of Bône to return goods seized from a Catalan galliot stranded in that port. But the governor ignored the order and, supported by the town's inhabitants, he sold the ship's cargo and either killed the crew or sold them into slavery. When a galley from Valencia, surprised by a sudden storm, attempted to shelter in the roads off Bougie, it was captured and the mayor imprisoned nine merchants who had gained the shore.[39]

The Muslim pirates of Africa, more frequently known at the time as Saracen corsairs rather than Barbary corsairs, did not owe any allegiance to the kings of Tunis or Tlemcen; they were warlords, adventurers, and bandits, answering to no one. No sooner had winter turned to spring than they would sally forth to attack the coast of Provence. They would avoid larger ships, or cities safe behind imposing walls, preying instead on fishing vessels and defenceless merchantmen. They would establish a camp in some rocky inlet and send expeditions into the interior to capture merchants and peasants. Marseilles was ever watchful for these raiders, cordoning off the port at night to prevent fishermen venturing out. Officers serving the counts of Provence, and authorities in towns across the region, kept a careful watch on the coast. In March 1395 an evidently well-informed Tuscan merchant was able to write that Moorish galleys were cruising off Majorca. Few doubted that they would next appear 'off Marseilles, as is their wont at this season'.[40] The following year a Saracen fleet captured a number of ships between Hyeres and Marseilles and their crews were carried off as slaves.[41] In 1320 African pirates captured pilgrims bound for the sanctuary of Montserrat. They were shackled and dragged through the streets of Bougie before being sold.

Watchtowers on Majorca were built to serve as lookout posts and their alarms sounded a number of times a year. But the Moors preferred to land at night, avoiding detection and thereby surprising their enemies. They attacked isolated houses or hamlets, killing the men, carrying off the women and children and, if there was time, making off with the harvest too. A poor man working as an artisan in Barcelona explained that he had fled from Lloret, a fishing village, because he was 'afraid that the Moors would seize him as there were houses there that were poorly guarded and so, one day or another, the Moors, or some other bad people, would come and put the place to the sack'.[42] Later the corsairs grew bolder and embarked upon more brazen expeditions, even attacking fortified ports and cities. In 1393 they swept into Syracuse, capturing the bishop; in 1406 it was the turn of Agde; in 1428 Capri; Malta in 1429; and Elba in 1443.[43] In 1447 a Tunisian fleet landed soldiers at Benidorm in the kingdom of Valencia; they looted the town and the surrounding area, carrying off hundreds of men and women. In 1456 another fleet, this time of between eight and ten ships, seized a number of Christian vessels off the Balearics, carrying off 85 prisoners.[44]

Bougie was a real haven for pirates. Its chief, Mohammed ben Ali Mahdi, was a true admiral, commanding a veritable navy in which different branches of service oversaw finance, arming and equipping of galleys, the recruitment of crews, and the distribution of booty – whether slaves of merchandise – between the various captains. He later established himself on the coast of Tlemcen too, where he deputised his authority to a Catalan renegade named Berthomeu Perpinya, and at Algiers. This latter place surpassed even Bougie by the 1460s. Part of his fleet set off from Algiers in 1472 to attack the Tuscan coast and again, in 1475, landed an expeditionary force at Fréjus. It was in 1503, however, that sixteen of his boats, carrying 500 men, arrived off Cullera, some fifteen leagues south of Valencia. The Moors landed, killed thirty inhabitants, kidnapped the rest, burnt the church, and made off with church silver and priests' vestments.[45]

Algiers witnessed the rise and fall of fortunes based on this clandestine commerce. Only in 1516, when the Barbarossa brothers – sons of a renegade Christian – renowned already for their successes against the Greeks and Latins, established themselves in the city, did Algiers take on the status of an important town. From then on hunting Christian ships took on a whole new allure.

The Pirate Emirs

The Ottoman Turks stormed into Europe in 1350 and established their capital at Adrianople in 1366. It was the first step in their conquest of the Balkans. Victorious over the Serbs at Kosovo in 1389, they then humbled a crusade led by Sigismund of Hungary and Jean de Nevers – son of the Duke of Burgundy – at Nicopolis in 1396. In 1440 their attempt to seize Belgrade failed, but Constantinople fell to them thirteen years later.

Domination of the sea would mean that the Ottomans could secure their communications with Asia Minor, frustrate Christian attempts to mount relief expeditions, and create opportunities to mount attacks on Italy. However, such a victory would not be won through a decisive engagement; instead, the Turks' desire to dominate the seas led to a veritable war of attrition in which pirates and corsairs were to play a major role.

The Turks established a number of key bases on the Anatolian coast and began to launch raids into the Aegean. Using small boats crewed by Greek or Albanian sailors converted to Islam, they raided fishing villages in order to bring back captives. As early as 1326 the doge of Venice warned officers of the Venetian fleet and governors of Venice's eastern colonies to watch out for the Turks 'who have rendered themselves masters of Asia Minor and who will soon contaminate and ruin the islands of Romania, principally those belonging to the principality of the Morea'.[46]

More than a century before the emergence of the Barbarossa brothers the poets (*ozan*) and chroniclers of the Ottoman court were lauding the exploits of their lords of the sea in the Holy War against the Christians. Based on accounts provided by sailors, warriors, and even prisoners, their exploits against the Byzantines were thus recorded for posterity. The *Destan d'Umur Pasha* – a vast poem more than 2,000 verses long – was the work of a man who had participated in Mehmet II's campaigns against the island of Lesbos and in Bosnia. As a reward for his labour he received an entire village. His poem celebrates the virtues – predominantly bravery and force – the audacity, and the cruelty of an invincible emir who, a century before the poem was penned, burnt, pillaged, killed, and carried off women and children, from the lands of 'those cursed dogs', the Christians.[47]

The poem's hero, Umur Pasha, was actually born in 1309, one of the emir of Aydin's five sons. He inherited the governorship of Smyrna from his father and, in 1327, launched a fleet of at least seventy-five ships against Tenedos, Gallipoli, Chios, and Samothrace. The following year, with just one vast galley and seven smaller vessels, he waged war on the islands nearest to Anatolia, notably Chios and Samos. During the course of this raid five large vessels (whether Byzantine, Genoan, or Venetian is not recorded) swept over the horizon towards him. They were immense and so tall in the water that 'each one could have been taken for a mountain, their sides were like fortresses and they carried enemies without number'. Miraculously, the wind ceased blowing, leaving the Christian ships becalmed and easy prey for the Turkish archers who, in their lighter boats, darted backwards and forwards at ease. For 'two whole days' they 'killed without respite those dogs, the sea was red with blood'. However, the Turks were too few in number to attempt to board the enemy vessels and so they withdrew, leaving a scene of carnage behind them, the sails and walls of the Christian ships being 'so covered in arrows that they resembled hedgehogs'.

Umur was a lord, and so led noblemen into combat. These men were true warriors of Islam versed in the ways of the Prophet, who 'waged this war in order to punish the nonbelievers'. Refusal to participate would have been a dishonour. In 1339 Umur threatened Piraeus and Athens and intensified his attacks on the Morean coast. He also struck the Cyclades, which belonged to the Sanudi, a Venetian family, and raided the Albanian coast before falling back to his base at Almyros. His ships were loaded with an astonishing amount of booty. 'Rich and poor were filled with joy by his gift. The whole of Aydin was overwhelmed by wealth. Happiness reigned. Lambs, sheep, ducks, and geese were roasted, wine flowed freely.' He gave his brother 'a number of moon-faced virgins, each without equal; a host of handsome boys to tend his horses; to this gift he added gold and silver and countless goblets.' One fifth of his booty, that which 'belonged to God', was distributed among orphans, the poor, and needy travellers. However, we must not forget that this was Holy War. The pasha-pirate took few prisoners – 'he cut off many heads and made blood run deep; he himself killed seventy Franks with his lance; he sent their souls to hell; none stood before him.'

In order to avoid the heavily-guarded Bosporus straits he managed to transport his boats (300 of them, according to the poem) overland – by means of a wooden walkway – into the Black Sea. There he unleashed a reign of terror as far north as the mouth of the Danube. He took Kili (Licostomo) and hunted down those inhabitants who tried to flee into the mountains or forests. 'They captured beautiful maidens and pretty boys without number and carried them back as trophies. They set fire to all the villages.'

The Byzantines, who employed all kinds of warlords in their service – Normans, Slavs, and even Turks – actually employed Umur at one point. Andronikos III presented him with the island of Qara Borum in 1336 as payment for his aid. Later John VI hired him to lead a fleet of mercenaries. The poem claims that 'the emperor and his son submitted like slaves and accompanied the pasha' when he sailed into the northern Aegean. Umur was retained in Byzantine service for a number of years, and, along with another Turkish corsair – Suleiman Bey – and a Bulgarian pirate called Mumcila, fought for John VI wherever required. Pope Clement VI launched a crusade against him, calling upon Christian knights to seek out and destroy this chief of corsairs, even though he was an ally of the Greeks. Heading eastwards, the crusaders attacked Smyrna and, on 28 October 1344, captured the town and its port but not its principal hilltop fortress. A few months later, however, they were defeated in battle and a good number of their leaders were killed.[48] In June 1346 a second expedition brought reinforcements for the beleaguered Christians, but most returned home following a minor victory over the Turks.[49] The real significance of these two crusades is in their demonstration that the papacy – and many Christian princes – were already well aware of the grave dangers posed by such Turkish lords as Umur.

Umur Pasha himself was killed by an arrow in June 1348 whilst trying to retake Smyrna from the Franks.[50] Others, however, maintained the struggle thereafter and continued to make their presence felt. In 1399 three Turkish ships established themselves in the Gulf of Patras, where they taxed ships as they passed back and forth. In 1402 Turkish ships sent a Venetian galley to the bottom as it passed between Tinos and Mykonos. At about the same time they swarmed around Crete, watching Venetian galleys coming and going, hoping to surprise one at a decisive moment.

As time wore on the Ottomans strengthened their position in the Aegean and developed a formidable fleet. Each victory seemed to offer them new and better ports, well-furnished arsenals, or sailors accustomed to raiding and piracy. In 1462 Lesbos fell to the Turks. They threw out the Genoese Gattilusi, seized their ships, and recruited their Greek and Albanian sailors after converting them to Islam. Among that body of men was the father of the Barbarossa brothers, who would begin their careers on Lesbos before launching themselves west to win their astounding reputations.

War and Conquest

Throughout the 1450s naval warfare, for the Ottomans, meant not only raiding and piracy but also full-blown conflict, involving grand fleets and hundreds of ships. With Constantinople vanquished in 1453 and newly peopled with crowds of immigrants from Anatolia, the Sultan and his warlords announced their bloody intention to wage war on Christians throughout the Mediterranean, and even to seize Rome. Above all, they sought to push the Latins out of their possessions in the Levant. No island, no land, was safe. Alerted by displaced populations, and urged to strengthen his defences, the king of Cyprus attempted to develop a new system of watchtowers to replace the old Byzantine defences, and doubled his coastal guard. The towers communicated by means of smoke during the day and fire at night: 'Every half-mile two villagers, furnished with wood, watched out for ships approaching the island; if they saw any they were to make as much fire as possible. After the going down of the sun, each sentinel was obliged, upon discovering something, to make a fire which would burn for as long as it took to say six paternosters.'[51]

Above all it was Venice which suffered from the developing threat. The Adriatic, which *La Serenissima* proclaimed was 'the gulf of Venice', was now threatened and exposed to raids from both the Turks – now masters of Albania and the Peleponnese – and Dalmatian pirates, the Dalmatian Illyrians having been celebrated seafarers since Roman times (*gentes Illyriorum latrociniis maritimi infames*). Known by the Venetians as Uskoks or *Uscocchi*, the latter could field a force of up to a thousand armed men at any one time. Having established themselves at Signa, near Fiume, in an uncultivated land devoid of forests but inaccessible from the interior, they terrorised the seas as far south as Ragusa. Their favoured boats were *brazzere* (from the island of Braza), each of which had six to eight rowers, who were changed every hour if necessary to keep the crews fresh. Their haunts resembled those of the North African pirates, overflowing with refugees from lands conquered by the Turks, renegades from Italy, and even deserters from the Venetian fleet. These Uskoks were, of course, enemies of the Turks as well, but the majority of their victims were most certainly Christian. They were well-informed about the departure of Christian ships from various ports, knew their routes, and sometimes were even informed as to their cargoes. Venice first tried to drive them off by sending squadrons of barques, then *fustes*, and finally galleys against them. But all was to no avail – the vessels were ambushed one after another, and were all lost.[52] Durazzo, a Venetian possession, was being slowly strangled by the Uskoks, and the Venetians eventually had to reinforce their Adriatic fleet.

As early as 1415 Turkish ships attacked Venetian galleys around the island of Tenedos. On this occasion the Venetians only escaped by darting into the Golden Horn at Constantinople, where they remained, in a state of siege, for twenty-six days. Another Venetian vessel was pursued for three full days in the Black Sea before being able to take refuge in the Samastro sound, where it waited for four days before the corsairs lost patience and abandoned the chase.[53] The Signoria of Venice summoned the Captain General of the Gulf (*ie*, the Adriatic) and placed him in charge of a fleet bound for the Levant, ordering him to proceed to the Aegean where 'a great number of Turkish ships contaminated the Euboea straits'. Intelligence had made it clear that the Turks had a number of vessels operating in the area, and the admiral was ordered to sweep them from the seas and re-establish the security 'so essential for the merchants'. He was also directed to send Captain Silvestro Morosini to attack the Turks based around Modon, and from Negroponte to Thessalonika. Venetian merchant ships returning from Constantinople were to be escorted safely home.[54] The fleet consisted of between six and ten well-armed galleys, each carrying fifty swordsmen and fifty cross-bowmen. Watchtowers, observation posts, and spies were told to be vigilant, although the distances involved complicated the receipt and despatch of orders. Venetian representatives and colonial officials were ordered to maintain their ships in a state of readiness. On Crete, a place of primary importance, four additional galleys were fitted out: two joined the Captain General's fleet, one was despatched to Euboea, and the fourth was retained to patrol north of the island and to defend Candia.[55]

As storm clouds menaced the horizon Venice liberally spent her riches on galleys – fast and relatively light vessels – and cogs of the kind which could be seen travelling between Beirut and Alexandria carrying cotton. The latter were huge ships with three decks and immense castles on poop and prow. Each could carry between 100 and 150 armed men, and carried a number of bombards to frighten off or crush the opposition. In 1406 workers in Venice's arsenal laboured for four months in order to build two cogs, each carrying four bombards – of 600 paces range – and 150 soldiers, doctors, surgeons, and barbers.[56]

Venice saw her possessions in the Aegean ravished and depopulated, whilst both land and sea became hazardous. Representatives in the Peleponnese and on Coron, Modon, and even Crete were not free from the threat of raiding. Protecting such an extensive and isolated island empire demanded special measures. Crete, in particular, suffered from raids mounted by the Asapi, a kind of Ottoman warrior, and as early as 1398 its governor was obliged to prepare a galley to be sent *ad damnum dictorum Turcorum et Asaporum*. He also warned *et possunt esse Asapi tam Christiani quam Turce et alia nationis*.[57] On Coron the harvests were brought into the fortress to safeguard them, whilst on Tinos and Mykonos the senate was forced to admit that it would be impossible to levy taxes on domestic animals as the bulk of them had been carried off by the Turks.[58]

In 1470 the Venetian garrison on Negroponte was attacked by an enemy force which had disembarked from 300 enemy ships. After putting up a stubborn resistance they were overwhelmed by a second assault. Thousands of Greeks were sold into slavery, whilst all Latins on the island were massacred on the spot. Kaffa, the Genoese base in the Black Sea, fell just five years later. The only Christians remaining in the Levant thereafter were on the larger islands of Rhodes, Cyprus, Chios, and Crete.

Rhodes: Last Stronghold of the Christians

The Knights Hospitaller of the military order of Saint John of Jerusalem had been evicted from the Holy Land in 1291, but in 1310, after a siege lasting two years, they had seized the island of Rhodes from the Turks. Their victory was aided by a Genoese corsair, Vignolo de Vignoli, and Rhodes soon established itself as something of a pirate's haven, from which soldiers of the faith issued forth to aid other Christians in their struggle against the Ottomans. Rhodes itself remained in a state of perpetual alarm:

> Nobody dared to tend the land or to live very far from the cities and castles. The soil, rich and fertile, could have produced all kinds of fruit but the fear of the terrible enemy meant it lay fallow. One night rumours that a huge Turkish fleet was not far off rang through the streets. The entire population took to their arms.[59]

It was hoped that God, the saints, and the angels would bestow protection. At Patmos, which also belonged to the Knights, the population affected not to fear the Turks at all, as they had John the Evangelist to watch over them, as he had for centuries. Tradition had it that whoever attacked or maltreated them would be unable to quit the island unwounded. A story was even told about a servant of the Hospitallers on Rhodes who was actually an enemy passing himself off as a Christian in order to spy on them. It was said that when he reached out and touched a venerated holy relic, the skeletal hand of some saint, 'the traitor was grabbed by the saint, who wouldn't let go; the traitor recognised his crime and his sin'.[60]

The Hospitallers waged a constant war against the Turks which was 'as violent as it was just'. They had some fifteen huge dogs which roamed free within two or three miles of the fortress on Rhodes. If these happened upon Turks they would career back to the fortress, raising the alarm; but if they chanced upon Christians they would welcome them and escort them on their way.[61]

The Knights also maintained garrisons on islands much closer to the Anatolian coast: at Simi, where 'the inhabitants are of such bad disposition that they are as bad as the Turks, even refusing to buy back slaves that are clearly from Simi itself'; at Tilos, where 'the harvest is kept underground in caverns to avoid it falling into Turkish hands'; and at Astipalia, Khalki, and Kos. They even established fifty knights and a hundred soldiers in the fortress of Saint Paul at Bodrum, on the mainland opposite Kos, and these set out on daily expeditions to take prisoners. In addition they hired and equipped Catalan, Castilian, and Provencal ships, which mounted lengthy expeditions against the Turks:

> We climbed aboard a Basque or Spanish ship full of soldiers, cannon and other weapons. The Grand Master of Rhodes had also supplied

several of his knights and his nephew the Grand Prior of Puglia. The ship mounted a raid against the Turks. The captain sought them out for several days, changing course this way and that and making a number of detours.[62]

Whilst the Pope ineffectually preached crusades in a virtual vacuum, unheeded by the kings, princes, and magnates of the west, the Christians of the east marshalled their forces to fight the Turks. The corsairs of Rhodes and the Knights of Saint John of Jerusalem were waging a very real war of survival. After the fall of Constantinople in 1453 they were all that stood between Christian Europe and the Turks.

However, it wouldn't be true to say that defending Christianity was the primary motivation of every Latin found in the Levant. This was particularly true of the Christian corsairs found in Venetian territory – notably at Coron and Modon, as well as on Crete and throughout the Morea. They recruited local fishermen, sailors, and villagers to sail and fight with them, but many Greeks refused to serve on the Venetian galleys and made their escape. Many fled to Turkish territory and later entered service with the Catalans, who would employ any kind of outlaw, be he a rebel or a thief.

The Hospitallers themselves remained constantly on their guard against the Ottomans and relied upon all kinds of alliances, compromises, and agreements to rally as much support as possible. Inevitably, they could not afford to be too selective. Their harbouring of pirates, however, was considered a threat to the fragile peace treaties that existed between the Christian powers and the Turks. The Venetians, who were utterly dependent on such treaties if they wanted their trade to prosper, eventually grew impatient and threatened the Knights with reprisals. In 1437, and again in 1454, the Grand Master was forced to agree that he would banish the corsairs from his territory. But in reality nothing was done, by him or by his successors.

A mere two weeks after the fall of Constantinople, Sultan Mehmed II demanded that the Knights of Rhodes pay him tribute. This attempt at intimidation, however, met with no success. The Knights merely played for time. Pierre d'Aubusson, elected Grand Master in 1476, set about strengthening the island's defences to such good effect that a Turkish expeditionary force of 100,000 men commanded by the renegade Manuel Palaeologus – a descendant of the Byzantine emperors – was utterly defeated on 28 April 1480. Further attacks were bravely met by the Knights, while the island's inhabitants, Greek and Jewish women, and those belonging to holy orders, tended the wounded and repaired breaches in the walls. On 27 July the Turks re-embarked and sailed away, and on their way back to Constantinople were attacked by a Catalan squadron, losing a number of ships and men.

For forty more years the Hospitallers maintained their hold on the island of Rhodes, despite ever stronger attacks by the Ottomans and an ever dwindling supply of aid from the west. It was in 1520, however, that the Grand Master of the Order, Philippe de Villiers de l'Isle-Adam, got wind of preparations being in hand for the most serious attack to date, and called upon Martinengo – one of the greatest specialists in siege warfare – to come to his aid. However, Martinengo was based on Crete, and the Venetians ordered him not to abandon his post; when he subsequently did, the Venetians confiscated his goods. The Turkish threat finally materialised on 24 June 1522, when 200,000 soldiers, including 18,000 Janissaries and 60,000 pioneers, launched their attack. For six months the siege was prosecuted by means of cannonades, sapping, and mining. Then, on 1 January 1523, Sultan Suleiman, his troops having suffered heavy casualties, agreed terms for the surrender of Rhodes. All the Knights and 5,000 of the island's other inhabitants were allowed to leave, the majority heading for Candia on Crete.[63]

Egypt Conquered

In the year 1480 the Sultan launched thousands of his warriors against southern Italy. They seized Otranto and destroyed it almost completely, massacring the population, razing churches, and setting fire to palaces. But the raid, which had been well planned, and executed with almost total surprise, was not followed up by any long-lasting conquest. True, it sent shock waves all the way to Rome and seemed to confirm every Christian's worst fears. But, attacked by resolute forces, the Janissaries gathered their survivors together, embarked their wounded, and sailed away. For the Sultan, his commanders, and his viziers, the operation was something of a lesson. Rather than risking their forces on grandiose expeditions in the east, they felt that now was the time to extend their empire westwards. The first step along this road might be to flush Christian merchants out of Cairo and Beirut.

For several centuries the Mamluks of Egypt and Syria had been subjected to attacks by the Franks. This was in part due to their weakness which, in turn, was brought about by internal dissension and faction fighting. The idea of launching a new crusade still captivated a number of Christian potentates, who foolishly believed they could seize and hold Egypt. In 1365 Pierre de Lusignan, king of Cyprus, seized Alexandria with a mighty army. His troops pillaged the town for a week before the bulk of them deserted, abandoning the king and leaving him with just a handful of loyal followers. Even so, the Cypriots continued to be mesmerised by the idea and, despite reprimands from Venice, mounted periodic raids.

Along the Egyptian and Syrian coastline, and even within the Nile delta, fear of Frankish pirates haunted villagers and fishermen. The slightest rumour usually led to panic and widespread suspicion of strangers. Men openly discussed the notorious exploits of these Christian pirates who swarmed over the seas 'daily committing crimes, robbing and kidnapping whosoever they came across. They attack Moorish ships and Moors on the coast, killing whoever resists.'[64]

The Christians, especially, the Venetians, despatched their galleys to Alexandria and Beirut in order to load them with spices and cotton. The captains of such ships, along with the merchants they carried, sometimes behaved like true pirates. They seized ships, sometimes within the harbours themselves, kidnapped unfortunates, and stole any merchandise they could get their hands on. As a result, during the winter of 1381–2 Genoese and Venetian merchants were arrested, their goods confiscated, and debts they were owed cancelled. Genoa despatched an emissary on the first eastward-bound ship, and in May 1383 an ambassador was sent out escorted by Admiral Pietro Piccono. All was in vain, and confusion prevailed. Only armed Christians, prepared for a fight, dared to set foot ashore. Once there, the slightest misunderstanding could lead to an outbreak of violence. By way of reprisal, or perhaps as a precaution, the governor of Alexandria seized all the Christians he could lay his hands on. The infuriated Franks, whether soldiers, sailors, or merchants, attacked Tineh in retaliation, taking some hundreds of its inhabitants prisoner. These were dragged to Damietta and held hostage until their families could bail them out. It was certainly a faster way to make money than trading. A Genoese squadron commanded by Niccolo Maruffo, at least ten galleys strong, sacked Sidon in Syria but failed, on two separate occasions, to take Beirut.[65]

The Catalans, ostensibly in Alexandria to sell cloth, also indulged in piracy. Chased out in 1424, they returned after the treaty of 1432 and, deaf to calls for peace and order, carried on attacking Muslim vessels off Egypt and Syria. One owner of a merchant ship from Barcelona actually had an Egyptian galley boarded and seized its crew. The Sultan of Cairo responded by having the ship's goods seized and confiscated all the goods in the Catalan warehouse in Cairo. In total it cost the Catalans 90,000 ducats.[66]

Suspicion was followed by conflict, conflict by reprisal. Christians, Venetians, Genoese, and men from Languedoc, however well intentioned, were roughly handled. The inhabitants of Montpellier even protested their case to the king of France:

> The merchants and traders of the town have suffered considerable loss in Alexandria, in which aforementioned town they, as well as those from other regions, have been killed or imprisoned in Alexandria in horrible and inhuman prisons. From thence they have been led to Cairo and have suffered much distress on account of the Saracens, who have stripped them of all they have, costing some 40,000 francs in all.[67]

The king, Charles VII, managed to restore peace. Jean de Village, chancellor to Jacques Coeur, was sent as part of a sumptuous French embassy in 1447 and obtained authorisation for the French to visit Mamluk ports. Sultan Said Jakmak (1438–53) received the officials well, showering them with gifts: balm, silver plate, Chinese porcelain, spices, almonds, and sugar. Village mediated a treaty between the Sultan and the Knights of Rhodes and also managed to lift the ban on Venetians which had been imposed a few years earlier.

However, profit was not as easy to come by as it had previously been. Well before the Portuguese discovery of a passage to India, the Mamluk economy had been in steady decline. Terrible epidemics (in 1468 a plague is supposed to have carried off 200,000 victims), the neglect of arable land, the sudden and capricious devaluation of the Egyptian dinar, and clumsy intervention by the Egyptian state had all taken their toll. Financial officials, securely installed in Red Sea ports, checked cargoes and prices, even frisking Arab merchants to check whether or not they were concealing merchandise on their persons. For Muslim and Christian merchants, sailors, and travellers, the journey from Alexandria to Cairo was an adventure bestrewn with hurdles and, at best, could waste both time and money. 'The officials gnawed at our bones, ceaselessly harassing us and tormenting us. Every hour, if not more frequently, new ones would arrive and put us through the same ordeal.'[68] Suffering from corruption, anarchy, and the cumbersome weight of its own state apparatus, Egypt was becoming more and more restrictive and less and less respected.

Everything clearly demonstrated the weakness of Egypt's industry and the paucity of its economy, a situation aggravated by incompetent officials becoming increasingly greedy and tyrannical. It was said that the Sultan let them grow fat at the expense of his treasury. His Mamluk troops preserved a fragile peace on the coast and in the Nile delta but Bedouin tribesmen from upper Egypt openly attacked even escorted caravans.[69] Few dared venture out from Alexandria or Cairo or travel by land or by sea without a strong escort of horsemen. These latter were garrisoned at Tineh, a fortress originally constructed by Sultan Baibars (1260–77) on the eastern side of the delta.[70]

Added to this, war between the Ottomans and Mamluks was inevitable. The Turks, having vanquished the Christians at Constantinople, indulged themselves in planning grand designs and demonstrating their power. After seizing Negroponte from the Venetians in 1470 they sent a squadron of some twenty or thirty ships into Alexandria and feted their triumph with salvoes of artillery, dancing, and warlike songs. Christians and Egyptians alike were intimidated.[71]

The Ottoman Sultan Selim I desired war. He accused the Egyptians of siding with his enemies the Persians by supplying them with arms and allowing their troops free passage through Egyptian territory in upper Mesopotamia. The Turks even contested Egypt's right to govern Medina and Mecca.[72]

The Sultan of Egypt, Kansuh, responded by marching out of Cairo on 17 May 1516 at the head of a vast army. The troops, preceded by three magnificent war-elephants, marched into Syria. Selim's troops were neither as numerous nor as well versed in the arts of war as the Mamluks, for the latter's exploits were legendary throughout the east. Yet he could call upon artillery infinitely more powerful than anything the Egyptians had – 800 pieces, of which 150 were of substantial calibre, served by veteran gunners. The two armies clashed north of Aleppo at the battle of Marj Dabik, fought on 23 August, and Selim triumphed. His victory owed much to the defection of the Mamluk governor of Aleppo, Khairbak. Kansuh died that evening, some say of apoplexy. The Mamluks were paralysed and the state, once so well organised, collapsed into chaos. Cairo had to wait forty days before confirmation of the disaster arrived. A new Sultan – Tumanbey, formerly secretary of state – wasn't appointed until early October, but on taking power he threw himself into the task of rallying the army and appointing new commanders and new governors. He even set about casting cannon but had difficulty finding sufficient gunners, the Mamluks themselves refusing to serve such dishonourable weapons. Slaves and former slaves were quickly pressed into service.

As Selim marched into Egypt each battle seemed to be decided by an artillery duel. The Ottomans, of course, had the upper hand, and some Mamluk emirs defected. On 23 January 1517 the Janissaries broke into Raidaniyah, the last defence before Cairo, and then pushed their way into the capital, fighting through the streets. They pillaged and burnt the place for three whole days. Tumanbey fled into the desert and managed to gather one last army about his standard. Selim, whose envoys were all brutally massacred, surrounded the Egyptians and in the ensuing battle 3–4,000 were slaughtered and sixty emirs captured and beheaded. Tumanbey sought shelter with an Arab chieftain, but was betrayed by him and delivered up to Selim. He was hung on 13 April 1517.

Now complete master of Egypt, the Ottoman Sultan spent several months in his new territory. He only departed for Asia in September, leaving Khairbak – the traitor from Aleppo – and several other Mamluks to govern in his name. Syria, with the exception of Aleppo, was given to Mamluk Djanbirdi, the man who had betrayed Tumanbey.

Selim's death in 1520, and the accession of Suleiman I, was followed by considerable disorder, and a number of revolts broke out in Egypt. Grand Vizier Ibrahim, 'the handsome Greek', husband of Suleiman's sister, reimposed order. On 25 March 1525 he entered Cairo at the head of a beautifully equipped army and was acclaimed by the population. He overhauled the country's administration and army, putting an end (for the time being) to Mamluk domination and imposing Ottoman rule through a *beylerbey* appointed by Constantinople. Meanwhile, all the leading families of the new Ottoman province sought to improve their position by marrying into Ottoman families.

Chapter II

The Barbarossas and the Turks

Even before Cairo fell to the Ottomans, Aroudj, the eldest of the Barbarossa brothers, had seized Algiers. The Turkish conquest of the Maghreb was as brutal, and as bloody, as the earlier Arab conquest. It was accomplished not by large armies, nor by set-piece battles or sieges of forts or castles, but rather by relentless corsair raids followed up by waves of veteran soldiers, amongst whom the Janissaries took pride of place.

The commanders of these corsairs had learnt their trade in the eastern Mediterranean before turning their attention to Africa, and had fought against the Knights of Rhodes and the Venetians in the Aegean. Their warships and galleys were initially produced in the arsenals of Anatolia or Istanbul. They were crewed by hardy seamen, the majority of whom were originally from either the Balkans – especially Albania – or from former Genoese or Venetian possessions. Some were renegades in the true sense of the word, while others had been seized from their families when infants.

The father of the Barbarossa brothers was Jacob, an Albanian who had been taken prisoner on Lesbos and had converted to Islam. He had four children: Aroudj (or Ouich), Elias, Isaak, and Kheir ed-Din ('the pious', or 'the fruit of Islam'), who were subsequently known as the Barbarossas on account of Aroudj's red beard. All four became sailors and corsairs. Elias was killed in a combat off Crete, whilst Aroudj was captured by the Knights of Rhodes. Legend has it that he escaped and fled to Egypt on a barque. In reality, however, the governor of Aladia paid his ransom and Grand Master Pierre d'Aubusson had released him. He resurfaced on

Lesbos, commanding a galley, and soon joined forces with Isaak and Kheir ed-Din, helping to lead dozens of ships as they headed west.

Aroudj, Algiers and Tlemcen

Diego de Haedo records the commencement of Aroudj's road to notoriety thus:

> Soon after his departure from Istanbul, he encountered some Christian sailors and soldiers. He ambushed them but soon recognised them to be former fellow-corsairs. He persuaded them that it would be beneficial if they joined forces with him, bringing their galliot with them, for there was much plunder to be had from Christian states. Seduced by thoughts of great profit, they joined him on an expedition to Tunis. As he sailed by Lesbos, he learnt that his father had died; taking his two young brothers with him, who were both miserable, he asked nothing more than that they join him in his enterprise.[1]

In 1502 or 1503 he, Kheir ed-Din, and Isaak appeared off Djerba. Few knew where they had come from or what they were; fewer still could guess that they would become renowned warriors and captains. They initially waged a hazardous form of warfare at the head of a small band of loyal followers, but soon they were taken into the service of the Maghreb princes, for whom they seized slaves, ships, and merchandise. As their prestige increased they also became active in politics, playing upon the rivalries of princes, backing pretenders, or siding with one faction against another. Then everything changed.

The brothers had always worked hand in hand with the Turks, sending reports back to the Sultan – which exaggerated their own role – and showering him with gifts. In return they received his assistance – possibly galleys, certainly men. Consequently at some point between 1518 and 1520 they and some of their faithful companions found themselves at the head of a force of 2,000 Janissaries. These redoubtable warriors, whom the men of Algiers and Tlemcen accused of smoking hashish and drinking *maslach*, had been sent by Selim to wage war on the Moors. 'Barbarossa had more than 1,000 Turks under his direct control and had acquired wealth and riches,' records Haedo. 'He thought, like the Spanish who own mines in the Indies, only of acquiring more.'[2] His troops lived off the populace, spreading terror throughout the land through their plundering and killing sprees. However costly and bloody they might have been, the victories won by the Barbarossa brothers, and their seizure of power in the North African kingdoms, were nothing short of a victory for the Ottoman empire. As corsair captains they never ceased to refer to themselves as officers of the Sultan, responsible to Istanbul, even whilst commanding personal forces more than capable of overwhelming the king of Spain's armies and fleets. In short they were governors of Ottoman provinces, and admirals of the Sultan's fleets.

Now master of the arsenals at Djerba, and commander of an ever-expanding fleet, Aroudj and his younger brother Kheir ed-Din took service with the king of Tunis.[3] Their ships and galleys were based at La Goulette, where they were supplied with all their needs and their crews were brought up to strength. However, it is not clear whether the brothers were allies or faithful servants of the Tunisian king or whether they ruled the city by proxy, receiving men, money, and orders from Istanbul. Either way, they set about the conquest of the neighbouring principalities, executing those who dared to resist. It was this pro-longed campaign in North Africa, rather than their raiding at sea, which earned the Barbarossas their reputation as great warriors, as cruel as they were courageous.

But their piracy continued unabated too. In the summer of 1504, off the Maremme coast, they seized two Papal galleys and the *Cavalleria*, a Spanish ship. The latter, bound for Naples, was carrying 300 soldiers and sixty Aragonese nobles:

> Some said that the ship's captain, a slave, scuttled his ship and allowed it to be flooded so that it could be treasonably delivered up to the corsairs. Some older Turks and the renegades declared, however, that the ship had suffered badly in the storm, and that it was leaking badly; the soldiers indeed couldn't leave the pumps for a moment, or they should perish. This made fighting impossible and it was cruelly necessary to surrender.[4]

Aroudj also seized Djidjelli without too many problems. He then arrived before Bougie in August 1512, having come to the aid of its king, who had been chased out two years earlier by the Spanish and had been a refugee in the mountains ever since. Aroudj's forces – twelve galliots, numerous pieces of artillery, and a thousand Turks – joined forces with 3,000 of the king's soldiers. Eight days of bombardment followed. The tower, erected by Pedro Navarro, had been virtually reduced to rubble by this onslaught when a Christian roundshot suddenly took off Barbarossa's left arm. He collapsed and his army lost courage. A second assault failed in 1514, the rebuilt tower proving too much of an obstacle. The arrival of Spanish reinforcements, in the form of five ships commanded by Martin de Renteria, temporarily put paid to any further attacks. Cara Hassan, one of Barbarossa's companions who had served at his side for many years, had meanwhile deserted and installed himself in Cherchell, where he was warmly supported by the local Moors and by Muslim refugees from Granada, Valencia, and Aragon. Barbarossa waited for Hassan's absence from the town, then seized it, obtained its submission, and beheaded Hassan upon his return.

King Selim Eutemi cordially received Barbarossa in Algiers in 1516, and the population accorded his troops a triumphal entry. However, more and more Janissaries continued to arrive, and just a few weeks after the sumptuous celebration Aroudj seized the palace and the city. He had Selim murdered in his sauna. His widow, Zephira, killed herself rather than submit, and her companions were tortured to death. The Janissaries and corsairs sacked the city thoroughly: the women were raped, and those who resisted were killed. Houses and shops were pillaged. Nothing was done to end the carnage. Instead, like a true tyrant seeing plots against him everywhere, Barbarossa methodically sought out those who opposed him and executed them in public places. Algiers was his.[5]

In 1512 the Beni Zyane, lords of Tlemcen, sought an alliance with the king of Aragon in order to counter the threat of attack by the kings of Tunis and Fez. The terms of the alliance included the liberation of Christian slaves, whilst the Aragonese king received twenty-two Arab horses, a young lion, and a golden hen with twenty-six chicks fashioned from the same metal. However, the death of Tlemcen's ruler Bou Sian (Abuter) towards the end of 1516 plunged the state into a grave succession crisis. Aroudj seized his chance.

He began by securing his hold on Algiers. Some twenty suspected ringleaders of a rebel faction were arrested one Thursday as they came out of the mosque, and were swiftly executed. Their heads and corpses were then exposed on the city walls before being thrown onto a rubbish dump. Only then, with his rear secure, did he feel strong enough to sally forth on campaign. He gathered an immense host about him, consisting of more than a thousand Turks and Janissaries (many of them Albanian), plus tribesmen from the interior following the banners of their chieftains, and Moriscos from Spain. In the summer of 1517 he scored a decisive victory over the king of Tlemcen in the Chelif valley and took the port of Tenes. Between Tenes and Oran his army defeated the royal troops again. The king himself sought refuge behind the walls of Tlemcen but was set upon by the population and killed, the people – having heard what had happened at Algiers – being determined to welcome the conqueror. The city's governors, and the king's advisors and officers, were carried through the streets, insulted and abused, and delivered to the executioners. Those who were not beheaded were drowned. None were spared. Those who had had a presentiment of what was to come had already fled to Oran, where the Spanish governor, the Marquis of Comares, had formed an alliance with Abou Hammon, nephew of the late king of Tlemcen.

Meanwhile Barbarossa showered the inhabitants of Tlemcen with his bounty. Seizing the king's treasure – and, as was his wont, having the king's seven sons hung from the ramparts – he ordered those who had pillaged the palace to return what they had stolen. He imposed heavy tributes on the city's Moors, rewarded his supporters, and had the city walls, and those of the casbah, repaired.[6]

For the Spaniards and their Moorish allies were on the warpath. Their forces were advancing towards the fortress of Beni Rached, which was held by Aroudj's brother Isaak. He had gathered about him a band of adventurers from Greece and Albania, but was, in the event, overwhelmed by an uprising within the fort. The Moors had been ceaselessly provoked by the garrison and took the opportunity to kill every corsair they could lay hands on.

Abou Hammon and the commander of the Spanish forces, Martin de Agote, soon arrived before Tlemcen. Aroudj had meanwhile almost exhausted his resources in trying to maintain his hold on a city which, though it had initially welcomed him, had grown tired of his yoke and was determined not to be governed by the Turks. He consequently fled in May 1518: 'He took advantage of a dark night to save himself from the wrath of the inhabitants, escaping with his Turks and Andalusians. He took as much treasure with him as he could manage, making great speed in the direction of Algiers.'

However, twenty-five miles from that place, close to Debbou and the Huexda river, he was intercepted by the Spanish and killed. His head was exposed on the great gate at Oran before being taken down and shown to tribal chiefs, whilst his body was nailed to the walls of Tlemcen, illuminated by four burning torches. Spain celebrated as though waking from a nightmare: festivals, cavalcades, and processions followed one after the other. The captain who had struck the first blow on Aroudj, Fernandez de la Plaza, was ennobled at once, his coat of arms showing the corsair's head, scimitar, and banner. Barbarossa's cape was given to the monastery of Saint Jerome at Cordoba.[7]

The Other Barbarossa: Kheir ed-Din, Lord of the Sea

Of the four Barbarossa brothers, Kheir ed-Din was the only one remaining. He outlived his elder brother by twenty-eight years, and it is largely because of him that the name Barbarossa achieved its legendary status. For many writers that name was synonymous with exploits on the high seas; it was feared everywhere and was everywhere victorious. In honour of his brother's memory he dyed his beard and hair with henna. He was a talented captain and was responsible for inflicting a crushing defeat on the forces of Charles of Spain beneath the walls of Algiers. Charles had gathered an expeditionary force of 5,000 men and a fleet of thirty ships, eight galleys, and several brigantines at Naples. This force, commanded by Hugo de Moncade, a Knight of Malta, managed to successfully disembark, but the fleet was decimated by a sudden storm and the army was almost overwhelmed by determined assaults mounted by the Turks, Moors, and local tribesmen. Christian casualties were heavy, including large numbers killed and captured, and Moncade only eventually got away, on 20 August 1518, with a dozen ships and a handful of men in a pitiful condition.[8]

Kheir ed-Din crowned his victory by breaking what power remained to the Moors. He obtained reinforcements – 2,000 Janissaries – from Sultan Selim and campaigned remorselessly in Kabylie. It was a war of conquest for the Turks, but was waged in a singularly cruel fashion.

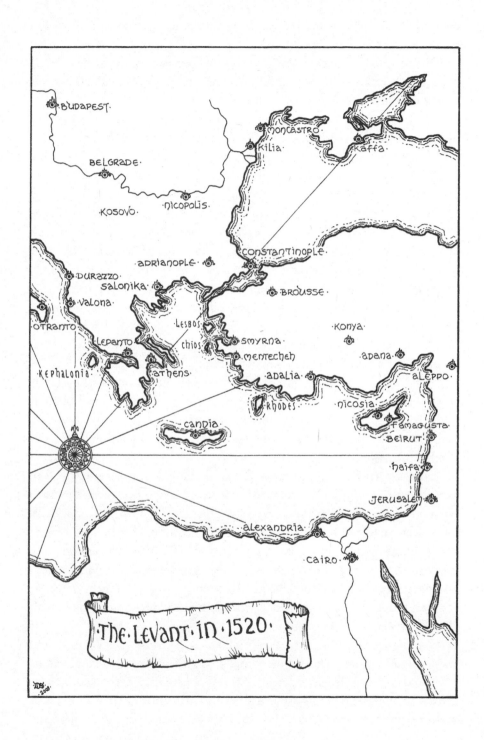

·THE·LEVANT·IN·1520·

Persecutions of Moors and Jews were accompanied by mass executions of notables and tribal chieftains.

This second Barbarossa was much better known as a pirate than his elder brother had been. Whilst a veritable lord of the sea, attacking not just individual ships but whole fleets, he also governed a state which largely lived off the spoils of naval warfare. Since 1514, whilst his brother had been unsuccessfully besieging Bougie, he had been seizing Tunisian ports, establishing arsenals, and repairing walls. He made Algiers his capital, his centre for re-armament and recruitment, and a market for the sale of booty and slaves. He trusted only those who had faithfully served him for some time. These were from the east; some were born as Muslims, while others, from Georgia, Crete, and Albania, were recent converts. Whatever their origins these became the city's new aristocracy. Their subjects were less fortunate, being faced with hefty contributions, harassment, and the arbitrary confiscation of wealth and property.

Barbarossa and his corsair captains attacked Sicily and the coasts of Italy, and in 1519, with twenty-five galleys, they cruised off Provence, between Toulon and Hyeres. They took Collo in Africa in 1521, pushed inland as far as Constantine the same year, and seized Bône in 1522.

On 21 May 1529 the formidable Spanish fort of the Peñon, on the islands commanding the approaches to Algiers, finally surrendered to him. For fourteen years it had held out against assault after assault, but had succumbed in the end to a devastating artillery bombardment. The victorious Barbarossa executed the fort's governor, Martin de Vegas, before his Janissaries. Other Spaniards who survived the battle were employed in rebuilding the minaret of the Great Mosque, which had been damaged by artillery fire. The Turks achieved a second great victory the same year, when they defeated a fleet commanded by Portundo – a Basque knight and general-in-chief of Spanish galleys – off Formentera on Majorca. Barbarossa captured seven galleys and brought back Portundo's son and all the galley captains to Algiers as captives. A few months later he accused them of taking part in a plot against his person and had them sliced to pieces with knives.[9]

Now, however, a leader emerged who would thwart the corsairs and the Turks of Algiers. Determined, and as fortunate as he was audacious, he would inflict a decisive defeat upon his enemies. Born in 1466 to an illustrious Genoese family in Oneglia, on the Ligurian coast, his name was Andrea Doria. By 1529 he was already a renowned captain, celebrated

68

for beating off corsair raids against the villages of the Italian coast. He had been taken into Papal service, and assisted the king of Naples in his attempts to defend his kingdom against the piratical scourge. Between 1503 and 1506 he was back in Genoese service, undertaking to recapture Corsica from rebel forces. Ten years later, in command of a fleet in which his own family and close supporters played a dominant role, he took an active role in attempts to sweep the Turks from the Mediterranean. In 1519 he achieved a striking success off the island of Pianosa, to the south of Elba, defeating a Turkish fleet which had been raiding Provence.

Francis I made him captain general of his navy during France's war with Charles V. In 1528, however, he refused to participate in a French siege of Naples, sending his cousin Filippino in his stead. Rumour had it that he was dissatisfied with the honours bestowed upon him, whilst others declared that he was opposed to French policy towards his native Genoa. Either way, Doria went over to Charles V's service, even returning his Order of Saint-Michel to Francis. Charles V declared him his 'General of the Seas' and showered him with honours, making him Marquis of Tursi – and later, in 1532, Prince of Melfi – and a knight of the Order of the Golden Fleece. Upon his return to Genoa he was hailed as a hero but was quickly sent to support imperial troops as they invaded Provence. He achieved his status as a hero and champion of the Christian faith by his relentless war against the Turks. Constantly at the head of his ships, he led his fleets against the African coast.[10] His vessels, many of which were equipped with twenty or more cannon, were crewed by oarsmen who were either criminals or volunteers (*buonavoglia*) from Genoa, Greece, and Dalmatia.[11] Whatever their origin, they were barred from blasphemy.

In 1531 Doria's men landed at Cherchell. Apparently 'Christian prisoners themselves told me that they had written to the prince [Doria] and informed him that it would be easy to free them and to demolish the mole which has only just been begun'.[12] The attackers seized a number of galleys moored in the port and liberated a few hundred slaves. However, shortly after this successful expedition he ceased troubling the Barbary coast and switched his attention to harassing the Turks further east. He took a number of fortified places, defeating the Sultan's garrisons and fleets along the Dalmatian and Albanian coast as well as on Coron and Modon.

Meanwhile Sultan Suleiman, who had succeeded Selim in 1520, had signed a peace treaty with Emperor Charles V in 1530 in order to gather his forces to deal with a threat from Persia. He summoned Kheir ed-Din and despatched him, with a strong fleet, to subjugate rebellious Syria. Barbarossa had achieved the status of statesman by this time, residing in his palace of Aya Sofia whilst in Istanbul, and using his considerable power to influence those around him. He was an ally of Grand Vizier Ibrahim and his supporter, the sultana Gülbahar, a former Circassian slave. This faction bickered with an influential group led by the chief eunuch, Amber Agha, and the sultana Roxane, herself a former slave. Born into the family of a priest on the banks of the Dnieper, she had been kidnapped as a child and sold at auction.[13]

Italy Threatened, 1530–5

Barbarossa was no longer acting as a corsair, mounting raids and punitive expeditions. Instead his ambition had launched him beyond the Tyrrhenian Sea and his major concern revolved around securing the Maghreb kingdoms. He was, of course, an officer of the Sultan, and directly under his orders, and he was an Ottoman enforcer, despatched to overcome rebellion, defeat enemies in the Balkans, or fight the Christians in the Mediterranean. He organised and commanded fleets and armies and he formed or broke alliances.

As lieutenant-general of the Ottoman navy, receiving a pension of 2,000 ducats, he oversaw the building of an entirely new fleet – one better than any the Turks had previously launched. Built with wood from Anatolia, iron from Bulgaria, hemp from the Crimea and Greece, oakum from Macedonia, and tallow from Thrace, this fleet was constructed by talented artisans. Heavily armed galleys – each with three decks, and with their hulls protected by sheets of lead – were produced by the dozen. On 21 June 1534 Barbarossa's own magnificent fleet of forty such galleys weighed anchor and sailed forth. His mission was, it was said, inspired by Grand Vizier Ibrahim's desire to capture Giulia da Gonzaga, widow of Vespasian Colonna, lord of Fondi, and carry her off for his harem. This beauty, much celebrated among western magnates, had gathered a circle of philosophers, poets, and artists about herself at Fondi, and it was there that Barbarossa launched his initial assault.

Legend has it that Giulia escaped miraculously, half naked. Truth is rather more prosaic – sources show that she was in fact at Sperlonga, not Fondi, on the night of the attack. She hastily fled from the castle there, seeking refuge in the night. Much later a nineteenth-century engraving would show her mounted on a black horse at the head of a band of soldiers, dressed in white and illuminated by the glow of fires, sword in hand. A strange image indeed of a woman who would end her days in a Roman convent.[14] Twenty thousand Janissaries had, however, landed near Terracina and had attacked Fondi, desecrating churches and the Colonna tomb and carrying off women and children.

Upon his return to Algiers, after this long absence, Barbarossa was hailed as a hero. His attention, however, now turned back to African affairs, and in particular the long-desired conquest of Tunis. In January 1533 the Tunisian king, Moulay Abou Abdallah, a life-long enemy of the Turks, died, setting in motion a grave dynastic crisis. Despite his youth – a mere twenty-one – the king's youngest son, Moulay Hassan, had all his brothers assassinated and their heads paraded through the streets. Just one, Rachid, escaped, and he quickly sought out Barbarossa. The latter's Janissaries, along with Spanish renegades, seized Bizerte and La Goulette before finally capturing the casbah at Tunis on 28 November 1534. The struggle had been brutal, thousands had died. Two hundred captives had even been hung from the walls of La Goulette.

Moulay Hassan now called upon the Italians and Spanish for help. Charles V responded, sending 25,000 men and a 400-ship fleet commanded by Ferdinand of Toledo, the Duke of Alba. The fleet left Barcelona on 31 May 1535 and was joined by twelve Papal galleys and a huge carrack belonging to the Knights of Malta before anchoring beneath the walls of La Goulette on 15 June. Charles V ordered an assault to take place on 14 July, and La Goulette fell to the Christians before Barbarossa could carry out his threat to have 20,000 Christian slaves within the city murdered.

A hard-fought battle, in which the Spanish were victorious, followed on the plains, and the Emperor, accompanied by Moulay Hassan, was able to enter Tunis on 6 August. Hassan recognised that he was Charles' vassal and agreed to the release of Christian slaves, to respect the Catholic faith, to grant licenses for trade to Spanish merchants, and to send an annual tribute of 12,000 gold pieces, twelve falcons, and six 'Moorish' horses.[15]

For a time it was believed that Barbarossa had perished in the fighting, just as his brother had been killed in 1518. There were consequently joyous celebrations, processions, and devout services of thanksgiving. Many towns presented dramatic spectacles – many in rather poor taste – or plays, ballets, and dances. On Majorca a condemned criminal was dressed up in Turkish attire, complete with turban and red beard, and was beheaded in a public square. However, Kheir ed-Din had not died. He had fled the field of battle accompanied by a handful of loyal followers, and galloped for Bône. Very much alive, he took to the offensive in 1535 and was soon bombarding Mahon on Majorca, which he sacked, carrying off its inhabitants and selling them in the markets of Algiers.

The Great Game: The French Alliance

Three years later, in 1538, Francis I, king of France, sided with the Turks. A French squadron, commanded by Baron Saint-Blancard, arrived in Tunis looking for Barbarossa. From there it sailed to the Balkans where, finding him, it requested his assistance and offered to wage war alongside him. During the winter of 1543–4 this Turkish fleet established itself in the port and city of Toulon. Then, accompanied by the French vessels, the Turks cruised all along the Italian coast, pausing to pillage, burn, and destroy fortifications and towns, taking hundreds, even thousands, of prisoners. This lamentable campaign ended at Istanbul, where Antoine Escalin des Aimars, Admiral of France and Baron of La Garde, otherwise known as Le Paulin ('the foal'), signed further agreements with the Turks.

These events created a storm of protest at the time, and generated lively opposition, especially as nothing concrete was actually gained by France. But it was the product of long gestated politics. A Franco-Turkish alliance had actually been signed as far back as 1520, when the king of France had needed a powerful partner to menace Italy and deflect imperial attention from French attempts to conquer, or reconquer, Milanese territory. In order to maintain those accords France had spent vast sums; embassies saturated with riches had been despatched to Central Europe to win over princes and nobles and have them side with

France against the Emperor. In addition, intelligence, supplies, weapons, and artillery were sent to Algiers.

The Embassies

Francis I had won the battle of Marignano in September 1515 and believed himself to be master of Milan. He met with Pope Leo X and solemnly promised to participate in a crusade. He also signed a treaty with Charles I of Spain. However, upon Charles' election to the throne of the Holy Roman Empire (where he became Charles V) in June 1519, Francis seems to have erased all thoughts from his mind but the desire to fight him. He abandoned the idea of a crusade against the Muslims and, instead, entered into negotiations with them. In 1520 a French ambassador, Guillaume de Bellay, was ordered to Tunis in order to persuade the corsairs 'to multiply the difficulties of the Emperor in his kingdom of Naples'.[16]

The Turkish alliance played such a prominent role throughout Francis's reign that it had an irrevocable effect on his policies. His problem was that he met such severe resistance in Italy that he was forced to turn to allies outside the peninsula in order to support his schemes. Alliances with Florence, or with the north Italian principalities, had been the traditional recourse of the kings of France, but their assistance was no longer sufficient. Perhaps the election of Charles V was only the final straw in this process. This event, however, was certainly vital to France's interests. Francis has been portrayed, by countless authors, as being gripped by the fear that France was now completely surrounded by enemies and that his country would be divided into pieces; this impression would certainly be magnified by a quick glance at a map showing the relative position of both sides. However, such an impression would not take account of the fact that Charles himself had tremendous difficulties in trying to maintain his incredibly dispersed possessions. Fernand Braudel, Jean Dumont and, more recently, Pierre Chaunu have shed new light on this issue and quashed this superficial explanation with the effective observation that 'the hydra-like House of Austria is nothing more than historical fiction'.[17] France was a compact mass, relatively easy to defend and free from internal squabbling and revolt; quite unlike anything the Emperor had. But Francis' policies were dictated not by a desire to defend his borders, but rather by the need to ensure the success of his grandiose schemes in Italy.

The only way to make his Italian dream reality was to find an ally capable of opening a second front in Central Europe and, simultaneously, of supporting the French against Italy and Spain. What matter if that ally was Turkish and Muslim, the sworn enemy of Christianity? These were nothing more than 'calumnies attempting to prove that a prince should not seek from a prince who does not share his own religion'. Francis set his counsellors, and writers in his pay, the task of proving him right, using historical examples from Greece, Rome, and the east. This resulted in a stream of, on the one hand, rather laboured accounts and, on the other, deliberately falsified facts.[18] Some drew attention to aspects of the comparatively recent history of the kingdom of France, noting that between 1450 and 1460 Charles VII of France and the king of England had resisted the Pope's appeals for a crusade to support Constantinople. They much preferred to pursue their own wrangling and their war against each other. Refusing to fight the Ottomans was therefore deemed acceptable; actually allying with them was just one step more along this well-trodden road.

The treaty, when it was signed, was a total alliance granting both sides whatever they wanted. Francis apparently neglected to recall that the Turks themselves wanted to conquer the whole of Italy and force it to submit to their laws. Selim had sworn to take Rome and have the Pope chased out, just as his ancestor Mehmed had taken Constantinople – the Second Rome – and done away with the Byzantine emperor.

No sooner had Charles returned to Spain following his coronation and begun attempts to put down the Comunidades revolt that had broken out in Castile than the king of France marched an army of 12,000 infantry and 30 guns, commanded by Lesparre, to the Navarrese frontier. In October 1521 Admiral Bonivet, leading a body of Gascons and German Landsknechts, seized Fontarabia. However, the defeat of the Comunidades revolt by forces loyal to the Spanish crown deprived Francis of his hopes of supporting them. His one consolation was to shelter a number of fugitive rebels, the most notable of whom was a certain Ricon who had been involved in negotiating a secret treaty between the rebels and Lesparre and Bonivet. From the autumn of 1522 Ricon and his secretary, Tranquilo, were pressed into action as secret envoys of the king of France, visiting Central Europe, the Balkans, and the Ottoman Turks.[19]

Francis provided aid to the Sultan during his campaigns in the Balkans and Central Europe. He even wrote to the 'Moors of Africa'. Missions and aid granted to the Emperor's enemies manifestly assisted the Turks during their attempts to overrun Hungary and make their way to Vienna. For, like Rome, Budapest and Vienna were expendable so long as Francis achieved his objective.

Ricon was most energetic in counselling the king, and advising his ministers of ways to weaken the House of Austria. He was ever ready to journey to distant lands – such as Poland and Hungary – for talks and negotiations; he enlisted the support of John Zapolya, voivode of Transylvania, as well as a number of Bohemian nobles. Other French emissaries, kings' men every one, journeyed to Bosnia and Croatia, hoping to incite the Turks to invade the lands of Charles' brother Ferdinand Hapsburg, Duke of Carniola and Styria: 'The King of France has schemed with Count Christoph de Frangebambre [Frangipani] who, with his men, has come to the aid of the Turks in Bosnia, near Croatia. They wish to enter my territory and make war on me.'[20] The Frangipanis, or Frankopan, were a Croatian family related, albeit remotely, to the Frangipani of Venice. They were dedicated enemies of the Hapsburgs and always on the look-out for allies. Francis I entrusted them with handling several diplomatic negotiations, some of which were of astonishing complexity, but many of these schemes came to nothing. The Franco-Turkish alliance, still secret, was, however, firmly established.

The disaster at Pavia on 24 February 1525 – a battle in which the king of France was captured – quickened the pace. Louise of Savoy, the king's mother, despatched an envoy to the Sultan to appeal for aid as soon as she heard the sad news. This time there was little that was secretive about the mission: twelve envoys (the name of the most notable has remained a mystery) were sent off bearing sumptuous gifts (a huge diamond, a golden sash, and four chandeliers) as well as a treasury for expenses which included 20,000 ducats for tolls and bribes and 10,000 for the purchase of horses. A few weeks later Giovanni Frangipani arrived in Istanbul himself, bearing letters from Louise and Francis. The latter had been penned by the king in December 1525 whilst he was still a captive in Spain. Both letters described the mistreated prisoner's humiliation, the countless wrongs he was forced to endure, and an illness which put his very life in danger.[21] In fact, his woe was but short-lived. On 14 January 1526, by virtue of the Treaty of Madrid, he was set free, promising in return to renounce his claims on Italy and to have his troops participate in a crusade. But he had absolutely no intention of keeping these promises.

The Turks, meanwhile, were on the warpath in Hungary, winning a signal victory over King Louis II at Mohacs on 22 March 1526. Louis died on the field of battle. Chroniclers (primarily Venetian and Turkish), ambassadors at Istanbul, and Grand Vizier Ibrahim were unanimous in declaring that the overtures of the French ambassadors, and their assistance and insistence, played a fundamental role in the Sultan's decision to go to war against Hungary. Frangipani, who had been in France since April, rushed eastwards to congratulate the Sultan. Francis, meanwhile, sought to justify his policies, especially to the princes of Germany. He pretended that he had not intervened directly, going so far as to deny that, in 1529, he had sent Ricon to Zapolya and paid him 40,000 *ecus* (or was it 100,000?) to enlist Turkish help. But when, on 8 September 1529, the Janissaries had marched into Budapest, Ricon accompanied them.

1529 was also the year in which the Spanish fort of the Peñon, opposite Algiers, had succumbed to fire from artillery which Kheir-ed-Din had fortuitously 'seized' from French ships which 'just happened' to be passing by. Barbarossa had, the previous year, sent rich gifts to the king of France – lions, tigers, monkeys, thoroughbred Arab stallions, and silks. Such a coincidence could hardly pass without comment, especially in Spain. It seemed that the foundries of Algiers lay in France.[22] In early May a Jewish spy arrived in Oran announcing that a French ship had docked in Algiers and that its crew were busy teaching the corsairs how best to seize hold of fortified places.

Sultan Suleiman's attempt to capture Vienna the same year failed and, on 14 October 1529, he raised his siege and marched back into Hungary. He now dreamt of beginning the great offensive against Rome – invading Italy and waging war at sea. He sent Barbarossa weapons and munitions and, in March 1531, sent Ambassador Giorgio Gritti – brother of Luigi Gritti, governor of Hungary and Doge of Venice – to France.[23] The alliance was confirmed. Barbarossa was to invade and desolate Italy, distracting the troops of Charles V, whilst the king of France – whom Barbarossa referred to, innocently, as the 'Bey of France' – marched in and defeated the Milanese.

The next few years saw the continual peregrinations of ambassadors. Ricon was received at Belgrade in July 1532; Turkish ambassadors led a hundred chained French slaves into Puy on 16 July 1533 and had them ceremoniously released; and Ricon met Barbarossa in Africa before proceeding to Rhodes and then Aleppo for a meeting with Ibrahim in the spring of 1534. Two French ships unloaded twelve excellent pieces of artillery, as well as powder, along with the metal to produce more of the same. In November 1534 a Turkish embassy arrived in France, disembarking from eleven wondrous triremes. Passing through Chatellerault, they arrived in Paris and proposed an economic treaty of alliance. The Frangipanis had also been kept busy.

Jean de la Forest, 'a gentleman from the Auvergne, secretary to Chancellor Duprat, Cardinal and Legate, nurtured in literature by Jean Lascari, being Secretary to King Francis I and Knight of Malta', left Paris in February 1535 accompanied by his cousin, Marcillac, and a citizen of Ragusa.[24] At Algiers they joined Barbarossa and accompanied him as far as Istanbul. 'Some said he bore no presents, whilst others are assured that he presented an excellent clock to the Sultan'.[25] They had arrived in the city on 13 June, having travelled with Barbarossa's fleet – which was 'in bad condition' – and a ship from Tunis carrying horses – more presents for the Sultan. La Forest earnestly desired to meet this monarch, being prepared to travel as far as Baghdad in order to see him. He subsequently grew more patient and settled down to await the Sultan's return. He lodged in a country house just outside Pera on the far side of the Golden Horn so that he, like other Europeans, 'would not be exposed to the coarseness of the Turks'. He made it clear to the Turks that the French were busily arming thirty-six galleys, two large vessels, and numerous galliots; others were expected from Normandy and Brittany. The fleet would make war on the Genoese.

In February 1536 La Forest obtained an agreement, known as the Capitulations, which made generous financial concessions to the French and provided for the liberation of a number of Christian slaves. It was bizarre that the banner of the king of France would now be the sole protection from the exactions of pirates and tax officials. Meanwhile the Franco-Turkish alliance was barely mentioned, being glossed over or, worse, lied about. The Capitulations were also shrouded in dishonesty; none of those responsible mentioned that the terms had been granted in return for aid supplied in the form of ships and guns. The treaty was presented in such a way as to suggest that it had been worked out in order to provide French commerce with protection. This trade was, of course, considerable and, so the story went, Marseilles and much of the country depended upon it; but to say that the French crown's sole concern was to safeguard it was going a little too far.

In any case, the trade was in decline and had lost some of its importance. The French themselves did not play a significant role as merchants in the Levant and the French kings were largely limited to politics when discussing issues in that region. During Charles VII's reign much had been made of Jacques Coeur's 'galleys of France' and their voyages into the Levant but, propaganda aside, they were of little consequence. Just two galleys per year, both of slight tonnage, had been despatched, whereas Venice and Genoa could each boast of 5,000 or 6,000 tons of shipping heading eastwards in the same period. It might be added that the French ships were limited to visiting Alexandria in Egypt, whereas the Italians anchored in Syrian ports, Istanbul, and along the shores of the Black Sea. Charles VII saw the galleys more as a gesture so that he could pose as the rival to the great maritime states of Italy. There was no concern for trade; the ships merely served a political role. Charles had toyed with an alliance with the Sultan of Egypt, who might serve as an exclusive ally of the French or even an arbitrator between the warring powers of the west. Charles had also had some dealings with the Turks, having written in 1456 to the 'Grand Karaman' of Konya to recommend his vessels to him and allow their entry into the ports of Aramon and Selefkie.[26]

The Turkish Fleet in Toulon, 1543–4

In 1537 Baron Saint-Blancard, Vice-Admiral of Provence, sailed from France with a squadron of twelve galleys carrying supplies for a hundred Turkish ships which would then, in turn, raid Puglia, Sicily, and Spain. On 15 August, having 'set sail in the Marseilles roads', he passed Toulon and the Îles d'Or. From there onwards the pace quickened as the admiral sought to conceal his vessels from Spanish galleys and those belonging to the Knights of Malta. He sheltered them off deserted shores and islands far from the main shipping lanes. He took on water from villages or towns that were remote and could boast of few defences. He swept into the Iron Gulf, beneath the mountains of Corsica, before moving on to Sardinia. There he took on water from streams running down the sandy shore.

Then he passed the islands of Toro, Veau, and Vache, and weighed anchor off the island of Zimbe where there were 'winds which were so hot as to have come from, or passed, a huge flaming fire'. The admiral intended to rendezvous with Barbarossa off Tunis but, unfortunately, he wasn't there. He was away fighting in the waters off Preveza, in the Arta Gulf on the coast of Epirus.

The Frenchmen went off to look for him, heading first for Cape Bon where, in order to please the local Moorish notables, his men attempted to pass themselves off as Spaniards. The plan misfired, however, when the Moors 'saw some of us dressed like Frenchmen, especially one in boots, a Turkish cap, and with a beard and long whiskers, and they wanted to beat him and behaved in a manner which showed they did not trust us'. Other Moors at Hammamet and Monastir, supporters of the Turks, welcomed the travellers with open arms and 'volleys of musketry and the galloping and leaping of horses'. In exchange for powder the travellers were given bread, mutton, beef, and fruit. Finally, learning that Barbarossa was cruising off the Balkans, the French set sail and headed east. At one point they were forced to shelter on an island, which they called 'Conilliers', for two weeks. Here they hunted the vast numbers of rabbits to be found there, snaring them or bludgeoning them to death. After that their voyage took them to Malta, Cephalonia, and Zante before they finally came across Barbarossa on 10 September at Preveza. This spacious and grand harbour, with its well-defended entrance, was filled with Barbarossa's fleet and numerous ships loaded with biscuits for the Sultan's army. A Turkish captain, dressed in a wolf-skin, with a cap of the same, informed them where they should go to find the camp.[27]

In the end Saint-Blancard only managed to persuade the Turks to part with a handful of their ships so that they could join him. Nevertheless, this was the first time that the two countries had created a joint force. The captains shared information and worked on possible plans of action together. The Franco-Turkish alliance was no longer confined to the realms of diplomacy. When news of the French expedition leaked out the whole of Europe leapt to condemn it, and in February 1538 the Emperor, the Pope, and Venice formed the League of Nice to counter the Turks. Francis, caught between counsellors in favour of the alliance and those – notably Montmorency – who were appalled by the scandal, dithered aimlessly. In the end he agreed to meet Charles V at Aigues-Mortes. The meeting, which took place on 14 July 1538, was an anti-climax; Francis remained aloof, mouthing empty pleasantries.

On 27 September, off Preveza, Barbarossa at the head of 122 sail defeated a Christian fleet consisting of thirty-six Papal galleys, sixty-one Genoese, fifty Portuguese, and ten sent by the Knights of Malta. No French ships were involved, but the battle bought time for Francis. He met with Charles again, this time in Paris as the Emperor was on his way to Ghent. The meeting took place on 1 January 1540 and Charles later proclaimed that the two monarchs were of one accord – never to trust the Turks. There would be no war between them. When the Sultan heard of this he was outraged, cried treason and rained down insults on the name of the king of France, calling him an ingrate and a scatterbrain. At the same time he ordered Ambassador Ricon and his entourage of Frenchmen to be massacred. Ricon saved himself by explaining that the Emperor was merely passing through France and that the meeting was of little importance; he underlined his words with rich and bountiful presents to all those of influence at court. For example, the Sultan's brother-in-law Loufty Pasha, 'in order to gain his favour and affection for the king, and to have him forget the Emperor's passage through France, received diverse kinds of robes, cloth of gold and silk and the sum of 300 golden *ecus*'. Mohammed, the 'third pasha', also benefited from 'robes costing 150 *ecus*', as did Rostan 'a kind of noble lord and the sultan's bascha' so that he could 'better understand the reasons for the emperor's passage'.[28] The king's men worked hard in his cause and soon the storm passed and the alliance was once again confirmed. Ricon, who was nothing more than a Spanish adventurer of rather slight means, was feted in France for this achievement and showered with honours and rewards.

Shortly afterwards he was once again sent on a mission, not, this time, on behalf of the French king, but for the Sultan himself. He arrived in Venice on 14 January 1541. The doge and senate refused point blank to see him and were adamant in their support of Charles V. He was dismissed, but the Venetians did provide him with an escort of fifty cavalrymen so that he might avoid falling into the hands of Imperial agents. Eventually he made it to Blois, met with the king and, that July, set off once again for Istanbul. However, as he was crossing Italy, making his way along the Po, he was apprehended by men of the Marquis del Vasto, a Milanese governor, and was killed on the spot. News of his death was kept secret for two months; some thought he had been taken prisoner and sought to have him released. The king, however, knew better and lost no time in selecting another ambassador. This was Le Paulin, the Admiral of France. He too tried to treat with the Venetians but again was unsuccessful; he continued his journey, finally meeting up with the Sultan at Buda on 2 September 1541.

In October Charles V commenced an expedition against Algiers, where his fleet arrived on the 23rd. He was accompanied by an immense force, consisting of 516 vessels carrying 12,300 sailors and 24,000 soldiers. Two days before its arrival there had been a storm, and the sea was still sufficiently unsettled to cause some delay in disembarking the army. When the men finally got ashore they took up a position on some heights above the town, but the torrential rain, and pestilential fevers, soon rendered their position untenable. It proved impossible to get adequate supplies or reinforcements ashore, and 'no army was ever in such a pitiful plight as the Emperor's one; the food that had been taken ashore had been consumed in three days and it was not known how we would supply the soldiers battered by cold and hunger'. It was a disaster. The Spanish, soaked by downpours and trembling with fever, were surprised by a sortie from the town led by Barbarossa's sixteen-year-old adoptive son Hassan Agha. They were driven off towards the coast in disorder or cut down and massacred. The survivors, saved by a rearguard composed of the Knights of Malta, who lost a good number of their brethren, retreated in terrible conditions to Cape Matifou. Here they found their fleet, reduced by 150 vessels lost in a storm on 3 November.[29]

Two years later the Spanish launched another offensive. The Count of Alcaudete, governor of Oran, had, for a number of years, been trying to get his hands on Tlemcen. He had actually forced the king, Moulay Mohammed, to come to an agreement by menacing him with just 600 men and four pieces of artillery. The king promised to become an ally and vassal of the king of Spain, to supply food and livestock, and to treat Barbarossa and his corsairs as enemies. In addition, the king would pay a tribute of 4,000 doubloons, two horses, and a dozen falcons. But the treaty was never implemented. So Alcaudete went back to his lands around Montemayor in Andalusia in search of support from his family and faithful supporters. His sons assembled vast stores of food – biscuits, wine, salted meat, and oil – and equipment at Cartagena and Malaga. Volunteers poured in and before too long a fleet of twelve vessels was ready to set sail from Cartagena. On 10 January 1543, accompanied by the acclamations of an enthusiastic crowd, the ships raised their anchors and slipped out of the harbour. Storms twice dispersed the fleet before it reached Oran, where it managed to disembark 1,200 infantry and 1,700 cavalry. Moulay Mohammed, meanwhile, offered Alcaudete a bribe of 200,000 ducats, then 400,000, to desist. But Alcaudete sallied forth, winning two battles before entering the city of Tlemcen on 6 February. He found the place abandoned and partially pillaged. The Spanish finished what others had started, although they could find little booty, and Tlemcen was laid waste for many years to come. On their march back to Oran, however, Alcaudete's force was vigorously attacked, losing nearly 2,000 men.[30]

With Algiers saved, and the Spanish army in North Africa worsted and reinforcements from Andalusia temporarily unavailable, the Turks thought that now, more than ever before, they might be able to complete their domination of the Mediterranean. Perhaps, too, they might be able to stage major offensives against Spain and Italy – to invade and conquer rather than to raid and ambush. In April 1543 Barbarossa sailed westwards with 110 galleys and forty galliots. Le Paulin, the king of France's ambassador, accompanied him and witnessed his brutal raids against La Puglia, and in Calabria and Sicily. The Turks pillaged Reggio, abandoned by its garrison, and captured the city's Spanish governor, Diego Gaetano. His daughter was kidnapped for Barbarossa's harem.

The king of France, having heard that 'the Turkish army, led by Barbarossa, was soon to arrive in Marseilles for his service', hastened to send a prince of royal blood out to receive the corsair 'and add the forces of the west to those of the aforementioned army'. The twenty-three-year-old Francis of Bourbon, Count of Enghien, was selected for the task. The count entered Marseilles to an enthusiastic welcome and a salute of artillery salvoes 'the thunder of which was so great that women carrying child and wet-nurses had need to shelter in the cellars'.[31] Then, in mid-July, the Turkish fleet sailed into Marseilles and was welcomed in magnificent style, in the king's name, by Enghien and his squadron of fifty ships. Fanfares followed cannonades and acclamations and the reception was rounded off by a huge feast, the food for which had been provided by the king. Enghien and Barbarossa, accompanied by a squadron under Le Paulin, then sailed forth to lay siege to Nice, which was then a possession of the Duke of Savoy. Barbarossa anchored at the port of Villafranca, seized the town, and promptly burnt it. 'From there, the

Turks, passing through mountains that were savage and steep, debouched onto the plains before Nice and lay siege to the place. They opened a tremendous fire on it with an artillery that Barbarossa had had manhandled through the mountains as their steepness had prevented other methods.'[32] The town suffered a relentless bombardment for nearly two weeks before offering to capitulate on condition that the Turks gave their word not to pillage it or to carry off its inhabitants. But the Turks continued their assaults, at one point attacking the citadel, which was held determinedly by Simone de Cavoretto – a Knight of St John all too familiar with Barbarossa's prisons – and his men. The Duke of Savoy and the Marquis of Guast, governor of Milan, meanwhile hastened to organise support.

However, the relationship between Le Paulin and Barbarossa was growing uneasy, and their troops were quarrelling. They were soon threatening not to support each other: 'The Turks were growing angry and bitter with us to such a degree that we were constrained not to supply them with ball and powder.' The situation steadily deteriorated until Barbarossa, 'seeing this, and that winter was drawing on, decided to make sail for Constantinople whilst his army remained secure in the port of Villafranca'.[33]

On 8 September 1543 the two fleets raised the siege, and went their separate ways shortly thereafter. Barbarossa carried off 300 children and monks and nuns from the villages around Antibes before anchoring off the isles of Sainte Marguerite near Cannes – not, as the king of France had wished, in the straits of Villafranca. The French had wanted their allies to follow them and now sharply accused them of treachery. Some even suggested that they had signed a pact with Andrea Doria, for 'the raven does not peck out the eye of the raven'.[34]

Francis I, however, was most accommodating. If Barbarossa promised to serve him the following spring, Francis, for his part, promised to supply him with all the food he needed and to reinforce him with 'such a splendid and brave a host on land that he would be master of the sea; and after that he had served the aforementioned monarch [Francis] he would aid him with all the support to see him back to his kingdom of Tunis.'[35]

It was decided that the Turks would winter at Toulon. The city's elders were therefore informed by royal proclamation that 'the city should be emptied of all malevolent persons, any disobedience to be punished by hanging'. The very same day they rushed a message to

Jacques de Roconi to plead with the governor of Provence 'to obtain provisions to supplement the store of fruit in the town, olives as well as others'. They also contacted the lord of Pensin – a consul – and two leading figures in Cannes and Antibes to treat with the Count of Enghien and inform him 'that they did not intend to move anyone out of the town except for those women and children who so wished to go'. It was apparently indispensable that heads of families and artisans remained in place and that 'sufficient policing be carried out to prevent disorder and inconvenience'.

On 14 October 1543 200 Turkish galleys anchored in the bay and a force of 30,000 men swarmed into the town. Barbarossa and his close associates established their quarters in a soap factory which had been transformed into a sumptuous palace. For six full months – until April 1544 – Toulon was transformed into 'a vast seraglio like Constantinople'. The cathedral of Sainte-Marie-Majeure was transformed into a mosque and the tombs of the city's nobility were desecrated and pillaged. The officers of the French squadron and those of Barbarossa openly fraternised and accompanied each other to interminable banquets, or on strolls through the streets. Men and women, whether ladies of the Provencal nobility or from the harem, exchanged gifts. The governor, Adhemar de Grignan, forced a much inflated Turkish currency on the city's population, and that of the surrounding area, whilst simultaneously promising to indemnify citizens who had been robbed or despoiled of their goods. He also prohibited Christian funeral rights for those Christian slaves who perished in the city's prisons. Men and women captured by the Turks were ferried over to the isles of Hyeres and auctioned. The Janissaries made a point of kidnapping young men from the city and surrounding countryside and pressing them into service as galley slaves in the fleet. There was a terrible shortage of wood and the city gradually ground to a halt, it being 'sterile and so lacking in revenue that it was altogether impossible to feed the citizenry'.[36]

The king's soldiers and sailors were gradually weakening as time wore on, and their effectiveness was compromised by the presence in their ranks of a good number of Florentine adventurers – many of whom had been exiled by the Medici – such as Leone Strozzi, a prior of the Hospitallers of Capua and commander of a small squadron of three galleys: his own, Baccio Martelli's, and Guidetto's *La Guidetta*.[37] The French and Florentine factions had fallen to bickering, conjuring up intrigue, casting libellous aspersions, and indulging in dark calumnies. But they were united in their inability to tolerate the arrogance of the Turks or, perhaps more accurately, the bravery of the Turks in battle: 'The Turks troubled our men greatly; they were, I believe, more than our equals for they were robust, obedient and more patient; they thought of nothing but war. Barbarossa was sour and angry with us because we were not sending him balls and powder'.[38]

With the arrival of spring the ships had to be prepared for the long-awaited joint expedition. But should it be against the Emperor in Italy? Or should Tunis be recaptured from the Spaniards? Arguments ensued, and the treaty between His Most Christian Majesty and the Sultan was first compromised, then jeopardised, and finally rendered meaningless. Francis I received affront after affront, followed by uncompromising resistance. From Toulon a steady stream of complaints, recriminations, appeals, and requests for money reached the ears of the king and his bureaucrats. The city council charged Le Paulin to travel to Lyon, then to Paris or wherever was necessary, to 'make known [to the king] the present true plight of this place of Toulon, the vast quantity of olives daily consumed by the foreigners and other things besides'. He was above all to inform him 'of the burdens placed on the shoulders of the farmers who, in accordance with the king's command, have Turks billeted upon them, for which reason they are constrained to live outside their dwellings and thereby endure much hardship'. He was instructed to obtain 'letters of favour, or those carrying exemptions'. The embassy cost the representatives of Toulon the princely sum of 125 golden *ecus*.[39]

The king kept the embassy waiting for quite a while. Then, on 20 April 1544, he consented to acknowledge Toulon's suffering. Because it was ringed by high mountains, he observed, 'the whole area around is so sterile and so wanting in revenue that it is impossible for the inhabitants to feed themselves without dependence on the traffic and trade of merchants'; but this was now impossible as, because of 'the quartering of the army of the Levant [there is no mention of the Ottomans], they have been obliged to leave their houses and residence, making it impossible for them to continue their trade in goods.' The king therefore exempted the city from taxes and contributions.[40]

Meanwhile the corsairs and Janissaries were being paid not by their captains but by the king himself: 'They came here today to see me three times, shouting that they have been dragged here from Constantinople and that I must order it so that they are paid as they have nothing to live on and that they will go back to their boats if they are not'.[41] Barbarossa, for his part, protested that he was neither being helped nor given any consideration. The king was procrastinating about whether to send troops for the reconquest of Tunis, and Le Paulin was obliged to step in to calm the troubled waters: 'I endeavoured to make him understand the causes preventing us from assisting him, and also reminded him of the great expense Your Majesty is daily going to.'[42]

Barbarossa was no longer so keen to fight for an ally who was so evidently hesitant. He considered returning to Constantinople or undertaking some other venture, and asked the Sultan to recall him and thereby free him and his forces from this predicament. He then seized the French fleet of fifty-two vessels, obliging Le Paulin – the 'Marquis of the Golden Isles' and 'Captain-General of the Army of the East' – to follow him wherever he decided to go.

Francis I finally agreed to permit Barbarossa's departure, and was obliged to pay a high price to secure it – 800,000 golden *ecus*, and great quantities of silk, cloth, food, and munitions: 'At Toulon there were thirty-two treasury officials filling sacks with 1,000, 2,000 or 3,000 *ecus* continually for three whole days and for the best part of the nights'. The king had delivered 87,440 quintals of bread and biscuits to the city through the winter; he would now have to deliver 200,000 more.[43] Inevitably, Barbarossa took his share. The areas around Toulon were reduced to borrowing in order to survive, whilst even the richest of officers, such as Leone Strozzi, had suffered irrecoverable losses.[44]

Meanwhile the good people of Toulon were counting their costs, assessing the damage, or listing the 'supplies issued to the Turkish officers before now'. They had, in fact, been keeping very detailed records:

I purchased a young goat and gave it to a renegade living in the house of Louis Cochon, it cost six gros; I gave two such goats to the sergeants of Barbarossa's guard. Then I brought in three hundred Seville oranges on 25 March and presented them to Barbarossa's ambassador and to Gaffer-Agha. Then, on 15 March, I brought in 1,500 apples. Then I gave a *quartin* of oil to Mustafa and to the sergeants guarding Barbarossa's door.

The MARINE *Quarterly*

Hope Farm, Lyonshall, Herefordshire HR5 3HT UK   (0)1544 340636

Your subscription to the MQ expires with this issue. If you would like to renew, please visit our website, or complete the form below and return the card with your cheque.

Sam Llewellyn, Editor

I enclose a cheque for £48 to renew my subscription to the MQ

Address . . . .

. . . .

Postcode . . . .   Telephone . . . .

Or renew at www.marinequarterly.com

Another account recorded that 'I paid Jean Julien of Garde and Pierre Viole, a muleteer, for the hire of their beasts for three whole days to transport Barbarossa's servants and a consignment of baggage.'[45]

A Time of Shame, 1544–55

Throughout this time, to backtrack a little, Barbarossa's lieutenant Salah Raïs, accompanied by numerous French soldiers and galleys, was raiding and pillaging the Catalonian coast. They sacked a number of ports, among them Palamós, Ampurias, Roses, and Cadaqués: 'Frenchmen and Turks were fighting side by side, demolishing the doors of houses with axes, bursting in and looting and pillaging'.[46] On 26 May 1544 Barbarossa finally left Provence, and his two squadrons – his own and that of Le Paulin – set sail for the east. French noblemen were crowded aboard, some reluctant participants whilst others were highly enthusiastic. The vessels sauntered towards Italy where, instead of seeking out and fighting stubborn battles with imperial troops, they attacked and burnt towns and villages incapable of putting up any meaningful resistance. They quit the Îles de Saint Marguerite with a squadron of eighty or a hundred galleys carrying heavy artillery, and then spent the next fifty days in a leisurely cruise towards Reggio in Calabria. Once there they razed everything to the ground that they could not actually carry off, and also kidnapped men, women, and children, bound them in chains, and dragged them onto their ships.

Jerome Maurand, a priest from Antibes and the almoner for the French galleys, has left us a long and doleful account of this terrible voyage. It is one of the only authentic accounts, if not the only such account, by an eyewitness who saw and noted the deeds of the corsairs on a daily basis.[47] On 7 June, at Talamone, after having seized everything he could get his hands on, Barbarossa had the corpse of Bartolome Peretti – who'd had the audacity to attack Lesbos some time before – dragged from its tomb, exposed to public view, and then horribly mutilated. The tombs of Peretti's servants and officers were also desecrated and their corpses were cut into pieces and burnt in the town's squares. Some 150 Turks marched out to attack a country house in the hills, dragging back with them men, women, young girls and boys, in huge numbers. At Porto Ercole

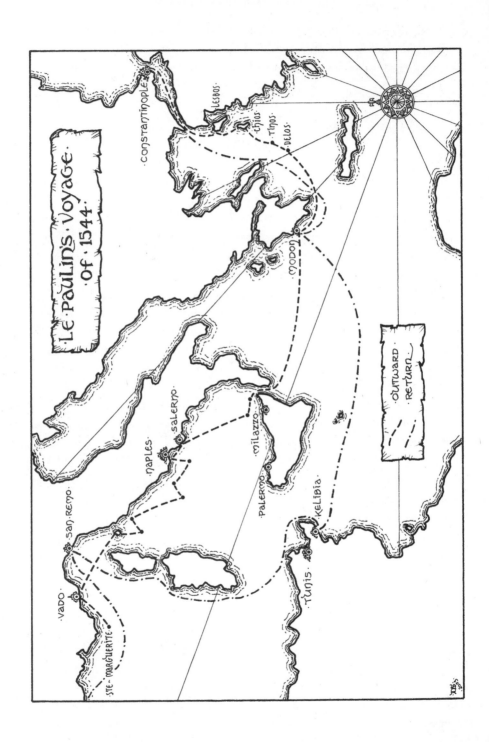

Le·Paulin's·Voyage·of·1544·

OUTWARD
RETURN

Constantinople·

LESBOS·
·Chios·
·Tinos·
·DELOS·

·MODON·

·San·Remo·
·Naples·
·SALERNO·
·MILAZZO·
·PALERMO·
·KELIBIA·
·TUNIS·

·VADO·
·STE·MARGUERITE·

Barbarossa received the formal submission of the inhabitants; they delivered up thirty men in return for a promise to spare the port and town. The thirty were led off in chains, but that did not save the town. 'The citadel was seized and sacked and fire broke out in all four corners of the town; hardly a house remains standing and the fire lasted three days.' On the island of Giglio Barbarossa's corsairs seized 632 captives and 'cut off the heads of all the principal inhabitants'. His captains even anchored their ships off the mouth of the Tiber to take on water; however, no attempt was made on Rome itself.

Next he seized Ischia in the gulf of Naples. Lipari, an island off Sicily, offered 15,000 ducats to spare it a visitation, but the corsairs demanded 30,000, along with 200 boys and 200 girls. When this was refused the principal town was invested for ten days, at the end of which, having endured a dreadful bombardment, it submitted and was sacked and then burnt. The artillery which had defended it was carried off and put aboard the Turkish galleys. The entire population was dragged before Barbarossa, who had the old men and women beaten. The Janissaries, meanwhile, had discovered a crowd of other elderly men and women seeking shelter in the cathedral: 'They were taken out, robbed of their clothes and cut open whilst still alive. All this was done out of spite. When we asked them why they treated these people with such cruelty they replied that among them such a cruelty was deemed a virtue. This was their answer.'

As the king of France's ambassador, Le Paulin assisted the corsairs throughout this period. At one point he sought to justify his actions by offering Talamone and Porto Ercole to the Pope, who refused point blank to receive them. He also made it known that he had purchased some of the Turks' captives in order to release them. On 17 July, whilst at Reggio in Calabria, he received permission to leave the fleet and headed for Constantinople, arriving there on 10 August before Barbarossa. He had hoped to make use of this opportunity to complain of Barbarossa's conduct – perhaps even to be instrumental in his disgrace – and to obtain a direct promise of aid from the Sultan himself. In these hopes he was to be frustrated by Barbarossa's triumphant arrival with a vast amount of booty, the fruit of his raids in Calabria and elsewhere; indeed, so overloaded were his ships that their crews had had to throw hundreds of slaves overboard to avoid capsizing.

Francis I told the Sultan that 'he would not contemplate peace nor a treaty with the Emperor unless the Grand Turk consents and wishes to be included'. Nevertheless, he signed a treaty with Charles V at Crépy on 18 September 1544 and agreed to wage war on the Ottomans. But despite this turnabout he continued to hover indecisively between the two powers, sending ambassadors this way and that to justify his actions right up until his death in 1547. Jean de Montluc eulogised about him at Venice, endeavouring, before the city-state's senate, to prove that France had not been guilty of any wrongdoing. Had not the Emperor himself been attempting to negotiate with the Ottomans these past dozen years? Had he not offered them 'a vast tribute' so that they might spare the kingdom of Hungary? He advanced the theory that the Turkish army and navy had never wronged anyone and that, on the contrary, Turkish ships showed considerable courtesy and allowed the free passage of Christian vessels without molestation. If they had taken anything it was only sufficient to ensure that their men were fed. The relationship between Turks and Christians had never been so good! Then came his decisive argument. Had the king of France, in order to defend his frontiers, not been an ally of the Turks then Christianity would have been assailed by them and would have had to bear considerable losses: 'Therefore it was more useful to Christendom that they were employed in the service of His Majesty the King rather than that they marched, without restraint, against the Christians.'[48]

Kheir ed-Din didn't remain in Constantinople for long. He left in 1545 with a vague plan to wage war on the Spanish. He cruised off Bône and then suddenly veered off to attack Minorca. At Mahon he made one of his largest hauls of prisoners, making off, it was said, with nearly 6,000 victims. Then he sailed back to Constantinople, settling down to build a vast palace and new mosque in the Buyukdere quarter (which boasted 'a crowd of palaces, mosques and gardens and made it seem like the most splendid portions of Genoa'). There, in 1546, he died, carried off by fever, his passing being 'much regretted by the Turks who held him in such high esteem on account of his exploits'.[49] With the last of the Barbarossa brothers dead the most famous of the corsair captains had passed away. But others soon took their place. Although never destined to achieve the same legendary status, admirals such as Dragut, Piali Pasha, Salah Raïs, and Euldj' Ali[50] served the Sultan well, especially in North Africa.

In 1550 Kheir ed-Din's son Hassan, king of Algiers, inflicted a crushing defeat upon the forces of Tlemcen and Abd el-Kader, Lord of Fez and Morocco. But just a year later he was recalled to Constantinople, his name besmirched by palace intrigues in which Rostan, husband of Suleiman's daughter, played a prominent role. The French too had been hostile, accusing him of being malicious and perhaps even mad. The French ambassador, d'Aramon, had fervently wished for his disgrace and in January 1552 was congratulating himself on his own good fortune: 'Following my prediction about the former king of Algiers, the Sultan has at last deigned to recognise my description of him; he is dismissed and reduced to a living of two *ecus* per day for the rest of his life.'[51]

Appointed in Hassan's place as pasha of Algiers was Caïd Saffa, but he reigned for barely seven months before he too succumbed to court intrigues. He was replaced in April 1552 by the corsair Salah Raïs, who led his forces south and seized Touggourt by storm, selling 10,000 of its inhabitants into slavery. At Ouargla, deserted by its terrified inhabitants, he only managed to capture forty chieftains and some black slaves. These were promptly resold, making 200,000 gold *ecus*.[52]

Tunis and its Moorish king continued to defy the Ottomans. Supported by the Spanish, Moulay Hassan held out against all comers – among them his own son, Moulay Hamida. In 1542, with the aid of Andrea Doria, he had wrested control of Monastir, Sousse, Sfax, and Kelibia from the Turks and corsairs, but two years later he was defeated in turn by forces loyal to his son and was chased from the city. Moulay Hamida proclaimed himself king, changing his name to Ahmed Satan. He then surprised everyone by making a deal with the Spanish governor of La Goulette.[53]

Tunis was a city somewhat on the sideline of international events – an uncertain entity and, for the Turks, a potential conquest. Dragut would attempt to seize it but fail, losing Mahdia into the bargain. He also failed at Gafsa and fled into the interior, seeking refuge with Doria's galleys and only being able to regain Constantinople much later.

Despite the fact that operations against Italy and the Mediterranean islands could reap tremendous booty, Constantinople was loathe to mobilise its fleets or even those of the North African pirates for such ventures. Nevertheless, one such expedition was launched in 1552 commanded by Sinane, followed by another in 1553 under Dragut. These fleets sailed against Sicily and southern Italy before disappearing eastwards. The problem was that it took a good deal of trouble to sail from the Bosphorus to the rich pickings of the west, and the Ottomans now received but scant support from the French. Indeed, following their sojourn in Toulon the allies had begun to fall out. Although Le Paulin had managed to persuade Dragut to attack Corsica – despite pressure from Moorish envoys seeking an expedition against Tunis – the Turkish commander had either changed his mind or received orders countermanding the French request. The following year the Turks were quite content to cruise in the Adriatic, something which upset the French immensely and raised a chorus of complaints. The Turks were accused of desiring nothing but plunder, and it was claimed that Sinane and Dragut especially had been bribed by the Spanish.

The new king of France, Henri II, was not, however, troubled by such rumours and in 1555 he asked Suleiman to lead a force into the Mediterranean and wage a 'strong and most royal war' against the Spaniards. That same year Salah Raïs, Pasha of Algiers, laid siege to Bougie, a Spanish possession since 1510. He had managed to assemble an imposing force of artillery but his army did not amount to much.[54] This was due to the fact that just as he was setting out a French armada of twenty-four ships under Leone Strozzi had sailed into Algiers carrying letters pressing the pasha to supply men and galleys to the French king to assist him in waging war on Philip II, king of Spain. Salah Raïs obeyed, providing twenty-two ships, well equipped with men and munitions, and Strozzi led them off on a campaign against the coasts of Tuscany and Corsica. Three years later the French and the corsairs of Algiers would again unite, this time to pillage Sorrento and Ciudadela on Majorca. Subsequently the allies went their separate ways – the French to Toulon, the corsairs setting sail for the east.[55]

Dragut remained in Constantinople for some considerable time before taking over command of Tripoli. From there his troops attacked the Sheikhs of Djerba from the sea and advanced into the interior by land. He occupied Kairouan in 1558 and set up a regime in eastern Berberie supported by contributions levied upon the tribes of the interior. But he was never successful in his attempts to subdue Tunis or to expand westwards.[56] Salah Raïs did manage to seize Peñon de Velez in 1555 and, a year later, took Bougie from the Spaniards.

For the Turks, the final balance sheet of their military and political alliance with the French monarchy was somewhat disappointing. True, riches had been seized in the course of their various operations, but no long-lasting victory had been won nor territory conquered. Tunis, for example, remained in Spanish hands.

For the French, the results of this risky relationship were just as bad. A few of the king's officers and counsellors later expressed regret over what had taken place: 'I have always thought badly of these affairs and think they could have been better handled. Everyone thought the Turks would triumph, and we too, through their assistance. But this was not true.'[57]

Chapter III

Lepanto

In 1555 Salah Raïs, Pasha of Algiers, had begun his siege of Bougie, which the Spanish had held for nearly fifty years; his artillery devastated the town and soon reduced its two principal defences – the citadel, constructed following orders issued by Charles V, and the Vergelette fort – to rubble. After running out of food and munitions the governor, Don Alonso de Peralta, surrendered, realising that further resistance was useless. The terms of the capitulation stipulated that the garrison was to be returned to Spain, complete with arms and baggage, and that the inhabitants were to be spared and allowed to leave with their portable goods. Even so, Salah made a huge haul of booty and led 400 men, 120 women, and 100 children off into slavery.[1]

Charles V abdicated in 1556 and his son Philip II assumed the Spanish crown. Henri II of France desired peace so that he could preserve his possessions in the east and north whilst, if possible, continuing to hanker after Italy; to this end he negotiated compromise agreements and made huge sacrifices of revenue. Then, on 3 April 1559, he signed the Treaty of Cateau-Cambrésis which ceded Calais to France, along with some forts along the Somme, in return for the French relinquishing their pretensions in Italy. This finally ended 300 years of Italian wars, which had begun with Charles of Anjou's conquest of Naples back in 1260 and seen successive French armies drawn into ever more ambitious, and ruinous, enterprises.

In the Mediterranean Philip II launched his ships against those of the Barbary corsairs. In the summer of 1559 a squadron under Medina Celi, viceroy of Naples, supported by ships of the Knights of Malta, had seized Djerba. However, the squadron was surprised when quitting its moorings by a Turkish fleet of 100 galleys under Grand Admiral Piali Pasha. The Christians lost thirty ships and had nearly 500 men captured in the ensuing combat and only extricated themselves with the utmost difficulty. The Turks sailed into Djerba and pulled down the Spanish forts before making off, on 15 May 1560, with thousands of prisoners, among whom Don Sanchez de Leiva, general of Neapolitan galleys, and Don Beranger, general of Sicilian galleys, were the most notable.

The Siege of Malta, 19 May to 11 September 1565

The Knights of St John of Jerusalem had been chased out of Rhodes in 1522 and had sought temporary shelter in Messina until, on 4 March 1530, Charles V had offered them possession of the islands of Malta and Gozo and suzerainty over Tripoli on the African coast. Malta was, at that time, sparsely populated, lacking in resources, and prone to seasonal outbreaks of fever. Nevertheless, the Knights established themselves on the island on 26 October 1530, taking up residence in Birgu – the fortified old quarters dominating the port, protected by the fortress of St Angelo. This single act rendered the island the bastion and first line of defence against the Barbary corsairs and the Turks. The Knights quickly began to establish arsenals, fortified their cities and outposts, and equipped themselves ready for war. They lent assistance to Spanish and Papal ships and were, by necessity, aware of every attack and counter-attack mounted by the Ottomans. For Malta lay in the path of every Turkish raid or campaign westwards, and every time the Turks sallied forth, or returned east, they came across the Knights and their guns and ships.

Jean Parisot de la Valette served the Order faithfully on Rhodes and continued to do so on Malta. He had once been a slave of the Turks until he was freed in an exchange of prisoners. He had defended Tripoli against a Turkish assault in 1551 before being elected Grand Master of the Hospitallers in 1557. It was he who organised the defence of Malta. Anticipating an Ottoman attack, all of the Knights living abroad, even those who had remained behind in the Levant, were recalled. Meanwhile, La Valette, who could count upon some 800 Knights of the Order, along

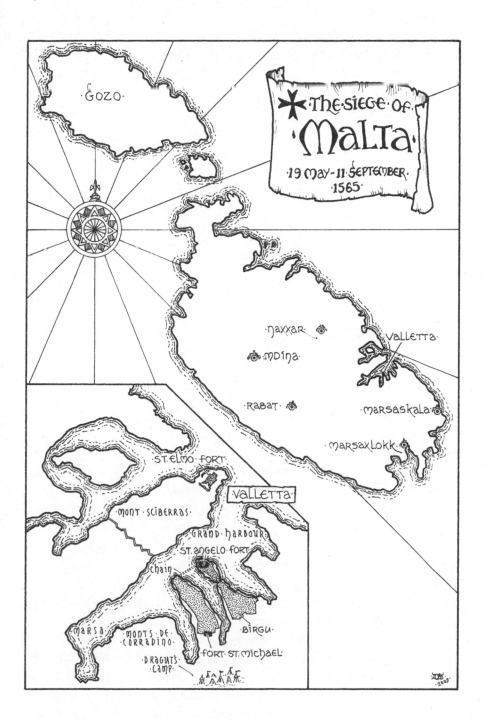

with a few thousand Maltese, hoarded vast quantities of grain and deposited it in Birgu's silos and warehouses.

In April 1565 Admiral Piali Pasha sailed out of Istanbul at the head of a fleet of 200 galleys and transports, the Ottoman force being under the overall command of Mustapha Pasha. The Turks disembarked on 19 May in the bays of Marsaxlokk and Marsaskala in the south-west and west of the island. Some said there were 28,000 Turks, others that they numbered 40,000. They seized Adrien de la Rivière, commander of a small detachment which attempted to flee but was overwhelmed. This unfortunate was tortured in an attempt to make him reveal the layout of Birgu's defences and the other fortifications. However, La Rivière tricked his tormentors into believing that the bastion of Castile, one of the best defended works on the island, was the best point to attack. Consequently the first Turkish assault, the most important in any siege, failed dreadfully, and the prisoner was executed.

The time won by La Rivière's bravery allowed the Knights to prepare themselves, while disputes arose in the Turkish camp about how best to attack Birgu and even when to attack. Some said an immediate assault was imperative, before the arrival of Christian reinforcements; others emphasised that they should wait and allow their own reserves, in particular Dragut's fleet, to catch up. Meanwhile they launched an assault against the fort of St Elmo at the entrance of the main harbour. The fort had been built but recently and its main defences faced the sea; this, it was thought, made the position vulnerable and, indeed, the Turks poured a withering artillery fire into the fort. Then, on 30 May, Dragut arrived with another twenty galleys and 1,000 soldiers. He urged the Turks on, hoping to take the island before the onset of inclement weather. Over the course of the next eighteen days the Turks fired between 13,000 and 15,000 cannonballs into the fort. The besieged garrison, cut off from all help and food, put up an incredible resistance, in many cases fighting to the death.

'On the morning of 16 June Mustapha launched a huge assault. A sea of howling soldiers, exhilarated by the chance of victory, threw themselves against the shattered walls but, after a battle which lasted six hours, they were bloodily repulsed.'[2] In this one attack the Turks lost 3,000 men. Five days later, on 21 June, another assault likewise failed. Then, on 23 June, a further attack was launched. The struggle continued for four hours before, finally, the Turks captured the fort. They found just nine defenders alive, all of them badly wounded, and massacred them on the spot. The corpses were then tied to planks and thrown into the sea so that the tide would take them beneath the walls of Birgu.

Meanwhile, help was a long time coming. In France 'a kind of secret society to come to the support of Malta was formed among gentlemen keen for adventure'. In all some 300 nobles, along with 800 soldiers, were mustered. Brantôme, who was among their number, adds 'we were left to our own devices, and we depended upon ourselves'. Their captain had, at his own expense, organised and armed a company of fifty arquebusiers. Everything was done in comparative secrecy so that neither the king nor the queen would find out 'for it was known that, if they did, their majesties would forbid such a thing'. However, before very long, 'the Grand Seigneur [the sultan] complained to the king and he, in order to reassure him, banished us and disowned us'.[3] Nevertheless, the adventurers left Moulins, passing through Lyons on their way to Provence, Rome, and Naples. There they embarked on a fleet of twelve or thirteen 'rather poor little frigates' which just about managed to carry them to Messina and, from there, to Syracuse. There were a number of great warriors in their ranks – Brantôme and his brother Baron Ardelay; Timoléon de Cossé-Brissac; Joseph de Bonifas de la Mole; the Count of Montesquiou; and Philippe de la Guiche, later Grand Master of the Royal Artillery. In addition there were a number of key Huguenots, such as the Marquis of Resnel and Claude and Clermont Tallard, who were outspoken in their condemnation of the French alliance with the Turks and recognised the Maltese as an essential bastion against the machinations of the Turks.

The Spanish, in Italy, dithered. The governor of Sicily, Garcia de Toledo, needed much persuasion to assist the Knights, arguing that he had no orders from the king and did not wish to take responsibility himself for committing forces to a rather risky enterprise. But finally he felt assured enough to despatch a small force of 800 men; these arrived on Malta on 29 June, a week after the fall of the fort of St Elmo. Despite the modest size of this contingent – which came to be known as the 'Little Relief' – it lifted the spirits of the besieged tremendously. Its arrival was accompanied by news that Dragut, one of the best Turkish captains, had been killed by a cannon-shot. Mustapha offered the Hospitallers terms for an honourable capitulation, allowing them to leave with their weapons and ships if only they would quit Malta as they had done Rhodes. However, his envoy was sent back unheard.

Shortly thereafter a Turkish attack on the rear of Birgu failed. The Turks had wanted to pass some smallish vessels over the Sciberra hills, allowing them to sail directly into the harbour, but the Christians had got wind of the project. Indeed, one of the Turkish captains, Philip Lascaris, a renegade descendant of the Byzantine emperors, betrayed his masters. He jumped into the water and, 'despite his heavy cloak, his caftan and his weapons', managed to swim to Birgu and raise the alarm. The besieged sallied forth and hastily erected a strong palisade across the Isla peninsula which would prevent the Turks from carrying out their plan. The Ottomans did launch their attack, on 15 July, sending 3,000 men to the south of Isla and against the fort of St Michael, but only a few hundred made it back to the Turkish lines.

At Messina, Giovanni Andrea Doria[4] was at odds with the governor, Garcia de Toledo. Then, finally, on 20 August 1565, Toledo issued instructions to Admiral Alvaro del Sando and his chief of staff, Ascania de la Cornia: sixty galleys and a few large warships were to transport 9,000 soldiers – just about all the available Spanish infantry in the region, some from Lombardy and others from Corsica – to Malta. Ten days later Doria's assistance was sought to reconnoitre the Gozo channel and prepare a suitable site for the landing. The Spanish fleet left Sicily on 4 September but was driven back by a violent storm and had to set out again a few days later. The troops were threatening to mutiny, whilst their captains were hinting that Garcia de Toledo was a traitor. However, the troops of this 'Great Relief' managed to land in the north of the island on 7 September, encountering little resistance as they marched to Mdina. The Turks, decimated by fever and irritated by cavalry raids against their camp, felt decidedly vulnerable; the rains of autumn were making it difficult for them to bring up their reserves. On 8 September, the day after the Spanish landing, they began to withdraw. The Knights reoccupied a number of positions, even installing a garrison in St Elmo fort. Yet Mustapha, alerted perhaps that the Christian relief force was not as vast as had hitherto been thought, recovered his composure and marched his men against Naxxar, to the west of Birgu, on the road to Mdina. His troops fought badly, discouraged by their reverses, and retreated quickly. They lost a good number of men as they fell back and, attacked from all sides, regained their ships only with considerable difficulty.[5]

The Christian triumph on Malta gave birth to hopes of victory elsewhere. The Knights celebrated their salvation with a Mass in the San

Lorenzo church, and 'passing past the harbour, a long and beautiful salvo of artillery and musketry rang out from the galleys, galleons and other ships present there in good number. The church was adorned with great tapestries and with portraits of all the Grand Masters who had served since the beginning of the Order.'[6]

For many years afterwards the pashas of Algiers, Tunis, and Tripoli continued to accuse the Knights of piracy and abominable crimes. They represented the Maltese as criminals terrorising, killing, and pillaging at leisure, desiring nothing more but to steal whatever fell into their hands. Such accusations were often repeated by those at the French court and by certain pamphleteers that they hired. Malta, so it was said, was nothing more than the haunt of brigands and would be better wiped from the map. This was, in truth, a handy way of excusing the French decision not to send aid to the besieged Knights.

In reality the days when the Knights had tormented the Turks by raiding the Anatolian coast were long gone. Now, isolated and exposed to Turkish attacks, weakened and ruined by the devastating siege, they were a mere shadow of their former glory. Mobilising enough men and sufficient vessels to join an allied fleet would have been something of a miracle – their participation in Christian leagues against the Turks would, from now on, be nominal.[7]

The Holy League, 1566–71

The Christians and Turks rearmed. The Pope and the Venetians gathered in their forces. In 1566 news of an alliance was broached: 'The hour has come for Christendom to act against the Ottoman power and for all Christian princes to fight and exterminate them'. The allies intended to raise the necessary money from 300,000 parishes and 150,000 monasteries, and the funds should be made available in a common currency – twenty-four carat gold.

Pope Pius V spent a year forming the Holy League. He first of all called upon Philip II to commit his forces (April 1570) and then, after numerous and ever more urgent embassies, obtained the support of the princes of Italy. The viceroys or governors of Milan, Sardinia, Naples, and Sicily pledged support, as did the dukes of Tuscany, Ferrara, Parma, Mantua, and Urbino. Surprisingly, given their traditional rivalry, Venice and Genoa also came on board.

Cardinal Alessandrino, nephew of the Pope, was brusquely dismissed by Charles IX of France and the king's envoy in Rome, turning a deaf ear to the subject of alliance, absented himself from court. François de Noailles, on the other hand, was more open with the Venetians, venturing to suggest that they should rethink their decision to join the alliance; and when the Holy League was solemnly announced at St Peter's in Rome on 25 May 1571 it was without the support of His Most Christian Majesty the king of France.[8] Indeed, 'the French continued to transport all kinds of food and munitions to Algiers, and informed the corsairs what was happening on land and at sea, advising them of where warships might be found and such like'.[9] They also continued to support anyone who presented a threat to the king of Spain's authority. The revolt of the Moriscos, which broke out in Granada in 1562, had been supported by the Barbary corsairs ('arms for the revolt had been gathered in an Algerian mosque'), while Moors and Turks were able to buy provisions and weapons from France: 'They came to Marseilles to replenish their supply of biscuits, and to take on board saltpetre and powder'. In 1563 Giovanni Andrea Doria seized a French ship, loaded with lead and munitions, bound for Algiers.[10]

In France opinion was clearly massaged by numerous publications favourable to the Turks; some were accounts of embassies, others were more general treatises on morals and religion. They included Guillaume Postel's *Concordance du Coran et de l'Evangile* (1543); Pierre Belon's *Observations sur le monde ottoman* (1553); André Thevet's *Cosmographie du Levant* (1564); and Nicolas de Nicolay's *Navigations et peregrinations orientales*. This last, by the king's own cartographer, was published in Lyon in 1568 and contained sixty-two engravings of Turkish costume.[11] The king's ambassadors and ministers were all, almost to a man, resolutely hostile to the Papacy. Charles de Marcillac, archbishop of Vienne, even called for a national council whilst the Council of Trent was still in progress. Of the rest, Jean de Montluc had been dismissed as Bishop of Valence by Pius V in 1566,[12] Claude de Bourg had signed the famous Capitulations with the Turks, whilst François de Noailles, Bishop of Dax, had also been dismissed by the Pope as a 'notorious heretic'; even so, the king retained him as a bishop.[13]

In 1568 the Turks of Algiers and the Moors had sought, with all their might, to support a Muslim revolt in Granada. They had supplied arms, ammunition, and men. Euldj'Ali had assembled an imposing force of 14,000 musketeers and 60,000 Moors and had loaded caravans of camels with powder and weapons, despatching the whole force to Mazagan, near Mostaganem, on the Gulf of Arzew. There they were to prepare an attack on Oran and against Andalusia. He sent forty galliots to cruise off Almeria, waiting for a signal from the rebels. However, plans for the revolt, which should have taken place during Holy Week, were compromised when the authorities seized an important cache of arms. Nevertheless, in January 1569 six Algerian ships landed a shipment of cannon and ammunition close to Almeria. An expedition consisting of more than thirty galleys and transports was scattered by a storm later that year, whilst in October a band of rebels at large in the mountains drew their strength from weapons supplied from North Africa and a small reinforcement of Janissaries. The following spring, that of 1570, Euldj'Ali was again preparing an expeditionary force to aid the Moriscos when he learnt that Don Juan of Austria was about to take the war eastwards.[14]

Meanwhile, another offensive was in the offing – a Turkish fleet had carried an army to Cyprus. The Turks landed in June 1570 and arrived before Nicosia, without having met much resistance, on 9 September. As winter approached Piali Pasha embarked his men and set sail for Constantinople. Then, in January 1571, another fleet –a much stronger squadron with 2,000 men, supported by impressive artillery – set off on the same enterprise. At first events did not go the Turks' way. However, they soon realised that the Venetian fleet of Sebastian Venier, which was perhaps awaiting reinforcements, was reluctant to attack. The Turks thereupon went onto the offensive, bombarding Nicosia incessantly and finally forcing the garrison of 8,000 men, commanded by Luigi Martinegro, to capitulate. The terms stipulated that the garrison, which consisted mainly of Venetian troops, should be allowed to sail freely away on 4 August. 'These articles were ratified by Mustapha, but it was clear he did not intend to keep to them.' Indeed, he allowed his troops to sack the town and to 'liberate all the Greeks and Cypriots found in the camp whilst killing more than 200 Christians from other nations who had ventured out on account of the truce. After which they seized all they could and took them, chained, aboard their ships.'[15] Tiepolo, the governor, was hung, whilst the proveditore, Marcantonio Bragadin, was tortured and executed in a public square.[16]

The immense forces mobilised by the Ottomans in 1571 had taken years to prepare and assemble. Such an armada was not destined to merely reinforce gains made in the west or in North Africa, or to raid and seize booty; this time it was intended that Italy and Rome should be attacked.[17] As far back as the fall of Constantinople in 1453 the Turks had blended their chants of victory with a new battle cry: seize, pillage, and subdue Rome, the capital of the Christians, the supreme goal of Holy War. Later, in 1537, Suleiman had assembled a vast host at Valona, opposite Brindisi on the Albanian coast. More than 100,000 men had chanted 'To Rome! To Rome!' to their Sultan. Only news of fighting in Central Europe had made him desist in order that he could rush his forces to another front. But it was to be but a brief respite for Christendom.

Ali Pasha, the sultan's son-in-law, left Constantinople at the end of September 1571. He raided Corfu, ravaging the island, before anchoring his fleet at the entrance to the Gulf of Lepanto. In Spain that spring, Philip II had finally – or so it seemed – quashed the Morisco revolt and was hastily assembling men, money, and ships. The entire nation was straining under an unprecedented financial effort; the Council for Crusades received 400,000 ducats in voluntary donations from the clergy and 300,000 in a levy from parishes.[18] Meanwhile the arsenals of Seville were working night and day.

At Barcelona Don Juan of Austria was assembling two *tercios* (regiments) under Lope de Figueroa and Miguel de Moncade. His fleet joined up with the forty-seven galleys of Genoa and, at Naples, the twenty-nine galleys of the Marquis of Santa Cruz. It was in Naples, in the church of Santa Chiara to be precise, that Antoine Perrenot de Granvelle, cardinal and viceroy, handed Don Juan the standard of the Holy League. It was in Naples too that Cervantes, a veteran who had already fought in the expedition of Marco Antonio Colonna[19] for the relief of Cyprus in 1570, signed up for the new enterprise. On 15 September 1571 he engaged to serve on board Francisco de Santo Pietro's *Marquesa*.[20] Giovanni Andrea Doria's forty-nine vessels joined the main fleet at Otranto.

The Christian combined fleet first made for Corfu, anchoring near the Gulf of Lepanto somewhere between the castles of Morea and Roumelia. In all it numbered 204 or 208 galleys, six or seven large galeasses, 100 transports or supply ships, and 80 brigantines.[21] Numerically the Turks were much the stronger, with 230 galleys which were sleeker and more manoeuvrable than those of the Christians and were each accompanied by one or two *fustes*. Both sides brought roughly 50,000 soldiers and sailors into the fray.

The Turkish advantage of numbers was offset by other factors, however. The Ottomans did not enjoy a unified command. Ali Pasha, admiral in chief, inspected the fleet and had his men dance and sing but, in reality, commanded but a hundred of the Turkish galleys. Euldj'Ali, king of Algiers, was in charge of a mightier force, and he very much wished to use it for his own purposes. Indeed, his men, far from being keen on fighting to the death, pleaded with him to lead them back to Africa and not to sacrifice them in vain in an enterprise of little particular relevance.

The command of the Christian fleet, on the other hand, lay firmly in the hands of Don Juan of Austria, the twenty-two-year-old illegitimate son of Charles V, who had spent the last four years waging war on the Barbary corsairs and Turks. Now he was responsible for the successful conclusion of this holy mission. For Don Juan, and the closest of his associates, the war with the Turks was far more than mere rivalry or a contest of territorial ambitions; it was firmly grounded in the belief that such a struggle was directly serving God and Christianity. Don Juan's own tutor, Ambrosio de Morales, was a close friend of Pope Clement VII's councillor Juan Guies de Sepulveda. This important figure was also chaplain and confessor of Emperor Charles V and author of *Exhortation à la guerre contre le Turc* (1530). Another of Don Juan's close companions was Alejo Venegas who, along with Alvaro Gomez de Ciudad Real, had written *La milice du prince de Bourgogne appelée Toison d'Or*. The chivalric order of La Toison d'Or, created by the dukes of Burgundy in 1430 and inherited by the imperial family, referred not to the golden fleece retrieved by Jason and his Argonauts from Colchis but, rather, to that of Gideon of Israel, whom God had aided to vanquish the Midianites and kill their two kings. Now it was time to do the same for Christianity.

The commanders of the various squadrons had, during the course of previous campaigns, demonstrated their aptitude and skill. They included such men as Luis de Requesens,[22] the Marquis of Santa Cruz and Commander of the forces of Castile; Giovanni Andrea Doria; Marco Antonio Colonna, Captain-General of the Papal fleet; and Giustiniani, Prior of Messina for the Knights of Malta. A number of princes were also serving in the fleet: Alessandro Farnese, Duke of Parma;[23] Francisco della Rovere, Duke of Urbino; Paolo Orsini, Duke of Bracciano;[24] Ottavio

Gonzaga, Count of Molfeta; the Marquis of Carrara; and, although he would not survive the battle, Francis, Duke of Savoy.[25]

The Christian forces were drawn from diverse nations and different origins. Don Juan's fleet counted fifteen Spanish galleys, thirty from Naples, ten from Sicily, 109 from Venice, twelve from the papacy, three from Malta, three from Savona, and twenty-seven from Genoa. Only three of the latter had actually been armed and equipped by the city's authorities, and were commanded by officers designated by those authorities; the others had been provided instead by the city's great families. Thus, for example, Doria supplied eleven, whilst such families as the Negroni,[26] Grimaldi, Lomellini, and di Mare provided a handful apiece.

Nevertheless, the allied fleet was very much aware that these diverse bodies needed to fight a combined, unified battle and that no squadron should wage its own war. Not that long ago an allied fleet, despatched to aid Cyprus, had fallen prey to in-fighting when, incredibly, the Venetians had opened fire on Doria's vessels. The Venetian Senate had rigorously investigated this shameful episode, and the guilty parties were pursued and subjected to the full rigours of the law. The admiral responsible was even thrown into jail.

To avoid a repetition of such behaviour, Don Juan took the clever step of not allowing any of the component nations to form a separate squadron. Instead each squadron consisted of a mixture of vessels from different countries. On the right flank, commanded by Doria, twenty-two Venetian ships would fight alongside six Spanish ones from Naples and five from Sicily, as well as two Papal ships from Civitavecchia. Each flew a green banner.[27] Other squadrons were organised in a similar way. The left wing, under Venetian command, consisted of fifty galleys and two galeasses, all flying yellow flags, whilst the centre, consisting of seventy galleys and two galeasses, flew blue flags. Finally, the squadron under the Marquis of Santa Cruz, general of Maltese galleys, which constituted the reserve, boasted thirty-one galleys flying white flags. Don Juan had, in addition to his plethora of sailors, some 7,000 Spanish infantry, 12,000 Italians, and 1,000 volunteers from across Europe under his orders. He distributed them throughout the fleet in such a way that 4,000 Spanish infantry were assigned to the Venetian galleys.

Don Juan promised that if victory was theirs he would set free such of his rowers as were criminals who had been condemned to the galleys, which gave them considerable motivation to do their duty. Aurelio

Scetti, a Florentine condemned to the galleys for murdering his wife, was on board a Sicilian ship.[28] In his journal, published a few years later, we are presented with a dramatic eyewitness account of the battle from the point of view of one such prisoner. He wrote: 'Besides the promises made to me by my captain, I had my faith in the grace of God and my prince. I told myself that it would be impossible after victory not to obtain what had been promised to us beforehand. To be sure, I took two Moors and said if I was not to have my liberty one way, I should have it by another.'[29]

The Turks, or rather their pashas, had more confidence in their ships than in those who served aboard them. That spring and summer had been spent in a veritable hunt for manpower so that the galleys could be provided with oarsmen, described as 'a pitiless quest to enslave men, whether Christian or Muslim, especially in Greece and its islands, areas already depopulated'. The admiral, Ali Pasha, was aware of his oarsmen's morale and their desire to flee at the first opportunity. On 28 September, just ten days before the battle, he ordered that 'Christian slaves should lie down if the vessel is boarded and should be killed if they lift their heads'.[30] These slaves would, as much as they were able, seek to avoid obeying their orders. All accounts speak of them attempting to save themselves by fleeing at the first opportunity: 'all in all they favoured our [Christian] victory and they fought accordingly'.[31]

7 October 1571

At dawn on 7 October the Christians began to deploy at the entrance to the gulf, where their enemies were waiting for them. It was a difficult manoeuvre against a stubborn crosswind and one potentially at the mercy of an enemy which could attack at any moment. But the risk paid off. The Turks, anchored in the gulf, didn't lift a finger to prevent the Christian move and soon found themselves hemmed in and incapable of manoeuvring. Ali Pasha, ignoring advice from many of his captains to position himself within the protection afforded by the forts along the coast, stuck religiously to the Sultan's orders to employ all his forces. Euldj'Ali, with a numerical superiority of three or four galleys against one, failed to defeat Doria on the right flank but then managed to drive a wedge between the Christian right and centre. Moving rapidly, his light galleys threatened to take the Christians from the rear: 'He manoeuvred his galleys as a horseman does a circus horse. He charged backwards and forwards, firing his cannon and muskets to left and to right.'[32] The Maltese galleys, attacked from all sides, were soon riddled with holes and perforated by arrows: 'Giustiniani's ship, the *Capitaine*, surrounded by seven enemy ships, couldn't hold out any longer. Even before the Turks managed to board, all the Knights were dead or mortally wounded. The enemy finished them off with a general massacre.' For the Christians this was the crisis of the day:

> The blare of trumpets and the rumble of drums grew terrifying. Worse still was the noise of muskets and shot and the thunder of the artillery. The shouts and cries were horrible and the clamour was so intense as to make it seem that one was caught in a hideous nightmare. Clouds of arrows rent the air which was poisoned by artificial smoke so dense as to seem like some terrible fog.

Don Juan had kept his reserve, the squadron of Santa Cruz, out of view. Now he released it to crash into Euldj'Ali before attacking Ali Pasha's ships, which were boarded and then sent to the bottom. The standard of the Holy League soon flew from the masthead of the Sultana, the Turkish admiral's ship. The admiral himself had either been killed before his ship was boarded or, according to some witnesses, had died during the struggle.

> The sea, for nearly eight miles around, was littered with masts, debris, oars and a vast quantity of corpses. Men wept, shouted, cursed and cried. This scene of monstrous fantasy swept us into an alien world. Turks who could not swim for the shore or who did not wish to throw themselves into the water, continued to fight. Those who no longer had weapons seized hold of whatever they could lay their hands on; they even threw oranges and lemons.[33]

Rather than support his comrades, and more intent on saving his ships, Euldj'Ali abandoned the struggle and fled. Passing along the coast and through the Turkish ships, he took his remaining thirty galleys northwards towards Petala and Santa Maura and then as far as Modon. From the point of his departure the battle was decided in the Christians' favour.

It was a resounding victory, resulting in the almost total destruction of the Ottoman fleet. The Turks had lost some fifty galleys destroyed by fire or sunk, while another 150 ships had been captured and their crews taken prisoner. As many as a hundred vessels were burnt after being captured, as it proved impossible to haul them all away. The Turks had also lost some 30,000 men killed and 5,000 taken prisoner, whilst 15,000 Spanish and Italian captives were liberated.

The Christians mourned the loss of 7–8,000 men. Of these, some 2,300 had been lost from Venetian galleys, either drowned or killed, including thirty nobles. Seventeen of these were commanders of galleys either destroyed or heavily damaged by the Turks.

A few days after the battle Marc Antonio Colonna was charged with the distribution of the booty made that day. This consisted, in the main, of 130 galleys, 117 pieces of heavy and 256 pieces of light artillery, and 3,500 slaves. Don Juan was awarded a tenth of this booty as well as sixteen galleys and 720 slaves.[34] Colonna was also given the task of escorting the most important of the Turkish prisoners to Rome, to deliver them up to the Pope so that he might 'do with them as he saw fit'.[35]

Victory

To suggest that Lepanto was an empty victory, or that it was flawed, and that thousands and thousands of men had perished for nought, neglects to consider the object of the Turkish offensive. The Spanish and Italians had been living, for decades, with the fear of seeing their cities sacked and their men, women, and children abducted and sold into slavery. The people of Corsica, Sardinia, and southern Italy – and even of Rome – had good reason to believe that the Turks were seeking to subjugate and conquer their lands, to turn their churches into mosques, and to forcibly convert them to Islam.

In truth, the suggestion that Lepanto was a hollow victory emanated principally from those territories which were either not particularly menaced or had not joined the Holy League, or had even been allied to the Turks and hostile to the king of Spain. For these, the fact that King Philip II, the Pope, and the Knights of Malta, had emerged as great heroes was too much. They felt the need to cast aspersions on the achievement and to diminish its significance as much as was possible.[36] Elsewhere reactions were more positive, and the victory at Lepanto, which halted the Ottoman invasion of the west, was widely greeted with relief and rejoicing.

Marco Antonio Colonna entered Rome in triumph at the head of a mighty procession, in an ostentatious ceremony reminiscent of ancient times. A thousand young people, from many different professions, filed past, banners blazing, to the tune of drums and fifes, 'their horses champing at the bit, a cohort of Roman nobles dressed in violet, each escorted by liveried servants'. Then came a dozen 'captains of the people', followed by their valets, dressed in crimson, and the Pope's cavalry squadrons beneath banners and standards seized from the Turkish fleet. Colonna himself, dressed in golden brocade, moved through the crowd like Caesar accompanied by his senators. The Christians rejoiced, Rome gave thanks.

Glorification of the victors went hand in hand, as it did in ancient Rome, with humiliation of the defeated: 'After the victory parade came that of shame and defeat: the lamentable convoy of 500 Turks, roped together, four by four, with nooses round their necks. Wagons followed in their wake filled with weapons, clothes and other booty from the Turks.' The Turkish seigneurs, hands tied behind their backs, stumbled along, not looking at the crowd which hurled insults at them. But it was the songs of deliverance, in gratitude of grace, that rose above the cacophony of triumph. 'The crowd shouted and cheered. Pious women said their rosary; it was once a rosary of prayer for success, now it was one of gratitude for victory.' Triumphs, festivities, and jubilant celebrations were organised across Italy by the Pope, the Doge of Venice, by princes and dukes, and by the king of Spain. These were not dry and dusty organised events but enthusiastic celebrations, occasions of public joy.[37] 'Christianity cannot believe its own good fortune.'[38] Spain and Italy celebrated in a thousand different ways because 'it was a great day for Christians; for all the nations of the world, who had thought the Turks invincible, were now disabused of this error and the Turkish beast had been tamed'.[39]

Earlier Spanish operations against the Turks in North Africa had given rise to the publication of various accounts, many of them by participants. Captains and Knights took up their pens in an attempt to describe the triumphs of the victors and the unhappy fates of the defeated and the prisoners. This had been the case following the taking of Tunis in 1535, the unfortunate expedition to Algiers in 1541, and that against

Djerba in 1560.[40] The day following the success at Lepanto witnessed the similar hasty writing of reports by Castilians, Italians (especially Venetians), and Knights of Malta alike, which sought to offer blow-by-blow accounts of the battle and to describe the merits, glories, and sacrifices of the fleet.

On 31 December, on Corfu, the Venetian Girolamo Diedo dedicated a long account of the battle to Marco Antonio Barbaro, Duke of Pliano and Tagliacozzo,[41] a relative of Andrea Barbaro, killed on his galley, and of another Barbaro who succumbed to a wound in his eye. The account was long, detailed, and immediate, and amounted to more than forty pages. Francesco Cornaro, the Venetian governor of Corfu, had asked him to draw up the work, and he did so meticulously, drawing on every source he could and including every detail. He outlined how Venice had been drawn into the war after surviving many setbacks and defeats in the east and in the Adriatic, and also included a vast body of information from the Spaniards and the Maltese. His assessment of the Christian fleet was, of course, slanted towards the exploits of the Serenissima's vessels – the 108 galleys of Sebastian Venier coupled with the twelve galleys of Marco Antonio Barbaro. He described and compared the Christian and Turkish fleets, attempted to analyse the effective strength of both, as well as their morale, and sought to throw light on the experiences of men on both sides, before concluding with an explanation as to why the Christians triumphed.

In contrast to this serious history the battle also gave rise to countless songs – soldiers' songs, popular songs, and ballads. Each exalted the defenders of the faith, and the sacrifices of men caught up in the struggle against enemies intent on pillaging, burning, and destroying. Don Juan, right from the start, was the central figure, the popular hero. He was, for many, the champion of Christ and everyone's idol. Examples of this kind of song are the *Chanson sur la victoire de seigneur Don Juan*, composed in 1572 by Herrera, and the short piece in which 'the army of the Holy League, like the Israelites throwing off the Egyptian yoke, march forward as with the prophecies and conquer the Holy Land':

Sing to the Lord, he who has vanquished
savage Thrace
You, God of Battles, you are our right.
You have bettered the forces of the Pharaoh
A ferocious warrior.[42]

Popular songs of the period, whether simple songs of victory or homages to heroes, poems, sonnets, and ballads, were issued in vast numbers – so many that it is impossible to catalogue all of them. Most disappeared relatively quickly, leaving hardly any trace. For Italy alone Eugenio Masi published in Milan, in 1893, an in-depth study of a hundred songs on the battle, and Giovanni Battista Quarti devoted an entire book to popular songs about Lepanto in 1930. In fact this latter study was devoted almost exclusively to songs collected just from the Veneto, Padua, and Forli, whilst others from the Papal States, Naples, and the Italian principalities were not included. The 310-page work had carefully transcribed all the songs and was minutely documented, covering some fifty songs in all. These varied from brief ballads of just one or two verses, to more weighty attempts of 150, 270, and even 320 verses, some set to music. Some were the work of celebrated writers of the period, whilst others were the work of obscure poets. These included Giovanni Battista Donato, the illegitimate son of a Venetian patrician, himself a man of letters who spent much of his time on his estates near Caorle. Another such was Manoli Blessa, another Venetian, a singer and dancer and sometime court jester, who lived on his wits as far afield as Crete and Corfu. There was also Agostino Rava, an honourable citizen of Vicenza, member of the Olympic Academy, and author of a lament on the death of his patron, Contarini, killed in the battle. Finally there was, Luigi Groto, known as the Blind Man, versed in law and Greek, player of the lute, and president of the Academy of Illustrious Men of Adria, in the Po delta.

A few of the songs, in truth, were little more than slogans: 'Long live the Christians who, in just a day, destroyed the armada of the Turkish curs'. Others, such as the *Pianti e Lamenti di Selim*, the *Canti reprehensibili*, and the *Essortazioni*, dwelt at length on the woes of the 'invincible' Turks and the Sultan, revelling in their humiliation. Selim's name is constantly cited, as a byword for bloodthirsty tyranny bloated with pride. One of the most virulent of the songs was directed against the Sultan's captain Euldj'Ali ('Occhiali' in the lyrics), urging that he be exiled and mockingly observing that 'You have no more galleys, no more fleets to go a-raiding; all your men are slaves. Listen, swinish brute, if Heaven is closed to you, so is the Earth and even Hell, peopled with beasts like yourself, will refuse you; where then will you roam?'

All these songs and lyrics illustrate one thing quite clearly. For the people of Italy the Turks were no distant threat, but one which caused a constant and general anguish and malaise. That is why, for Italians, Lepanto could not be considered an empty victory.[43]

A Fragile Peace, 1571–81

It proved impossible at first to pursue Euldj'Ali across the Peleponnese. The evening of the battle, and the following day, was spent reforming the fleet, dividing the booty, and welcoming those Christian slaves who had survived the bombardment, drowning, or execution by their overseers. More than 20,000 men were landed on the Adriatic coast and cared for in improvised hospitals. But winter was approaching and the Spanish fleet was troubled by a storm as it made its way back to Messina. There it was welcomed by frenzied acclamations and *Te Deums*.

Almost inevitably, discord now began to show itself among the leaders of the Christian fleet. The question of how to follow up the victory generated a heated debate which, in turn, called forth embassies, letters to and from princes, kings, and the Pope, and sundry orders and counterorders. Captain Thome Cano, a counsellor of the king of Spain and subsequently author of a scholarly study entitled *The Art of Making and Arming Ships of War and Merchantmen* (published in Seville in 1611), thought Lepanto a marvellous, miraculous, and famous victory but regretted that discord, distrust, and jealousy prevented the reaping of 'the rightful fruits of victory'.

Indeed, the Holy League had now split into two opposing factions: one, following the lead of Philip II, hoped to consolidate the victory by turning on the North Africans and destroying the corsairs' bases; whilst the other, led by the Pope and the Venetians, hoped to carry the war eastwards, retaking some of the Venetian colonies and securing the rest, and striking a blow against the weakened Turkish empire. The *Serenissima*'s ambassadors remorselessly pressed Rome and the Italian states to such an extent that commentators in Spain and Italy reproached them for pursuing a futile dream of creating a great colonial empire in the east.

It was Philip II who ultimately gave up. In the end he maintained Doria at Messina to guard the straits of the Tyrrhenian Sea whilst a grand fleet of 280 vessels sailed east to confront Euldj'Ali, who was skulking from one harbour to another in the Peloponnese. The Spaniards, however, failed to take Modon and were unsuccessful before Coron. A few months later Venice decided that, rather than build more and more galleys and undertake risky adventures, she would prefer to make peace with the Turks and quit the League. By doing so they would at least guarantee favourable terms and lighter taxes for their merchants.

Even though virtually isolated, Philip II could still call upon considerable resources – 150 galleys, plus those of the Pope and the Knights of Malta. But now he turned towards Africa.

It was a moot point whether to attack Algiers or Tunis. A few months after Lepanto Philip gave careful consideration to an attack on Algiers, and gave up on the project only when he received reports that a considerable body of Moors and Janissaries had reinforced the town's defences. Their commander, Pasha Ahmed, was himself well-informed regarding Spanish intentions; some of the intelligence which he received was supplied by ships sent from Marseilles by Charles IX of France for that express purpose. In return an embassy brought the king handsome gifts – Arab horses, lions, tigers, and buffaloes ('a rather strange cow' according to the French observer).[44]

Don Juan took Tunis without too much trouble and was again greeted as a hero upon his return to Naples in November 1573. He left 7–8,000 men in Tunis along with numerous guns, a good stock of munitions, and specialist engineers to reinforce and improve the town's walls. In Constantinople the loss of Tunis, following so soon upon the heels of Lepanto, provoked despondency and a campaign designed to root out the corrupt, the incapable, and the negligent. Meanwhile, the city's arsenals worked night and day, arming dozens of galleys in a matter of months.[45]

In July 1574 Euldj'Ali, appointed Captain-General by the Sultan, arrived before Tunis with a fleet numbering more than 200 galleys, thirty galliots, and forty 'mighty vessels' manned by 5,000 sailors and carrying an impressive force of 40,000 men under Sinane Pasha, a renegade from the illustrious Visconti family of Venice. The Spanish garrison was virtually swamped but fought back vigorously, repelling daily assaults. The fort of La Goulette nevertheless fell on 23 August and Tunis followed on 13 September. The besieged had lost thousands of dead and the rest were dragged off into slavery.

The stubborn Spanish resistance at Tunis had at least diverted the Turks from attacking Italy. Their victory had been bought only at considerable cost, the Turks having lost more men at Tunis than the

Spaniards, a fact which, when coupled with the Lepanto disaster, made it a somewhat Pyrrhic victory. Spanish and Italian sources, although inclined to exaggerate, estimated Turkish losses in the expedition in tens of thousands. Cervantes wrote that they suffered 25,000 dead before Tunis itself. Cabrera de Cordoba, a chronicler and companion of Philip II, thought that 33,000 was nearer the mark, amongst whom many 'were captains and men of importance'. A Genoese merchant in Tunis itself thought that the Turkish loss amounted to 50,000 killed plus 15,000 dead of disease. Jean Dumont was perhaps right when he noted that 'the human cost of the war against Christianity was becoming prohibitive'.[46] The Sultan saw his forces wasting away and recognised that, since the rancour of 1544–50, he could no longer count on any military assistance from the French.

The kings of France were nevertheless still engaged in a diplomatic war in favour of the Turks, and continued to provide support to the enemies of Spain, Austria, and Rome. During the reign of Henri II (1574–89) French ships, on unofficial or official business, frequented North African ports and went on their way unmolested. Trade was good and food, weapons, and munitions changed hands. In Algiers, and in Constantinople, the French were treated as friendly neutrals, enjoying privileges and special treatment.

Morat Raïs, of Albanian origin, was one of the most famous of the Barbary corsairs and was a successful and renowned pirate. Diego de Haedo thought that he had 'punished us hard for our sins'. However, he had the temerity to hold up French ships on one of his expeditions. This was 'quite contrary to the orders of the Great Lord [Sultan]'. In 1578 the French ambassador was presented with Morat's head and wrote, indulgently, to his master in France that 'at the express command of the Sultan this Morat Raïs, a great corsair from the Barbary coast, and the principal author of the thefts and robberies, was apprehended and thrown into irons, his goods and slaves confiscated.'[47] On 25 January 1581 Henri of Angoulême, the governor of Provence and Captain-General of Galleys, wrote to thank the king of Algiers and to solicit from him a few further favours. He closed his letter with the telling 'You are doing me good service and I would be obliged if you would inform me if there is anything I can do in return'.[48]

Unsurprisingly, the disaster which befell the invincible Spanish Armada in 1588 was celebrated almost as much in France as it was in

England. A Spanish galeasse, harried by contrary winds, was blown on to the French coast, where Henri III, ignoring Philip II's protestations, liberated the ship's crew of 300 Turkish and Moorish slaves. These unfortunates were brought to Chartres Cathedral, where they prostrated themselves before their deliverer and offered up their thanks.[49]

However, such aiding and abetting of the Turkish cause was never actually supported by concrete action. No French captains or French fleets attacked the enemy or raided his coastlines. France was an accomplice, but it was not involved.

The Turks gradually made peace with the western powers, signing treaties one by one. In 1581 an Italian Knight named Maglieni, a hero of the fighting around Tunis and La Goulette, was sent by Philip II to discuss terms for a year's armistice. The Turks concurred and made this an annually instituted agreement and a lasting peace.[50]

Chapter IV

The Africa of the Corsairs

There was never any real lasting dialogue between Christian Europe and Barbary Africa, and there was certainly no theological discussion. Juan de Segovia's book, entitled *De mittendo gladio Divini Spiritu in corda Sarracenorum*, written in the aftermath of the Turkish conquest of Constantinople, was reasonably successful and gave rise to a certain amount of public debate about missions and conversion. In the book the author recommended that Arabic should be learnt and that a trilingual (Arabic, Latin, and Catalan) edition of the Koran should be produced. He also submitted that Holy War was 'theologically unacceptable' and that, in its stead, concord should be reached. He was not suggesting that Christians shouldn't fight to protect Christian lands overrun by Muslims, but, rather, sought to condemn overtly militant action waged in the name of religion.[1] Shortly after publication, however, when news of increased persecution of Christians in North Africa arrived, with details of the fate of missionaries, the evangelical ardour aroused by the book was somewhat diminished and plans to convert the peoples of the Barbary coast were aborted. The activities of the Trinitarians and Mercederians – two orders dedicated to buying back Christian captives from the Moors – were closely monitored. They were frequently suspected, but their spirit of 'travelling to the Moors' and seeking out martyrdom and beatification overrode such concerns.

Very few merchants, and very few slaves, ever learnt an African language. In part this was because North African society was so diverse.

There was a dearth of structure and a wealth of different languages – communities simply imposed their own, or adapted a local patois which suited their particular needs. The Moors typically made use of an Arabic dialect which varied from one region to the next. Most merchants and sailors were quite happy to confine themselves to buying and selling, restricting discussion to talk of prices and markets. If they were required to stay a little longer they would be accommodated among their own compatriots in the *fondouk*, limiting their contact with the locals to, perhaps, just customs officials or royal agents. Such officials made use of a special jargon, which they termed 'Frankish language' but which bore but a passing resemblance to any Western European tongue. Such a phenomenon can be found in any cultural melting pot where peoples speaking diverse languages come together to live and communicate. This particular jargon took words from Catalan, Spanish, Provencal, and, naturally, Latin, and blended them with a few Arabic phrases as well as with some Turkish and even some Greek, or close approximations thereof. It respected neither grammatical rules nor linguistic convention; but it did make its presence felt, and was in widespread use not just for trade and commerce but in everyday life too, being employed even by women and children throughout the region.[2]

No European merchant would willingly make use of the local currency: 'All the coins, *reales*, *ecus*, *solta*, are of uncertain value as the Pasha of Algiers raises or debases the currency according to his needs'.[3] They would, in preference, use Italian or Spanish coinage, most particularly silver *reales*, which were the most sought after by Arabic traders and could be used by them across North Africa and even as far away as India and China.

Nor could any European look upon the Maghreb in the same way that he could view the countries of Syria, Egypt, or the East. There they might marvel at the riches to be seen, or the elegance of the architecture, or at least of the profits which might be had from trade. Descriptive accounts of the Maghreb were exceptionally rare; there was no place of pilgrimage, no grand market for spices. Sudanese gold, or rather gold-dust, was bought at Honein or Oran, but trade for it elicited as much enthusiasm as trade for pepper or some other spice.

Eyewitnesses: Warriors and Pilgrims

Even so, to a number of Christians the Barbary coast was not altogether alien or remote. Warfare, raids, and the carrying off of relatives or neighbours made it impossible to avoid hearing about its foreignness, or its customs and way of life. And if merchants and sailors chose to be guarded about disclosure of information, and chose not to set their affairs down in writing, this was not true of liberated slaves, diplomats, and members of the religious orders. Such people were more inclined to put pen to paper, and their often precise descriptions serve as good source material. Captains, warriors, and soldiers also provided worthwhile accounts. Many set down lengthy descriptions of their campaigns, recalling particular circumstances and places. In addition they often sought to provide explanations for a defeat or a setback, and described fortifications and their state of defence, their own resources, and those of the enemy. From them we have a reasonable picture of the coast, as they discussed all the important positions along it, how to tackle them, and how to surprise them.

Luis del Marmol-Carvajal, a native of Granada, served as a cabin boy on one of the ships which took part in Charles V's expedition against Algiers in 1541. A little later he was seized and held as a captive for seven years and eight months in Taroudant and Fez in Morocco. He later spent a good deal of time living in Africa, and all this experience combined to make him an authority on that continent from the Barbary Coast to Guinea. His book, which was translated into French and published in 1667 as *L'Afrique de Marmol*, comprises three quarto volumes of astonishing density. It covers the history of various military campaigns, and provides descriptions of Barbary, Ethiopia, Egypt, and the Sahara.

The second volume, which is 600 pages long, describes the region's towns and villages, kingdom by kingdom. Some eighty-six chapters describe 180 Moroccan towns, 135 in the kingdom of Fez, fifty-eight in Tlemcen – including Algiers – and fifty-eight in Tunis. Naturally, a great number of these places would be almost impossible to trace today, and few of them appear in any other works on the subject. Thus, for example, in the kingdom of Tlemcen we have Micila, Migana, Yeteza, Zamora, and Necaus. The author's description of Algiers itself runs to about a dozen pages, that of Tunis some forty, and Djerba twenty. Marmol also talks about the people, their customs, and their costumes. But his is the only contemporary account which attempts a comprehensive history of the region's cities from Roman times onwards. The reader marvels, too, at the depth of detail when he describes the rise and fall of dynasties and tribes.

As a man of war he is especially particular when describing fortifications and defences, highlighting where such and such a position is weakest, and outlining the possibilities for hoarding food and water and positioning reserves. Regarding Bône, for instance, he observes that: 'There are neither wells nor fountains in the town or in the citadel; instead, there are great cisterns which store all the rainwater which is channelled off the roofs of the houses.' He also provides details of the mundane, such as markets, noting that at Bône 'the Berbers flock to a market at the city's gates on a Wednesday; merchants from Tunis, Djerba, Tripoli and even Genoa also come on account of the profit to be made there.' For Tunis, he relates that 'in the middle of the city there is a square surrounded by shops; it is always crowded and the perfume shops remain open until midnight as the city's women go to bathe at night.' At Djerba (which was captured in 1284 by Roger de Lluria, admiral for the king of Aragon, and held by the Catalans for a considerable period thereafter) there could be found 'a settlement inhabited by Turkish, Moorish and Christian merchants, as there is a vast market there every week, a fair at which all the resources of the land can be found; the Arabs bring their goods and their flocks, which the country has in abundance.'[4]

Francesco Lanfreducci and Gion Ottone Bosio were both Knights of Malta. The former was responsible for the Order's accounts and in 1599 became an admiral; the latter was the brother of Jacques Bosio, celebrated historian of the Order and author of its history from the eleventh century to the battle of Lepanto.[5] In 1587 they were ordered to compile a detailed report on Barbary, which was presented under the title *Costa e Discursi di Barberia* (or 'A Military and Political Report on the Coast of North Africa'). This was, in due course, followed up by more detailed monographs on Tripoli, Djerba, Tunis, and Algiers, as well as a three-page treatise on 'How to Curry Favour with the Bedouin Chiefs'.

The main report was designed to be of use to military commanders in the event of any planned attack on the coast. The authors sought to identify all the principal coastal features – promontories, islands, and shoals – with suggestions of how to avoid them. So, for example, 'in the kingdom of Tunis, there are three rocks twenty-five miles to the north-east of Kerkenna. The distance from Kerkenna can be measured by sounding. A mile is equal to a fathom's depth. If red sand is brought up from the seabed then you lie to the west; if shellfish are caught you are easterly.' And so on along the coast.

When it came to describing the cities and towns along the coast the two explorers-cum-strategists apparently relied on information provided by spies. These reports allowed the authors to hazard an estimate as to how defences were maintained and how best they might be assailed. At Djerba 'the taking of the fort would always be supported by Christians in the place; success would come to even a poorly equipped fleet if it arrived before the place in autumn or even winter and made use of secure anchorages offering protection. Galleys can come close up to land for the disembarkation of troops.' For Tunis success would be attained 'with 100 galleys and 100 sloops, and 20,000 men, sometime between August and the end of September, a period during which time it would be impossible for the Turkish fleet to intervene. Such an affair should not last more than twenty or thirty days as there are few defenders.' Whilst for Algiers, 'without a doubt if this place falls it will spell the end of the Ottoman dynasty'. But such an undertaking was by far the most difficult, considerably more so at the time of the book's compilation than when the Emperor had attempted it in 1541.[6]

Many liberated prisoners also recorded their experiences upon their return from captivity, so as to inform their fellow citizens of the strength of the Muslims and provide details of their leadership and their methods. Nicolo Carraciolo, Bishop of Catane, had embarked upon a galley belonging to the Knights of Malta at Messina in 1561 in order to attend the Council of Trent. Two days later the vessel was captured by Dragut and the bishop was dragged off, along with a number of other prisoners, to Tripoli. His loyal parishioners not only prayed for his deliverance but also set about raising money for his ransom, which the good cleric refused. He was nevertheless released a short time later for the considerable sum of 30,000 ecus; it was whispered that he had even agreed that if he ever became Pope, he'd pay the Turks an even greater sum. Whatever the truth of such rumours, the bishop was soon writing an account of his captivity, which, known as the 'Discourse on the State of Tripoli', he dedicated to the viceroy of Sicily. In this he outlined the city's defences and suggested a possible way to attack it. He also attempted to analyse the personality of the corsair Dragut, who reputedly made all Italy tremble and was 'brave, audacious, as enterprising as bold and who seized everyone he could, generals as well as soldiers'.[7]

Diego de Haedo, a Benedictine monk from a distinguished Basque family (one of his relatives was Archbishop of Palermo), was taken prisoner by the Turks in 1578 and spent three years in Tripoli. He had plenty of opportunity to familiarise himself with the lot of its Christian slaves, as well as to observe Moorish merchants and artisans and the Turkish officials of the pasha. He was, indeed, close enough to some to converse with them and to obtain sometimes contradictory information on the region's history. He was subsequently able to write a detailed account of the first Barbarossa's attack on Bougie in 1514 because, as he recounts, survivors of the enterprise had confided in him: 'Some of the older Turks told me that the true reason behind the abandonment of the enterprise was the departure of the king of Bougie and his allies'.[8] After his release he gathered additional material from other former captives and also drew upon the memoirs of the Trinitarians. The result of all this research was three major publications. These achieved considerable success in their day and are, even now, major sources for the history of the period. One of these – the *Topographia e Historia general de Argel*, published in Valladolid in 1612 – devotes an entire chapter to the captivity of Cervantes, as well as describing the fate of Christian slaves in detail.

Father Pierre Dan was the author of the *Commentaire des choses des Turcs*, dedicated to Charles V at the time he was preparing his expedition in 1541. Dan had dedicated his life to buying back Christian captives and, for half a century, had struggled hard to raise the necessary funds and carry out such difficult transactions. Paolo Giovo was another eyewitness who was more a humanist than a man of action. Born at Como in 1483, and educated in Florence, he later practised medicine at Rome. His first work was rather modest and bore the title 'River and Sea Fish', but he then switched to writing a chronicle of events in Italy, or rather an analysis of events in the peninsula, which was completed in 1547. The resultant history contained much on the Barbary Corsairs and the Turks, and also described their lands and cities. It was published in Lyon in two volumes in 1552 and 1565. A prolific writer, Giovo also edited the lives of noted contemporary figures and an elegy on notables from antiquity up to his own time.

The Cities of the Corsairs

The Saracen corsairs had various haunts dotted along the Barbary coast, such as Mahdia, Sfax, and Bougie, the very names of which sowed fear in the hearts of every Christian. The situation in Africa, with warring tribes and clans in the interior, guaranteed these bases a certain degree of independence. As far back as the start of the thirteenth century the arrival of Muslim refugees from Spain, fleeing before the Aragonese and Castilian *reconquista*, had added new strength to the corsairs. These Spanish Moors weren't always warmly received, and frequently remained on the periphery of North African society, but they brought with them long experience of commerce and financial matters. Such an influx of talent, well informed, as it was, on the strengths and weaknesses of the Castilian and Valencian coastline, could only be of benefit to the corsair community.

The arrival of the Turks and the Barbarossa brothers marked a second, more violent wave of immigration, one with dire consequences. These new overlords, comparative strangers to the region, set about extracting as much profit as they could for themselves, and took to the seas to find more. This phase was relatively short-lived, since these new corsair captains soon began to enter the Sultan's service as his official admirals and commanders, sending thousands of men to support his forces and building their galleys in his shipyards. The Andalusian migrations had had an impact on the development of the North African states, but the Turkish conquest was far more decisive, ensuring that they stopped short of being kingdoms in the true sense of the word and became instead mere provinces of the Ottoman Empire, governed from Constantinople. Transformed into colonies, the region found itself at the mercy of a power which sought to impose its rule by force as much as through agreement and treaty. The Barbary states were as much at the mercy of the whims and intrigues of the Sultan's court and seraglio as he himself was.

Only Tunis maintained its king and a semblance of independence before, in 1573, falling to Don Juan of Austria and then, a year later, to the corsair Dragut. It had long been a prosperous city, not only on account of the activity of its corsairs but also because it was a trading post, frequented by ships of all nations, and was an object of admiration to both Muslim and Christian travellers and explorers. One Italian pilgrim on his way to the Holy Land dedicated no less than eighteen out of thirty-six pages of his travel journal, written in 1470, to describing the city, its suburbs, its mosques, and its ports. He also described how the king governed, the nature of his people, how many men he could mobilise for his armies, and what monies he could collect. 'Tunis,' he wrote, 'is well fortified and has six gates and countless towers close upon one another. The walls enclose a square area with, in the west, a large citadel known as the Casbah. This is where the king resides for much of the year. The buildings thereof are, on the inside, of such astonishing beauty and luxury that I can barely describe them.' This citadel was divided into two distinct parts, the first of which was 'surrounded by the quarters of the king's guard, comfortably lodged with their families'. The second part was the actual royal residence.

Between the Casbah and the eastern gate were the *fondouks* of the foreign merchants, Genoese, Venetians, Pisans, Florentines, and Catalans. These concessions were square enclosures with but one entrance. The lake of Tunis, 'which stinks', was linked to the sea by means of a straight canal, as wide as the width of a galley, its banks supported by walls. South of this Goulette canal was a large tower, called the Rades, which protected the city's port and La Goulette against the incursions of pirates, brigands, and other enemies.[9]

Before the Barbarossas stormed onto the scene, and the dramatic expansion of piracy in the region, there was little of note to rival this kingdom of Tunis. There were a few nests of pirates, difficult to attack, protected by fortifications and with good supplies of wood nearby, but that was all. Mahdia, situated on a slight but rocky peninsula, and built on the remains of a Phoenician camp, had enjoyed its own era of glory, when its inhabitants had pillaged the cities of Italy to such a degree that they had been referred to as true descendants of Carthage. But now it was a 'mean little port with room for a handful of galleys'. In the same region, further northwards, lay Hammamet, which offered 'a beach backed by ramparts, pretending to be a mole'. Far to the south was Djerba, protected by treacherous waters, shifting sands and unstable channels, which boasted 'at least 100,000 inhabitants and brought in a revenue of 100,000 ducats'. However, Djerba did not offer sophisticated arsenals, nor could it supply sufficient quantities of wood and iron. Its shipyards were nothing more than a collection of shacks and ramshackle buildings. Large prizes, seized by the corsairs, could not even be brought into its harbour; booty was unloaded instead onto smaller boats and rowed ashore, while the captured ships were either burnt or sold off at Tunis, Tripoli, or even Alexandria. As an observer wrote in 1510 about Aroudj and his lieutenants: 'All his galleys were made from materials taken from ships captured as Gelves [Djerba] cannot supply trees fit for the construction of ships; they have just palm trees and olive trees.'[10]

To the west lay Honein, sometimes known as the royal port of Tlemcen. This was the place where the Catalans and Italians came to purchase gold-dust brought by caravan from the Sahara. But it was a rather insignificant square-shaped place measuring 320 metres by 350 metres. Its port was more impressive, being 50 metres by 85 metres, guarded by a rampart and with just one main point of entry – the 'Sea Gate' – just eight metres wide. The approach to this gate was hazardous, being rocky and exposed to sharp westerly winds.[11] Oran, before the Spanish conquest, regularly gave shelter to the corsairs, who often brought in wealthy prizes seized from Catalonia or the Balearics. Even so 'it was not a town which wallowed in abundance; the people subsist off bread made from barley'.[12]

Algiers the Great

Algiers, like Bougie (a 'big city, well populated and surrounded by vast walls') and Bône – and, indeed, like all the cities along the coast which had to protect themselves from attacks from the sea and from raids by Arab or Bedouin nomads – was well provided with strong defences. But this had not always been the case. Not many years before the zenith of the raiding corsairs, the city had been little more than a rather vulnerable port. Indeed, the harbour was not even protected by a mole but had to rely on a rocky isle called the Peñon.

Algiers had long been the haunt of pirates living off their plunder. It hadn't traditionally been a trading city and had no notable commercial links with Christendom nor, it seems, with the tribes of the interior. It didn't play host to a Christian community of Catalans, Italians, or merchants from Provence; there were neither consuls nor *fondouks* and, in these respects, it suffered in comparison to Tunis. The trans-Saharan trade routes, and the trade in black slaves and gold, was carried out without involving Algiers – most such activity took place on the Atlantic coast of Morocco, or at Honein, a port belonging to Tlemcen. Tunis and Tripoli played a part in it too, as did Alexandria in Egypt. Arab writers and geographers gave Algiers scant attention, deeming it sufficient to mention it but not to actually visit it. Reference was made to its corsairs, or to its gardens and sources of fresh water, but records were silent regarding its architecture or population. Jean Leon the African – an oft-cited source, and one perhaps over-praised – reserved his full attention for Tlemcen. Of Algiers he noted in passing only that the city's walls were 'splendid, extremely strong, made of huge stones taken from the ruins of the Roman city', and that the mosque was built on top of the ramparts, but little else.[13]

Aroudj, the oldest of the Barbarossa brothers, had quickly set about building a bastion and arsenal, assisted by an influx of Turkish Janissaries and pirates. But a problem remained whilst the Spaniards were masters of the Peñon isle and its fort: ships could only enter the port by running the gauntlet of the Spanish guns. Lighter ships preferred to beach on the shore near the gate of Bab el-Oued, while larger ships often anchored in a little bay close to Bab Azoun. Both were exposed to the mercy of the winds.[14] No sooner had Kheir ed-Din chased the Spaniards from the fort than he began construction of a proper mole that was partially supported by a string of small islands. Extending 300 metres, some of the stones from which it was built were obtained by demolishing part of the Spanish fort. Others were brought over from quarries outside the Bab el-Oued gate, whilst more material was obtained by knocking down what remained of the ancient city of Rusguniae on Cape Matifou, 'a limitless source for cut stones'.[15]

Streets, Markets, and Palaces

In the space of a few decades – fifty years at the most – Algiers under-went a complete transformation. Some eyewitnesses were convinced that the city was triangular – 'the walls climb up the slopes and meet, forming a triangle, which, from a distance, looks quite elevated' – whilst others saw it as an irregular rectangle.[16] One observer even thought its shape resembled that of 'a bow with its string'. All wrote at length about its

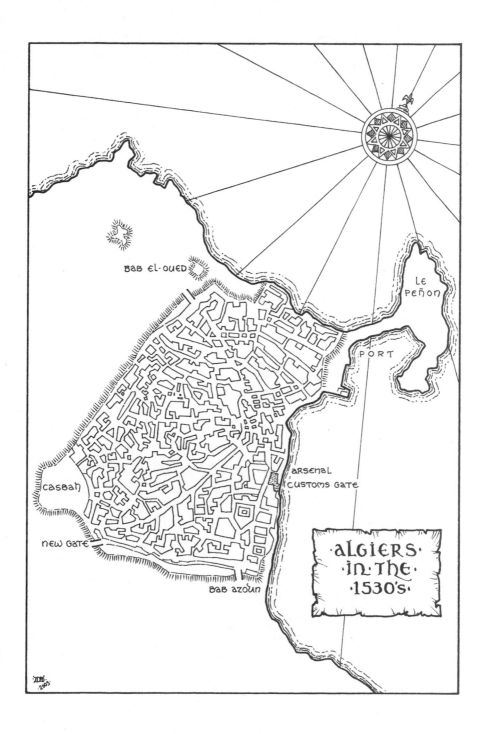

BAB EL-OUED

LE PEÑON

PORT

CASBAH

ARSENAL
CUSTOMS GATE

NEW GATE

BAB AZOUN

ALGIERS
·IN·THE·
·1530's·

walls, gates, and bastions, some even seeking to find the weak points in these defences and eventually noting that the aqueducts could be cut during a siege. Moats filled with water protected the well-maintained outer walls, as did the strong forts constructed along them at intervals. Diego de Haedo described the gates one after another, pointing out their strengths and outlining the role they played in the life of the city. Bab el-Oued was in the north-west; two smaller gates served the Casbah, as did the New Gate; and Bab Azoun served the south of the city. In the east, close by the arsenal, was the customs gate, through which the fishermen sallied in the morning. Finally, opening into the square of the 'Fishermen and Gunmen', was Bab el-Djezira, a gate of immense strength flanked by two towers, giving access to the port.[17]

Two new forts were begun at the instigation of the city's corsair admirals and pashas in order to strengthen Algiers' defences. The first was the Emperor's Fort, begun by Hassan, son of Kheir ed-Din, in 1545 on the spot were Charles V had pitched his tent during the fateful expedition of 1541. It consisted of a 'huge, strong tower' which guarded one of the principal roads into the city and one of the sources of the water that supplied six of the city's wells. The second, called the Bordj el-Ochali, Fort Bab el-Oued, or the 'Fort of the Twenty-Four hours', was begun by Mohammed, pasha of Algiers between January 1567 and May 1568.

In order to deter the raids of Bedouin and other hostile tribes and keep them at arms' length, the pashas of Algiers did all they could to ban the building of houses beyond the city walls. Haedo noted just one outside suburb, containing perhaps a thousand people, but Arab Ahmed had it demolished in the wake of Lepanto, fearing a Christian expedition and landing. Outside the Bab el-Oued and Bab Azoun gates there was nothing save some land given over to the Janissaries for duelling, and for the tombs of officials and governors.[18]

The city itself was split by a large boulevard which was 'almost straight', or at least a good deal straighter than the others, which the Knights of Malta called the *Statta grande del Soco*. This stretched from the Bab Azoun to the Bab el-Oued. Along it lay such important places as the exchange, two baths, a Janissary barracks, the bazaar, and the Batistan – an open square surrounded by the shops of merchants. The last was one of a small number of open spaces of note in this otherwise densely populated city. There were few gardens and a handful of small market places, lost in a jumble of streets and alleyways.

Suleiman the Magnificent was the driving force behind Ottoman expansion. His forces threatened Vienna by land and he actively supported the corsairs as they raided and attacked throughout the Mediterranean.

Charles V saw himself as Europe's bastion against the infidel. As such he waged a determined campaign, when not distracted by the French or by German Protestants, against Barbary's corsairs.

Aroudj and Kheir ed-Din Barbarossa, the redoubtable pirates. Vaunted Turkish admirals they were in fact the sons of an Albanian living on the Greek island of Lesbos.

Two contemporary images of Kheir ed-Din, the most famous of the Barbarossa brothers and the most successful Barbary corsair. He was attacking Italy as early as 1519 and would be a thorn in the flesh of Christian Europe until his death in 1546.

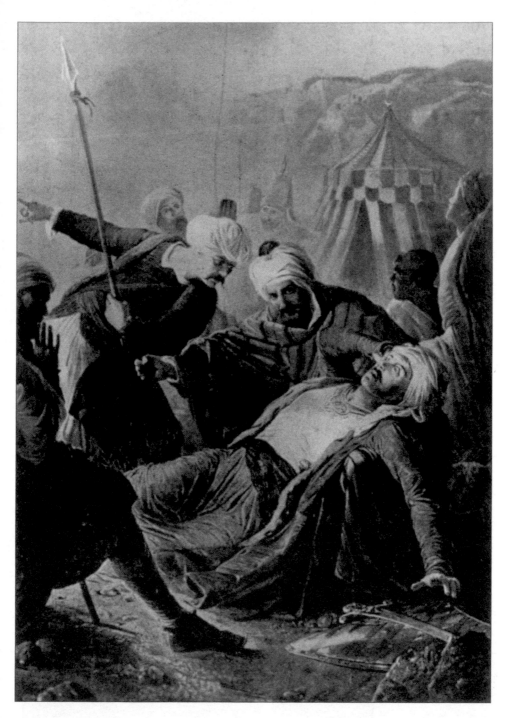

Dragut is mortally wounded during the siege of Malta. Dragut had started his career as a simple gunner but Barbarossa recognised his talents and offered him the command of a squadron. He was captured by the Christians and served some time as a galley slave. Escaping, he was again entrusted with command but died besieging Malta.

Left: Moulay Hassan. A Christian vassal and ally of Charles V, Moulay Hassan was for a time the despot of Tunis. Deposed by his son, who blinded him for good measure, he went into exile and ended his days living on a miserable pension in Italy.

Below: A sixteenth-century view of the slave market in Algiers. The city was 'well populated and surrounded by vast walls' and was the principal market for Christian slaves as well as the principal base for the corsairs. In that sense Algiers was the place where supply met demand.

Christian clergy buying back slaves from their Barbary masters. Between 1566 and 1592 the Papacy sent out 6,000 letters requesting donations for the release of Christian slaves. The Trinitarian and Mercedarian orders were the most active, however, raising money, travelling to Africa and negotiating the release – for payment – of captives.

Above and opposite: Tortures inflicted upon Christian slaves. Images such as these preyed upon the Christian imagination for centuries. Whilst most slave owners treated their captives as an investment, punishments for attempted escape, mutiny or crime could be barbaric indeed.

In May 1535 Charles V despatched a fleet to attack Tunis. After a bloody siege the Christians triumphed – entering the city in August – and dealt a serious blow to Ottoman ambition and corsair activity.

One of Jan Cornelisz Vermeyen's tapestries depicting the taking of Tunis in 1535. Vermeyen accompanied the expedition, making sketches, and his vast victorious scenes later decorated Charles V's palace in Seville.

A Portuguese squadron accompanied the Christian fleet in 1538 as it sought to track down and destroy Barbarossa's fleet. Here the Portuguese ships can be seen off Tunis.

Left: A contemporary map of Tunis. An Italian traveller noted that the city was 'well fortified and has six gates and countless towers close upon one another. The walls enclose a square area with, in the west, a large citadel known as the Casbah. This is where the king resides for much of the year. The buildings thereof are, on the inside, of astonishing beauty and luxury'.

Below: Barbarossa's fleet of galleys anchored in Toulon harbour in the winter of 1543. After wintering safely in the French port the corsair's ships would embark on a spree of raiding along the Italian coast. Not surprisingly this example of Franco-Ottoman cooperation shocked contemporary Europe and led many Frenchmen to question the wisdom of an alliance with the Turks and their Algerian vassals.

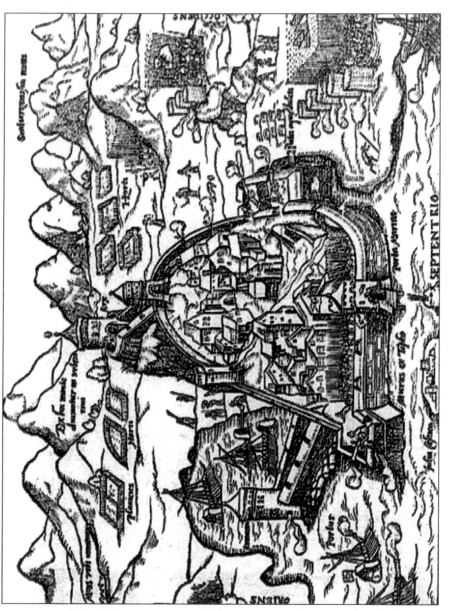

A depiction of Algiers in 1554 by Jean Bellere. A superb natural harbour, a strategic location and a strong tradition of piracy made it a natural base for the Barbary corsairs.

A Barbary brigantine chases a Christian vessel. Many of the corsairs' vessels were small, agile and superbly handled. The capture of a Christian vessel meant that the corsairs would profit by selling the cargo and selling the crew.

A Venetian galeasse combining sail power with oars. Venice was a pre-eminent maritime power but was so frequently troubled by pirates in the Levant that it ordered many of its merchant ships to sail in convoy.

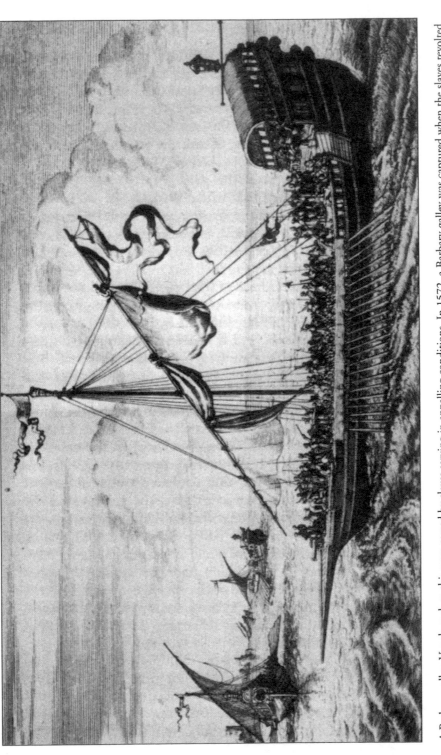

A Barbary galley. Vessels such as this were rowed by slaves serving in appalling conditions. In 1572, a Barbary galley was captured when the slaves revolted upon catching sight of a Christian ship: 'The galley slaves onboard were so badly and cruelly treated that no sooner had they caught sight of us than they jumped up, seized their captain and dragged him along the full length of the ship, administering so many blows to him that his soul departed for hell.'

The Knights of Malta had a substantial fleet of galleys, many of them powerful vessels like the one pictured here. Each galley carried 30 Knights – each Knight serving a six-month tour of duty at sea – as well as soldiers. The galleys were rowed by Muslim slaves and Christian convicts.

The Marquis of Santa Cruz. A key Spanish admiral, he commanded the reserve at Lepanto and played a pivotal part in the Christian victory.

Andrea Doria. This Genoese admiral served the Sforzas of Milan and the king of France before transferring to the service of Charles V in 1528. He was Kheir ed-Din's arch-enemy, victorious at Patras but defeated at Preveza.

'The houses ascend the hills by degrees, making a very respectable sight for they all have windows and one does not obstruct the sight of another. There are numerous palaces, and a modern fort constructed by the Turkish admirals or their renegades.'[19] As with many North African houses those in Algiers turned their backs to the street and opened inwardly on central courtyards. Some were veritable palaces, a fact which might not have been easy to identify by the casual observer on the outside, but which was readily apparent from the inside. One of the most elegant was the Dar Sultan el-Kedina, the residence of the king of Algiers until he was murdered in his bath by Barbarossa in 1516. It was also the scene of the death of Martin de Vegas, governor of the Peñon, who was beaten to death here in 1529. The palace was described minutely by Nicolas de Nicolay and was a veritable labyrinth, the unwary becoming easily lost. There were different wings of the residence given over to different functions, all wrapped around tiny courtyards boasting fountains. In addition there were countless antechambers with private apartments or reception rooms. The central courtyard was embellished with a large fountain whilst, in one of the corners, a wooden staircase led up to a gallery, richly ornamented and supported by marble columns.[20]

Opposite the north-facing façade, the only one visible from a distance, was a public square which teemed with activity and was 'a theatre in which deliberations, transactions and diverse acts of public life were enacted'.[21] Public notaries held office there, consuls were received there, Janissaries received their pay and criminals were tried and punished there. In addition it was used as a slave market for those Christian captives who no longer had a master; on occasion emissaries from religious orders would come with the intention of liberating slaves by purchase, citing names and attempting to pay ransoms.

Civil life took place in the midst of fear, generated by the Arabs of Mitidja who would intercept and rob caravans. But food at least was assured, as grain was stored up in vast magazines and water arrived in abundance from a reliable source about half a league from the city walls. As the city grew, along with its population, further sources were sought out. The city's first fountains had been established in locations indelibly linked with power: in the king's palace and in the adjacent square, in the courtyards of the three Janissary barracks, and in the residence of the pashas. Later a large fountain was placed near the port, to supply ships with water, and two others were created at the Bab el-Oued and Bab Azoun gates.

People

More than any other Mediterranean port, Algiers surprised and aston-
ished. It was crowded with all manner of people and with social and
ethnic groups distinguishable from each other through dress, language,
physical characteristics, and even hairstyle. Such groups occupied
different quarters of the city, speaking their own tongue and attempting
the language of others only with difficulty, if at all. The population was
often swamped and enlarged by waves of new arrivals, shifting the equilibrium of the social order this way and that. Peoples from far away
arrived to find themselves under the thumb of strange rulers with
different manners and customs.

Authors and witnesses couldn't help being dazzled and confused by
the diversity which pervaded every street, alley, or stairway; they
emerged charmed but a little breathless. As for attempting to estimate
the number of people in the city, it was nigh impossible. There were no
official statistics nor anything on paper that might provide a clear indication – not even a record of how much food was being consumed, by
which, through mathematical acrobatics, it might have been possible to
hazard some kind of guess.

Our main sources for information on the population are again the
accounts by captives or members of the religious orders. They – the
former especially – had time to observe people and places, to discern
differences in appearance or behaviour which might suggest social hierarchy, and to analyse reactions, understandings, and conflicts. Such
observers, however circumspect, uncertain, and cautious they felt they
had to be, offer occasional figures, if not for the total population, then for
the number of houses occupied by such and such an ethnic group.[22] These
groups were categorised, as far as was possible.

There were, for instance, some eight different types of Moors from
different regions, speaking different languages or dialects. Among these
the Baldis seemed to be the original inhabitants of the city, occupying
2,500 houses and owning many of the shops. Aroudj had granted them
immunity from taxation. Many owned fields close to the outer walls. The
Kabyles were a poor mountain people who hoped to make their living in
the service of the Turks. They worked the land too, and frequently

served aboard the corsair galleys as oarsmen. Among the Kabyles was a sub-category termed the Azuagues (or Zouaoua), an ethnic group from the kingdom of Beni el-Abas, near to Bougie. These proved excellent soldiers and were employed by the Turks in their garrisons at Bône, Mostaganem and, a little later, Tunis.

The Arabs, often called Bedouins, were nomads, and many preyed on caravans. Those who found themselves in the city 'had such a miserable life. They begged, and feared everything. They slumbered in the porches of houses, lying under sheep fleeces and few had other beds . . . Such scum, so vile, would prefer to die of hunger rather than work.'[23]

There were also Andalusians from Spain, consisting of Mudejares from Granada and Tagarins from Valencia and Aragon. Many of these were artisans, shopkeepers, moneychangers, or metalworkers. Some bred silkworms, others owned workshops devoted to weaving and spinning cloth.

Jews, according to our sources, were numerous. They originated from many regions but, increasingly, came directly from the Iberian peninsula. They wore different hats of different colours and styles according to their various origins and specialised and worked predominantly as tailors, grocers, jewellers, and goldsmiths. They also traded and engaged in commerce. They paid tribute 'and were held by the Muslims in such low esteem that a Muslim child could insult or injure them with impunity'. Even wealthy Jews lived miserably.[24]

The Turks themselves ('burdensome, hairy and common') weren't only Janissaries or soldiers. Some lived off their strength and hired themselves out for all kinds of tasks. There were others too, such as the Chacals, who had supposedly arrived in the city on ships and were of Greek or Balkan origin ('lively, clean and paler than the others') or else came from Anatolia ('larger, of browner skin, less tall and of less fine physical features'), who served as volunteer or salaried oarsmen on the corsairs' galleys. Some 1,600 houses were occupied by this group.

More than 3,000 houses – the figure can only be approximate – belonged to Turks who were neither Janissaries nor sailors; these were, on the whole, merchants who had set up shop in the souks of the city. These socialised with each other, keeping themselves to themselves, restricting their contacts to their children, their relatives, and their slaves. They kept few official records, but kept accounts on reams of oversized paper. Usury was forbidden to them by their religion; nonetheless they practised it 'and only paid in clipped coins or counterfeit money'.

The vast bulk of their trade went to Constantinople, where they sent coral, pearls, precious stones, Spanish gold, and other fine goods bought from the Moors.[25]

Finally there were the renegades – former Christians converted more or less against their will.

Some Islamic or North African circles maintained that it was wrong to keep men in servitude for longer than seven years and that, after that period had passed, the captive should be liberated and kept as a servant, well-treated and adequately fed. However, as far as we can tell the actual relationship between a master and slave was very different, especially in Algiers. 'It was only those who were without slaves who talked thus; those who had [slaves] thought and did the opposite.'[26]

Escape was rare. It would have been a miracle if a corsair's ship went down and the oarsmen managed to slip their chains in battle. Even if a slave could expect that his ransom would be paid, it would only be after long, tortuous delays. Hope would frequently disappear. The only solution which might enable a man to recover his dignity and status might well be to convert to Islam. In conquered territory in the Levant, and indeed in Spain, numerous inhabitants had submitted to the law of the conquerors and converted. A number of these converts in Granada and in Algiers and Tunis had renounced their faith in order to gain a certain amount of freedom, or, at least, to avoid the harsher fate of those who chose to remain faithful.

In Muslim Granada those Christians who chose to convert to Islam – the Helches – had played an important role in the city's administration, in the army, and in the merchant classes.[27] Diego de Haedo affirmed that such renegades were more numerous than the Moors, Turks, or Jews when he stated 'there was not a land in Christendom which had not furnished in Algiers a part of the renegade population'. All other contemporary authors agree, some even going beyond Haedo's statement. Father Dan dedicated at least fifty pages of his quarto volume of 1637 to describing their condition and influence; Nicolas de Nicolay, a somewhat better-informed source but one still concerned with astonishing his readers, attested that in the 1550s all the Turks in Algiers were in fact nothing more than Christian converts. Finally, a century later, Thévenot warned visitors that they should desist from speaking Italian in the city's streets if they wished to keep a secret.[28]

A number of slaves who had been captured young became Janissaries;

this was particularly true of children kidnapped from the Balkans. Others became apprentices or entered the households of rich masters as servants. A few children were even adopted by rich families and showered with generosity. Raised as sons, they were even allowed to inherit. Euldj'Ali had almost 500 of these 'renegades', more or less adopted, in his household. It might even prove possible for such young men, once converted to Islam, to marry the daughter of their master or of one of his neighbours.

Those with particular talents in business, or who proved to be effective administrators, could find themselves rapidly promoted by the pasha or by a merchant or captain. From then on wealth and fortune might smile down upon them. According to Haedo such wealthy renegades owned more than 6,000 houses in the city and in these 'dwelt the powerful, rich and influential of Algiers'. Of course, Christian captains and members of the holy orders who escaped the clutches of the corsairs had nothing good to say about such converts, who they regarded as 'the worst enemies of the Christians, cruel and more heartless than the rest'.[29] Few renegades thought of escape or flight, most being more concerned with making the pasha aware of their devotion and skill. Cervantes was twice betrayed by converted slaves before he finally managed to escape. But he does also mention that it was something of a custom for renegades who might one day wish to return home to press Christians who were about to go back to certify that they had rendered a service to them. Such certificates were sometimes produced by renegades serving on Muslim ships shipwrecked on a Christian coast. Such individuals might then make their peace with the Christian church. But many fled back to Barbary as soon as they could.[30]

War on Land and Sea: The Janissaries

Turkey's elite soldiers were frequently the sons of Christians residing in the Balkans. Torn from their families, they were converted to Islam and instructed in the military arts. When Kheir ed-Din found himself without reliable soldiery and threatened with the loss of Algiers, he obtained a promise of reinforcements from the Sultan. The Janissaries serving in the town objected, saying they would not allow into their ranks any renegade or anyone who had only converted to Islam as an adult; which objection was countered by a threat not to permit the Janissaries to serve aboard corsair ships and thereby obtain their share of the booty. Only in 1568 did Mohammed Pasha allow renegades into his Janissaries and, simultaneously, permit converted Jews to serve. This latter measure was quickly repealed, however, and a band of 100 Jews, who had already been paid, were dismissed. Rumour had it that they had only enlisted to avoid paying taxes.

The Janissaries didn't use halberds or pikes but were armed with arquebuses, and were proficient in using them. When on board ship they sometimes served as bowmen. They invariably served as infantry, only their captain (*boulouh-bachi*) being mounted. By way of recreation they preferred unarmed combat, wrestling, and racing horses; they disdained other forms of exercise. These activities were performed only on days that weren't Islamic holidays. In contrast to many of their contemporaries they rarely quarrelled among themselves, didn't carry daggers, didn't play at cards, and didn't blaspheme.

When the Janissaries grew older they became Spahis. As such they were still liable to take up arms for the pasha but were more frequently utilised on the city ramparts than sent on distant expeditions. The Spahis lived within the community, receiving pay of between twenty and forty doubloons a year and contributions of wheat, beef, or mutton, or even silver, levied from local Moors. Some chose to work the land with the assistance of servants and Christian slaves, tending flocks of sheep or herds of cattle, or selling grapes and figs at local markets.

There were about 4,000 Janissaries based in Algiers itself and another 2,000 parcelled out into garrisons across the region.[31] Those in Algiers were frequently called upon to serve in highly mobile columns of around 600 men sent into the hinterland for upwards of five months to raise taxes and live off the local population. They also stole what they could, menaced and threatened any who dared resist, kidnapped women and children, and returned to Algiers dragging behind them a huge train of camels and mules carrying their booty. A smaller number served aboard the galleys and took this form of combat to the shores of Italy and the islands of the Mediterranean.

Their supreme commander, the Agha, was all-powerful, more so than the pasha himself, and had the sole authority to command and punish his men. He was chosen from the most senior representatives of the warrior caste but was replaced once every three or four months, to prevent opportunities for intrigue and the growth of secret cabals. There were, inevitably, occasions when objections were raised to the promotion of those who should by rights have been given the post; indeed, in August 1578, four consecutive candidates were rejected, one after the other, when it was argued that their wives had been behaving in a frivolous manner.

Some 800 houses in the city were occupied by Janissaries when they weren't off on their punitive expeditions. Others were billeted eight, ten, or twelve in a room in purpose-built barracks. The three most important barracks, which all conformed to a specific plan – with rooms opening out onto galleries above a central courtyard with fountain – housed some 600 soldiers. Some Janissaries were thrifty, saving up their pay and using their booty to set up workshops making buttons or soft furnishings. Others moonlighted as tailors, potters, or rope-makers. Such endeavours were roundly condemned by the authorities, who sought to maintain a more martial demeanour. As a contemporary song records, such base behaviour would not do:

> Your soldiers are turned merchants
> With Baghdad turbans on their heads
> And their wares on their backs
> Dealers in curds
> Shouting 'figs from Smyrna'
> Your soldiers are mere grocers[32]

Another song describes a Janissary turned tobacco salesman:

> He tears his beard out when there's no custom
> He's pale and wan
> Before him lies snuff
> But he's not strong enough
> To grind any more
> He looks to the left and to the right
> Imploring God to give him sight
> Of a customer[33]

But other soldiers behaved with arrogance, living life to the full in a subjugated land. It was enough for a man to lay his hand on a Janissary, even if it was only to guide him on his way, for that hand to be severed. Whoever murdered a Janissary was burnt alive, or sliced into pieces whilst alive, or impaled. Janissaries looked upon it as their right to walk into any shop and pillage it of bread, eggs, or meat, threatening the owners with an axe if they protested; an eyewitness records that 'it was impossible to make them let go or pay for the wares'. They marched through the city as if on manoeuvres, looting cafes. Many became dissolute, drunk on brandy or wine, and abusive. They were feared by everyone and rarely restrained by their commanders: 'they live the life of dirty animals, behaving like scum, giving themselves over to indolence and to the infamous vice of sodomy; they purchase Christian children and dress them up as Turks. They also use Jewish and Moorish children, retaining them despite the pleas of their parents.'[34] Nor were Christian commentators – understandably disinclined to show them in a good light – their only critics. Moors, religious leaders, and conscientious soldiers all railed against such decadence, lambasting these indolent warriors who knew neither how to pray nor how to fight: 'I have seen the army,' wrote one, 'it is a bazaar.'[35]

The Captains: Piracy and Raids

No other port on the North African coast could boast the facilities and yards of Algiers. Stern directives had ensured that master carpenters and engineers maintained the city's arsenal to a very high standard. Timber was brought down to the yards on mule trains or wagons from the mountains near Cherchell, from the forests of Kabylie, and from the coast. The shipyard workers were nearly all Christian slaves, and the Janissaries' Agha served them three loaves of bread per day. A few corsair captains owned skilled slaves of their own, many of whom were Genoese. These served on board ship as master carpenters and were taken out on raiding expeditions to repair and make good any damage, their ships being anchored in coves or off beaches so the work could be undertaken. Turks served as caulkers or oarsmen.[36]

A special ceremony usually took place before the launch of a galley. Captains, dressed up in all their finery and wearing their best jewels, would look on with their entourages as two sheep were ritually sacrificed and thrown into the sea. Other ceremonies, perhaps less grand but still highly charged with symbolism, took place before the departure of the fleet. Friday was deemed the most auspicious day to commence an expedition and dusk was the preferred time. Thanks were traditionally offered up to Sidi Bacha, who was much venerated for having saved the city from Charles V in 1541. The common people, it was said, had attributed the actual miracle to his Negro slave, Youssef, but the city's notables had shied away from glorifying a black slave – one, moreover, who allegedly practised pagan arts from the dark heart of Africa; instead, Pasha Hassan Agha was persuaded that it had been Sidi Bacha who, night and day, had offered up prayers for the deliverance of the city and, on the appearance of the Christian fleet on the horizon, had invoked the devastating storm which had swept away the enemies of God.

The corsair captains armed and equipped themselves for raids, which were their preferred style of warfare. They had little time for the innovations which had been influencing seamanship for well over a century. Their ships were traditional galleys – fast, light, and capable of manoeuvring in shallow water – and they scorned the heavy ships, standing high in the water, beloved by other Mediterranean powers. Each corsair galley boasted a complement of around 200 oarsmen, sometimes more, who were tied to their oars and urged on by whips. As with all sailors of that epoch, the corsairs knew how to navigate their way across the open sea, making use of compasses, sundials, hourglasses, and astrolabes. When part of a fleet they made use of signals and signs to indicate their intentions. To deceive the enemy they flew false colours, disguised their ships as merchantmen, and used renegades speaking a Christian language to communicate with other ships.

Many of the ship owners were Moorish merchants or Turks who, one way or another, would invest a sum of money in the expedition. Captains hired their oarsmen out to these owners, most often at the rate of twelve pieces of gold per man per voyage. Moors who volunteered to serve on the galleys, sometimes known as *bonavoglie*, received the same sum as pay. All oarsmen also received a daily ration consisting of biscuit, oil, and vinegar. So too did the men-at-arms serving on board – either Janissaries or renegades from the Levant – although these did not receive a salary as such but were paid out of the spoils gained at sea or from raiding the coast.

Raiding wasn't looked upon as warfare but rather as an adventure, sometimes dangerous, often unhappy. Two ships or more would operate

together, falling upon fishing smacks, barques, and unarmed merchantmen. Christians called such attacks cowardly: 'It is like hunting hares or
rabbits; they pick one off here and another further on.'

During the summer of 1550 three notorious corsairs, famed for their
brigandage, watched as a fleet commanded by Garcia of Toledo sailed by.
These corsairs were known to the Spanish as Valledupar, Chamite (or
Mohammed), and Vagassidubriz – clumsy approximations which make it
difficult to chart their true identities – and commanded three galleys
which had been armed and fitted out at Djerba. In the wake of the
Spanish fleet came a frigate, loaded with supplies, which should have been
escorted by two galleys but which had been abandoned by them. The corsairs attacked it a few miles off Ischia. The Spanish captain and his six
arquebusiers abandoned the ship and its twenty-four passengers (mostly
valets but including a chaplain) and jumped into a barque. As they
sought to flee they were showered with arrows and forced to surrender.
The corsairs then spent five days on the island of Ventotenne, dividing
the spoils, before setting out on the prowl once more. Meanwhile, they
sent the captured boat off to Algiers, hoping to sell it; it didn't get far, as
it crossed paths with a huge Spanish vessel just off Capri, was recaptured,
and was towed off to Messina. The corsairs, meanwhile, cruised around
for a further fortnight, operating between Ponza and the Italian coast.
They struck lucky when they came across a large ship bound for Rome
with pilgrims. It took only a few days to sell these at Hammamet. Finally,
their expedition drew to a close with the pursuit of an unarmed merchantman which, being outrun by the lighter pirate vessel, only managed
to save itself by getting close under the guns defending Ostia. Its crew
then fled, leaving just the ship, which the corsairs stripped of anything
useful before making good their escape.[37]

Cervantes, who was shot in the chest and had his left hand mutilated
at Lepanto, served under Don Lope de Figueroa the following year.[38] He
was present at the battle for Tunis in 1573, then sailed to Genoa, Naples,
and Palermo before rejoining the garrison at La Goulette. Next, taking
advantage of a year's leave, he, his brother Rodrigo, and Pedro Diaz – the
fort's governor – embarked upon the galley *El Sol* and set sail for Spain on
20 September 1575, accompanied by two feluccas. However, the three
vessels were blown off course by contrary winds and ended up off the
French coast. There, he writes, 'in the waters commonly called the Three
Maries, two Turkish galliots appeared; one keeping out to sea, the other

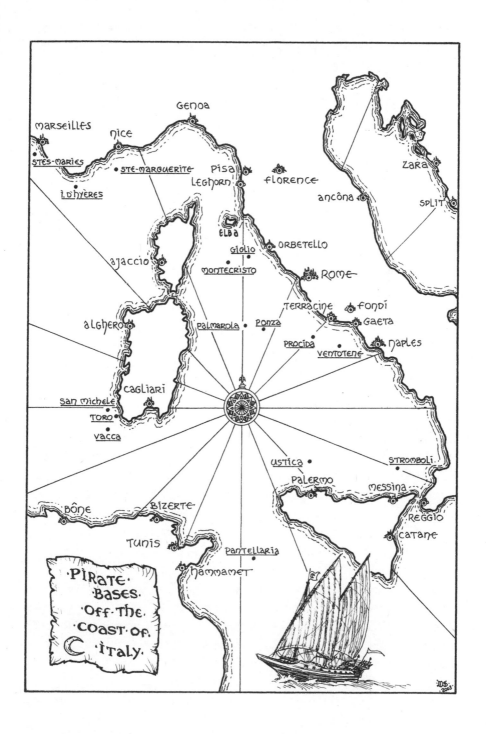

MARSEILLES
NICE
GENOA
STES-MARIES
STE-MARGUERITE
I.D'HYÈRES
PISA
LEGHORN
FLORENCE
ZARA
ANCÔNA
SPLIT
ELBA
AJACCIO
GIGLIO
ORBETELLO
MONTECRISTO
ROME
TERRACINE
FONDI
GAETA
ALGHERO
PALMAROLA
PONZA
PROCIDA
NAPLES
VENTOTENE
CAGLIARI
SAN MICHELE
TORO
VACCA
USTICA
STROMBOLI
PALERMO
MESSINA
BÔNE
BIZERTE
REGGIO
TUNIS
CATANE
PANTELLARIA
HAMMAMET

PIRATE BASES OFF THE COAST OF ITALY

crept close to the land and barred our progress. We were taken prisoner.'
The corsairs clambered aboard, with their captain Arnaud Mami at their
head, and set about pillaging their captives, who they stripped of their
clothes. They then filled the feluccas with as much booty as they could
hold and beached them, 'declaring that they would come back for them
and that they would serve to carry more galima, for that is what they
termed the riches they took from the Christians'.[39]

Sometimes prey wasn't always that easy to overwhelm and occasionally
it fought back. The corsair Vagassidubriz was once frustrated by three
Spanish musketeers; after having seen six of his men and two oarsmen
shot and killed, and others wounded, he turned tail and ran for Algiers,
where he sold the captives he had taken. Another incident in which a ship
escaped occurred in 1550. That summer the corsair Damergi seized some
sixty captives from Sardinia. Then, when off Lipari on his way home, he
gave chase to a Neapolitan frigate loaded with wine and foodstuffs. The
Neapolitan dumped his cargo and made off at speed to the little island of
Ustica. Damergi followed closely with his ship, marshalling his twenty-
two archers from Djerba, of whom he landed fifteen to confront the
Neapolitans only to lose them all in the ensuing battle. He made off in
shame, happy that 'at least he had prevented his oarsmen from throwing
the ship onto the beach and thus recovering their liberty'.[40]

Piracy of this nature, involving, as it did, long voyages far from home
ports, could only take place successfully if use was made of secret
refuges or collaborators. Such is the case with the episode Cervantes
described, where the corsairs beached the captured feluccas off the
Camargue so that they could return and collect them later. This might
suggest that the local population, and the authorities, had been ordered
not to interfere, or perhaps that they were even taking a share of the
profits. Corsairs certainly made use of islands which hadn't been conquered but where they could make repairs, take on water, oil, or fruit,
share out booty, and pay the men-at-arms. They might be welcomed
there or, at least, be able to shelter without fear of their presence being
denounced. Such islands as Formentera in the Balearics, San Pietro off
Sardinia, Lipari, Stromboli or Ventontenne, to the west of Ischia, served
such a purpose. Were such places like the Caribbean islands later became
for the Buccaneers? Probably not, as the corsairs did not winter there,
never established settlements, and only used such bases as temporary
sources of respite.[41]

THE AFRICA OF THE CORSAIRS

Corsairs returning from an expedition would announce their arrival in their home ports by firing off salvoes of cannon, these varying according to the quantity of booty they were bringing back. The return of a corsair's ship was invariably the signal for much rejoicing: the galley would be met by an enthusiastic crowd, and the Janissaries would be invited to interminable feasts. The festivities would usually be followed by the distribution of the prizes seized by the pirates. The pasha, as 'king of Algiers', generally took one seventh of the cargo, silver, cloth, and captives as his own share. The captains, and their associates, and those who had invested in the voyage, usually took the remaining slaves and cargo, whilst the silver was split between the men-at-arms.[42]

Moorish corsairs, sometimes called 'Saracens', grew increasingly rare as Turkish rule developed. More frequently commands at sea were given over to Christian renegades who 'were versed in the arts of navigation off the Christian coasts'. For instance, on 25 March 1578 Mami Arnaut, an Albanian renegade, set off on a raid. Serving under him were eight galliots, captained by Moussa Safi, a Turk; Morat Raïs, a French renegade; Gaucho, a Venetian turncoat; Youssef, another turncoat, this time from Naples; and Daourdi, Mami, and Dali Mauri, all Greeks. In his history of the Barbary Coast and its corsairs, Father Dan lists the names of thirty-five captains commanding Algerine galleys. Some twelve were Turks, one was a Jew, and one was Hungarian. Of the remainder, all were renegades: seven from Genoa, three from Greece, and two from Spain.[43] The existence of such former Christian captains gave rise to all kinds of legends and stories. Around the time of Lepanto, an Italian song exhorted Euldj'Ali to turn his back on Islam and come back to Christ:

Be baptised at once, for your own good
And carry the Spanish banners to Algiers
Hasten, now, for you should
Kneel before the Holy Father in Rome[44]

The corsairs' Christian foes, whether soldiers, counsellors of kings, or simple merchants and sailors, did not look upon their enemies as supermen or ghosts. They were all too real for that. And too well known. Having fought against them year after year, they could frequently identify them, knew their names, and could recognise their strengths and weaknesses. They also knew a great deal about their origins, their present rank, how they had obtained their promotion, and to what they owed their good fortune.

At Lepanto Don John and his captains were fully aware of which admirals commanded the Turkish fleet. All of the contemporary accounts detailing the course of the battle include a good number of names. Luis del Marmol-Carvajal's description the Ottoman fleet gives its exact disposition with the names of each commander of each particular formation. He noted that Memet Bey, Governor of Negroponte and Siroco, and of Alexandria, commanded the right wing of sixty galleys, whilst Euldj'Ali, again with sixty galleys, commanded the left. In the centre was stationed Ali Baba, supported by Fasta Bacha and his two sons. Barbarossa's son-in-law, commanding forty ships, 'supported the fleet', whilst the Governor of Tripoli, with twenty-two galliots, reinforced the right wing. In the aftermath of the battle Marmol noted down the enemy's loss, and could even name those who had been killed: '200 Turks, thirty of whom were governors of provinces, plus 160 beys and chiefs'. Then followed a list of the thirty most prominent captains, each given his rank. Thus Suf Aga was recorded as being 'the comptroller of the Grand Seigneur'.[45]

Another long and detailed account, this time by the Venetian Girolamo Diedo, rejoiced in the heavy Turkish casualties – 'perhaps 30,000 dead' – and crowed that the Turkish captains and chiefs 'had gone to join their damned Mohammed'. He gave the names of eleven such leaders, and listed their titles, role, and past exploits. Some were evidently famous for corsair raids whilst others had held high office in the Levant or Constantinople. He also noted down four others who had drowned and four who he remained silent about 'as they were too obscure'. Of the prisoners, Cara Mustafa and Mehmet Bey, son of Salah Raïs the king of Algiers, along with nine others were the most significant. Seven captains had managed to escape, among whom Casa Geli, a Corsican renegade, and Hassan Agha, a Venetian who 'had been a slave since childhood', were recorded.[46]

The Christians were sufficiently aware of their enemies' way of life to recognise their manners, how they ran their domestic affairs, and their relationship with their servants. Any reader of a Christian account can gain an insight into the personality of some of these people. Diego de Haedo certainly knew, personally, at least one pasha, and in his *History of the Kings of Algiers* gives a detailed portrait of another thirty-one kings, some of whom only reigned for a couple of months. For example, Hassan Pasha 'was small, fat and seemed dependent on remedies and herbs; his eyes were large and he had thick eyebrows like his father before him; his beard was black and he spoke with a heavy lisp ' Yussuf was 'immensely tall and dark; he had large eyes and a bushy beard. He left but one daughter to inherit his riches; she was known as Gorda on account of her girth.' Couca Mohammed was, apparently, a Turk of a common kind who died at the age of fifty. He was of medium height, but very fat, and pug-nosed. Rabadan Pasha was 'a man aged fifty-five, of medium build and of dark complexion. He had a thick beard and bulging eyes. He was a good governor, just, without malice, an enthusiastic reader of Arabic and Turkish religious books, something which used up all the free time he had after carrying out his duties.'[47]

Other writers, particularly military men, were more inclined to stress their enemies' exploits, extravagance, and caprice. Many of the corsairs forged significant reputations among their Christian foes, some almost achieving the status of the Barbarossas. Dragut was perhaps the most celebrated. Born in a little Anatolian village he had first gone to sea aged twelve, serving on board a galley under Aroudj at Djerba. Later, as a commander of galleys himself, but blockaded by Andrea Doria, he conscripted thousands of peasants and had them create a roadway along which he had his ships dragged overland on logs back to the sea. News of his exploits, his raids, and his captures, so incensed Doria that he fitted out twelve galleys in an attempt to run him to ground. Assisted by Berequel de Requesens, Captain-General of the Sicilian galleys, Doria finally captured his quarry off Corsica, and Dragut subsequently served as a Genoese galley slave for the next four years. He was then sold to the Genoese Lomellini family before being 'repurchased' by Barbarossa – in effect he was exchanged for the fortress of Tabarca and its lucrative pearl fisheries. For the next twenty years Dragut led his men in raid after raid against the coast of Italy, burning towns and villages and carrying off captives. He became famous for his audacity, and infamous for the many appalling massacres he ordered. Rumour had it that he had hundreds of Spanish soldiers serving under Alver de Saude, a lieutenant of the Viceroy of Sicily, killed in a single day. He then had their heads piled into a lofty pyramid for his own delight.[48]

Three other heads of state were as distinguished, all of them renegades. Euldj'Ali (sometimes known as Ochiali) was born in Calabria and worked as a fisherman. Captured by the corsair Ali Ahmed, himself a Greek renegade, he took to wearing a turban and was sometimes known as 'the bald'. Rabadan Pasha, born in Sardinia, was kidnapped and taken to Algiers at an early age. He married a young renegade Corsican, worked hard, obtained promotion, and ended up as governor of Tunis in 1570. Recalled to Constantinople, he was later despatched to Algiers and, in 1574, became its pasha and king. Hassan Pasha was a Venetian who had been captured by Dragut as he was serving as a clerk on board a Ragusan vessel. He was sold to a Turk in Tripoli before ending up in Dragut's own household. He then served Euldj'Ali, becoming his treasurer and trusted intendant. He too spent some months at Constantinople before being appointed the twenty-second pasha of Algiers in 1577.

There were, of course, lesser men who rarely commanded more than a handful of vessels. But even these were well known to any sailor. Amongst these were: Elie the Corsican, a sworn enemy of the Genoese, who, when captured by them, was crucified on the mast of his galley; Aydin, 'the scourge of the devil', from the Ligurian Riviera; Al Morez, from Crete, who was a great kidnapper of slaves; and Simon le Borgne, known as the Jew, who, on 25 June 1566, laid siege to Barcelona at the head of thirty vessels.[49]

Barbary Corsairs or Turks?

Corsairs and Janissaries frequently clashed in bloody struggles for power; intrigue went hand-in-hand with scuffles in the street and assassination. Rulers and captains were not rigidly defined classes. Rather they were splintered entities made up of numerous clans or cabals which thrived on disorder and constantly conspired. Algiers, like all North African ports, lived a precarious existence of fragile fortune. The hero of the hour might become the owner of a rich palace and possessor of fabulous wealth, but the next day he might lose it all and be tipped into the gutter, or, more usually, meet a bloody end in some squalid quarrel.

Rare indeed were those kings, pashas, or *beylerbeys* who could cling to power for a significant period. Between the arrival of the first Barbarossa in 1516 and that of Mustafa Pasha in 1596, Algiers had thirty-one rulers. The majority of these 'reigned' for but a few years, if not for a few months, before being overthrown in some plot or recalled eastwards when they ceased to please their master or when the vizier or favourite who was their benefactor died or fell into disgrace.

Time and time again the Janissaries would mutiny, demanding money when their pay was late. On 23 October 1534 Kheir ed-Din almost lost his life in such a revolt and only survived by paying them from his own purse. Just a month later there was another mutiny. This one was savagely crushed, 200 of the mutineers being killed whilst many others were hung on the city ramparts. During the winter of 1579 Algiers suffered from a famine which 'killed the poor Moors and Arabs like flies'. The Janissaries, poorly paid and badly fed, ran amok in the streets.[50] When no supplies arrived by sea they set about pillaging the storehouses, regardless of whether they belonged to merchants or to their own government. Hassan Pasha was in desperate straits and was unable to intervene. He even found it hard to obtain sufficient shrouds for the dead.

In 1578, further east, Janissaries had butchered Arab Ahmed, the governor of Cyprus, who they accused of not paying them regularly. He was first tortured before being cut into little pieces by his tormentors.[51]

Naturally such forthright soldiers could, and would, intervene directly in politics. They took sides, imposed their will, obstructed the pasha, and defied instructions sent from Constantinople. Between 1569 and 1571 even the famous and much respected Euldj'Ali, protégé of the Sultan, was prevented from going on a raid by his escort of Janissaries: 'He had fourteen ships prepared and laden with supplies but having been persuaded not to accompany them, he gave commission to the corsairs to themselves undertake the expedition at their convenience.' That April he fitted out as many ships as possible in secret and quit Algiers 'like a fugitive in order to escape the soldiers, and despite the sea being rough, headed for Matifou; he had stationed sufficient Christian rowers on each vessel to ensure his deliverance.' The Janissaries sent twenty of their principle captains after him 'in order to convince him to return or, if he refused, to provoke a mutiny amongst his soldiers and sailors on his ships.'[52] But they never caught him. Instead they attempted to impose a pasha of their own. This brought a swift response, however, and they were quickly attacked by the corsairs and troops sent by the Sultan. Peace was only restored when a new ruler, appointed by the Sultan, set foot in the city.

After the death, in 1545, of Hassan Pasha – the Venetian renegade, not to be confused with the son of Kheir ed-Din – the Janissaries elected one of their own, El Hadji ('the pilgrim'), as his replacement, without the authority of Constantinople. The Sultan mobilised Sidi Bou Trek ('lord of the roads') and his tribal followers against the upstart, who was now calling himself Hadji Pasha. A force under the Caïd of Miliana attempted to stop the tribesmen but was defeated and horribly massacred. Hadji Pasha himself then pulled together a force of 4,000 Turks and 500 Andalusians and, with the aid of other renegades and mercenaries, inflicted a crippling defeat on his enemy and returned to Algiers in triumph. Eight months passed before he was obliged to submit to the will of Sultan Selim II and allow Hassan, son of Barbarossa, to take his place.

Salah Pasha, king of Algiers, died of the plague whilst organising an expedition against Oran in 1556. His Janissaries then attempted to install a Corsican renegade called Hassan Corso on the throne. They sent urgent messages out to Ali Sardo – a Sardinian renegade – at Bougie, and Mustafa – a Greek – at Bône, to close their ports to the ship bearing Mohamed Tekelerli, the Sultan's nominee. These obliged, and opened up on the ship with artillery. In Algiers, however, the corsairs held the port and the surrounding district and sent out messages to Tekelerli bidding him welcome. On his arrival he seized Hassan Corso and had him put to death: 'After having stabbed sharp reeds into his fingers and toes they placed a red-hot iron crown upon his head. Then they impaled him alive on a sharpened stake by the Bab Azoun gate where he remained in public view, suffering the most dire agonies for more than half the day. He gave out the most terrible screams before dying of this torment.'[53] Ali Sardo of Bougie was also tortured to death, whilst Mustafa of Bône was condemned to be impaled but managed to save his life (in return, it was said, for a huge cash bribe).

However, the debacle wasn't over. Youssuf, a Calabrian renegade, and a follower of Corso, rallied a few supporters and succeeded in killing Tekelerli. Proclaimed pasha and agha in Algiers, he was much fêted, especially when he distributed 10,000 golden *ecus*. However, on the seventh day of his reign he died of plague.

It was, however, Constantinople that made most of the decisions. The Sultan proclaimed new kings and recalled them on a whim, before, perhaps, reappointing them. The destiny of the Barbarossas was largely decided at the imperial court, in the offices of the palace or in the harem. This was how Hassan, the son of Kheir ed-Din, managed to be made king of Algiers on three separate occasions. He was first designated as such in 1546, when his father bequeathed the title to him but, in 1551, he was relieved of his position due to the hostile attitude of Vizier Rostan, 'one of the three supreme pashas of the Great Divan'. Haooan initially attempted to resist his removal from office but then, resigned to his fate, journeyed to Constantinople and submitted to the Sultan's wrath. It was short-lived. Rostan died and in 1557 and Hassan was sent back to Algiers in triumph. Then in September 1561 his Janissaries turned against him and despatched him eastwards once more; but the rebels only held the city for five months before their leader died of plague, after which Hassan was soon back on the throne.

Those in the west who believed they could do business with the kings of Algiers, without bringing the Sultan into the equation, were deceived. In September 1538, for instance, Charles V attempted to open negotiations by sending his ambassador Alonzo de Alarcon to Kheir ed-Din. The latter, with his sights set on affairs in the east, promised not to wage war against the Spaniards and, in particular, not to attack Oran. Subsequently, however, it was discovered – thanks to reports sent by Dr Romero, a special envoy in Constantinople – that Barbarossa was double-crossing the Emperor: 'I can guarantee that he is a better Muslim than Mohammed,' wrote Romero. 'The negotiations are a front. True, weapons have not been sent from Constantinople but it is because the sailors complain that they are ruined and exhausted. Barbarossa has been to Turkey to attempt to remedy matters.' It is also important to remember that the Barbary kings were kept men; they were constantly under the surveillance of one of the Sultan's trusted advisors – a *sandjak*. During the Preveza campaign this was Suleiman Pasha. Others included Tupi Pasha, Rostam Pasha, and Mustafa Chelibar, all of whom received salaries from the Sultan. Many of Barbarossa's own commanders were kept in line by one further ploy – the fact that their families were all in Constantinople. 'Should any of the commanders come over to our [the Christian] side, their wives and children would be executed.'[54] Francis I, king of France, was no doubt aware of this situation but it did not prevent him attempting to ingratiate himself with such commanders, sending them guns, munitions, supplies, and advice. But if you really wanted to establish an understanding with the corsairs it was best to work through the Turks. Consequently the king's ambassadors mostly went straight to Constantinople, and not to Algiers or Tunis. All of the

Franco-Turkish expeditions against Spain's possessions in Italy set out from Constantinople and returned there. Pashas and admirals obeyed orders from Constantinople, not vice versa.

No Barbary commander could really expect to govern a city or a province along the Barbary coast without the Sultan's favour. The kings of Algiers were neither Algerian nor kings, but rather Ottoman-appointed officers in charge of the government. Their title of pasha (a term which had originated to describe the Sultan's viziers) simply marked their place in the imperial hierarchy. As far as Constantinople was concerned they were *beylerbeys* – beys of beys – a title usually conferred on the governors of conquered provinces. It was a particularly distinguishing title. The first *beylerbey* had been appointed in 1362, to rule over Rumelia (Thrace and parts of Macedonia). There were seven such officials in the 1540s and that of Algiers was no more important than any of the others.[55]

Euldj'Ali attempted to persuade the Sultan and his viziers to create a more potent administration on the North African coast, but to no effect. His son, Hassan Pasha, was ambitious and did little to disguise his thirst for power. The target of all kinds of plots and machinations, he fell in 1551, only to be reinstated in 1557. This time he was more successful – at least to start with – driving off the Spaniards and waging war on the Moorish tribes firmly entrenched in the mountains south of Bougie. These warlike chieftains had never acknowledged Turkish suzerainty and had managed to muster quite a sizeable force. Their leader had recruited a number of renegades from Algiers and was paying them handsomely; he had proclaimed a welcome to all fleeing Christian captives, even declaring that 'if they wished to remain Christian, he would leave them at liberty to do so, so long as they fought by his side'. Even so, Hassan with his 6,000 arquebusiers, 600 Spahis, and thousands of loyal Arabs, was able to crush the hostile Moors. Hundreds were left dead on the field of battle, and the Moorish leaders submitted. To cement the peace and firmly establish the Turkish yoke, Hassan set about forging alliances with the Moors living around Algiers and Kabyles. He married the daughter of the Moorish king of Koukrou and married his cousin off to her sister. He allowed warriors from Kabyles to enter Algiers and also permitted the enlistment of a 600-strong unit of Azuagues, soldiers from Koukrou. These latter 'came and went buying weapons, behaving as though the town was their own and raising suspicions amongst the Turks and renegades that the king of Koukrou was paying Hassan Pasha the respect he was due'. Indeed, there were accusations that Hassan himself wanted to be king and that the new alliance was in fact the first step towards a new dynasty. Such a thing couldn't be tolerated in Constantinople, where rivalries were only winked at so that the Sultan could divide and rule; nor was it acceptable to the Janissaries. The Agha finally resolved to ban the Azuagues from purchasing weapons and had them chased from the town. Hassan was then thrown into prison, manacled along with two of his relatives. After their palaces had been sacked the unfortunate trio were placed on board galleys and despatched to Constantinople, accompanied by a missive which 'listed the faults committed by them and of the suspicions to which these gave rise'.[56]

Dragut was hardly more successful. Despite his determination his kingdom to the east of Tunis (the principality of Lesser Syrte) was but short-lived. Chased from Mahdia by the Spanish in September 1550, and thrown out of Djerba six months later, he had no option but to place himself at the mercy of the Sultan and plea for his protection. But fortune would not smile upon him again. Instead, for many years thereafter, he was subject to capricious uncertainty. In June 1551 he served with Sinane Pasha, the brother of the Grand Vizier Rostan, cruising off the African coast. He then acted as *sandjak-bey* for the fleet based at Lepanto and Preveza (some forty or fifty galleys menacing Italy). In July, accompanied by the bey of Rhodes, he attacked Sicily and burned Augusta but stalled before Malta. Then, pausing to pick up a few thousand captives from Gozo, he made his way to Tripoli and seized the place after a nine-day siege. Yet however much he wanted Algiers, and however much he attempted to persuade the Sultan that he was the right man for the job, it was to no avail. Another corsair, Moat Agha, was elevated to that office instead. Dragut died a mere captain in the assault on Fort St Elmo on Malta in 1565.[57]

Spanish Possessions

The Spanish had a policy whereby, on the very day that some place or fort fell into their hands they would immediately set about reinforcing its walls and bringing in supplies, munitions, and food for the garrison. They would draw up a detailed plan of the town, the fortifications and defences, and the port and access to the harbour. On 12 June 1506, for example, Captain Juan Laso wrote to the king assuring him that he could maintain Mers-el-Kebir with 500 men until the arrival of reinforcements. Shortly thereafter the Marquis of Comares arrived and left a garrison of 5,000 men. At Bougie a garrison of 800 men was initially established and orders went to Valencia to supply them, as soon as possible, with a thousand sacks of corn and biscuits sufficient to last at least fifteen days. On 8 September 1531 Don Alonzo de Balzan penned a long account of the expedition sent against Honein. It had left Malaga with eleven galleys, two brigantines, and sufficient food for two months. On the way 250 soldiers had been dropped off at Oran. In Honein itself a garrison of 700 men – 400 of them arquebusiers – was installed with sufficient food for fifteen days. The matter-of-fact account was accompanied by a concise plan of the town and its port.

Four years later Charles V was fully informed about the capture of Bône in a detailed letter written on 29 August 1535, a mere five days after the victory. The Spaniards maintained a garrison of 800 men in the place, 200 of them established in the citadel and the rest in the town. Moors were barred from the citadel. Even so, the situation was difficult to say the least and the commandant was soon obliged to ask for assistance. Meat and grain in the magazines had gone bad and the soldiers were suffering accordingly. On 23 October the Emperor responded, writing from Messina:

> Only occupy the citadel and have the city walls demolished; maintain 600 men with you and keep two brigantines in the port; fortify the tower on the rock on the coast in order to protect the ships and keep between twenty-five and thirty soldiers in it: you must allow the Moors freedom and live in harmony with them. Pay them reparations, keep spies and agents among them. You will be sent a thousand ducats at once. Maintain sufficient supplies to keep yourself until the end of the year; you will receive more after that and subsequently every six months. Have your surplus troops embark for Mahon on Minorca. Forbid merchants to trade with Algiers and with other places held by the Turks. All traffic must pass though either Oran, Bougie, or La Goulette.

On 13 January 1536 the governor, Don Alvarez Gomez de Horozco, sent a minutely detailed report to his superiors, again accompanied by a plan. He couldn't resist pinpointing the precise place where the fleet of Caesar's lieutenant Publicus had anchored before setting off to destroy Scipio's fleet. But, in addition, he discussed all manner of affairs, from contracts drawn up with the Moors to details of purchases of beef and poultry.

On 26 October 1535, at La Goulette, Mendoza ordered a complete account to be taken of the state of the fort's defences:

> The work to reinforce the walls is well in hand. The arrival of Doria's fleet, which brought twenty-four barrels of water, made a great impression upon the Moors and it is scarcely possible that they shall revolt. Turkish vessels, which seemed to be preparing to attack, have now sailed off. Unfortunate is the news that the king of Tunis, our ally, is misbehaving. He seems determined to retain his Christian captives and to make them Muslim. The king of Constantine and the Arabs seem to be with the Turks. At what price should the food be sold to the soldiers? I have been informed of the cost for the bread and the wine, but not for oil, vinegar, peas, rice biscuits or cheese.[58]

Ten years would pass before the Emperor would again be informed about the state of the city's defences, this time accompanied by a most remarkable plan, skilfully drawn and labelled with a minute but immaculate hand. One such label read as follows: 'The grain silos are inadequate and too humid; it is proposed that the grain be shifted into purpose-built cellars below the munitions; two cisterns should also be sunk between the new stores.' On the left-hand side of the map was written: 'This little island is inhabited by the Moors who work in the fortress; on it can be found a mill and a few stables for draught horses.' Finally, above the map was written the legend: 'This bastion, the most ancient, will not suffice; a new wall must be constructed to support it. The houses which open out onto the main square are built side-by-side and form a kind of continuous rampart. The great buttresses which were supposed to be built here have remained nothing more than plans.'[59]

Spanish Colonies?

In the period immediately following their conquest by Spain it was suggested that Oran, Bougie, and Tripoli should be peopled almost entirely with Christians. King Ferdinand's letters to his royal governors make this clear beyond a doubt. Moorish kings and tribal leaders could retain their sway over the interior and over some of the towns but 'should we allow them to dwell in the coastal towns it will soon be impossible to preserve our conquest'. Later it was thought that the coastal districts could be settled by knights belonging to the Spanish military orders – the order of Santiago in Oran, that of Alcantara at Bougie, and that of Calatrava at Tripoli. Evidently some measure of settlement occurred, as Charles V later mentioned *caballeros comarcos* living in Africa, but it was of limited impact and scarcely featured in the records relating to either defence or population. Little of the élan associated with the Reconquista found its way over.

The Spanish authorities in Oran did bring over 600 artisans and merchants, confirmed Christians, who set about dividing up some of the city's best property as had been done before in Castile and Andalusia. Two hundred of these workers undertook to perform military service as cavalry, the rest operating as foot militia. But this, the only true attempt to establish a colony, was only partially successful.

Such footholds on African land could only be maintained at considerable cost, constrained, as they were, to be ever vigilant and ever ready to ward off attacks by Barbary corsairs, Turks, or Moors. The African frontier was expensive in terms of men and lives. Maintaining these bastions – many of which were poorly garrisoned and supplied – demanded considerable sacrifices from a Spain already deeply involved in transatlantic enterprise and the affairs of Italy and Flanders. It also necessitated diplomatic vigilance, the Spanish authorities keeping on the alert for signs of alliances between Moorish leaders, and playing on their rivalries with the Turks; either way the Spaniards had to be ever watchful for actions which might be the prelude of an attack or a defection.

Charles V was certainly aware of these difficulties, but it did not prevent him from seeing his holdings in Africa as another front in the war against the Ottoman Empire. To an extent he oversaw the conduct of the campaign by giving instructions directly to subordinates in the field and receiving information from a network of informants. On 7 November 1534 he himself wrote out orders to be given to Luis Presenda, a secret agent, to be despatched to Tunis. Presenda would proceed to Sicily and then pass himself off as a merchant, attempting to solicit from Barbarossa or the king of Tunis a safe conduct for a brigantine charged with merchandise. At Tunis he was to outwardly sell his wares but, at the same time, clandestinely seek out those close to Barbarossa. He was to be generous with presents and to throw expensive banquets according to the manner of the country. He was to attempt to excite the king against Barbarossa and to have him murdered, either by using poison or by having him strangled whilst he slept or was drunk – for he couldn't take his drink. Finally, he was to attempt to sow discord amongst the captains of the Barbary fleet. There then followed three questions, written out in the hand of one of Charles' advisors: Could he promise a pardon to those renegades who were to assist him? The response, written alongside, was 'yes'. How much should a Moor be paid to assassinate Barbarossa? The reply 'Between 4 and 5,000 ducats'. Could he present himself as an ambassador? 'No'.[60]

Letters from royal governors frequently mentioned their spies and agents. Such individuals were employed to keep tabs on the Moors and on the corsairs – an activity not without danger, as there were many false friends only too happy to denounce them. In Honein such spies were frequently drawn from Moorish thieves only too happy to sell intelligence. In La Goulette Mendoza kept two kinds of spy on his books: those who kept an eye on Algiers, in collaboration with Moulay Hassan, king of Tunis; and those who kept an eye on Moulay Hassan.[61] Such agents were plentiful and cheap as 'they were all poor men'. Their reports, noted down in official journals, came in daily and were sent off in summary form to the Emperor. He was therefore kept well informed about dynastic squabbles between indigenous princes, the marshalling of troops, and intrigues, exiles, and uprisings. On 11 September 1534 the king of Tlemcen threw El Mansour, brother of the ambassador at the court of the king of Spain, into prison and left him to die. It was noted that 'his numerous relatives, many of them important personages, have all fled'. In the same year a letter by Vallejo, royal governor of Honein, noted that:

I have received three reports in as many days from Moorish spies. The king of Tlemcen is preparing to attack us. Hassan, son of Barbarossa, has offered him artillery. Two Christian slaves have arrived here, they had been in Algiers where they had accompanied their master, a Turk. They say that six ships have set sail to go raiding against the Christians. The region occupied by the Turks is much agitated by a Moorish uprising.

Two weeks later Vallejo again wrote, confirming the king of Tlemcen's designs:

> I'm sure he would make war on the Christians if I did not know him to be a cowardly man, given over to vice, and one who is only seeking to extort some money. In the period that he has been on the throne he has married seven times and has done little but impose taxes on Moors, Jews, and Arabs.

More reasoned information, and certainly more politic, came from a report on the situation in Algiers drawn up around the same time. It included a kind of inventory of Turkish forces in the region. There were 1,800 troops in the city, a mere twenty-five, commanded by a renegade, at Tenes, twenty at Cherchell, 150 at Medea, 300 at Constantine, 100 at Miliana, and twenty at Collo. Algiers, the memoir stated, had 3,000 Moorish and 300 Jewish families. Eight galleys, replete with 300 Turks, had set sail to join the French fleet. Eight further vessels were anchored in the port, the largest of which pulled seventeen oars a side. Vast quantities of biscuits were being hastily manufactured at Algiers, Medea, and Miliana. 'Large caravans of camels and mules were arriving in the city carrying biscuits, these are being deposited at Barbarossa's residence.' There then followed all kinds of details on weapons, artillery, and defences, before the memoir closed with the observation that 'the Arabs are being treated so badly that they wish for Christians to become masters of Algiers; they know that in Oran Arabs come and go as they please, selling their wares for good prices and leaving again without being harassed.'[62]

In addition information could be gleaned from accounts given by people passing through the area. Those by Spanish soldiers or Knights of Malta were much prized in this respect, as they often included evaluations of the military situation and reports of troop movements. Lanfreducci and Bosio, for instance, reported that Algiers was 'stuffed with people'. The Turks had 13,000 soldiers and 6,000 Janissaries available as well as Mudejares and Granadan auxiliaries. In addition there were their allies the Kabyles, giving a total disposable force of 25,000 men. They also noted down the names of the principal corsair captains and, unusually, the names of those tribal leaders who were opposed to Turkish rule and who might be worth courting as potential allies.[63]

But would the Spanish be able to overcome their isolation? They knew who they could trust and, more importantly, they knew who they should be wary of. They closely monitored the movements of the French, for example. In May 1529 a Jewish spy in Algiers noted that a French ship had anchored in the port of Oran and that one of the merchants travelling on the ship had told Kheir ed-Din the best way to capture the fortress of the Peñon. In 1534 two French merchantmen had landed twelve or fourteen pieces of artillery along with powder and metal for the manufacture of guns. On 4 January 1535 Brother Juan de Iribes, who had arrived to organise an exchange of captives, penned a detailed note on the capture of Tunis by Barbarossa, an event which had taken place on 18 August 1534. He estimated the Turkish forces to have numbered 4,500 and that 2,000 Moorish men, women, and children had died in the fighting. On 24 August Jean de La Forest, an ambassador of the French king, had arrived from Constantinople and been greeted with open arms. He and Barbarossa had agreed that the latter was to join up with the French galleys at Marseilles. The combined force would then attack Genoa, after which the king of France would seize Milan whilst the Turks carried the war into Sicily.[64]

Misery and Setbacks

Whichever way you choose to look at it, Spain's ever-watchful garrison troops in Barbary suffered greatly. There was an excess of misery matched by a lack of supplies and money. In 1506, just a few weeks after the seizure of the city, the governor of Mers-el-Kebir was bemoaning the delays in supplying him with pay for his soldiers. In addition he had been forced to deal directly with two merchants based in Barcelona for the supply of a thousand *cahizes* (666 litres) of grain. Three vessels had been despatched, loaded with these and other supplies, but had had to seek refuge from a violent storm at K'saca 25 kilometres to the west of Milla.[65] Nobody seemed to know when they might venture forth again. Meanwhile the soldiers were murmuring: 'It's not Peru where you can go out and collect gold and precious stones; it's Africa and all we have here are Turks and Moors.'[66] To cap it all there was a shortage of drinking water.

Oran, at least, seemed to have some advantages. Raids into the interior brought in flocks of livestock whilst, below the walls, local traders sold meat, vegetables, and grain. But Oran was never really anything more than just a rather poorly fortified camp, and it wasn't unknown for soldiers to die of starvation. Promised convoys failed to get across the sea, the people of Tlemcen failed to deliver grain or, more frequently, corrupt suppliers cheated on their obligations.

In fairness, however, the officials responsible – the *provedores* – did their best for Spain's African 'frontier', responding to distress calls and attempting to ensure that each post held sufficient flour to last for at least four months. But it was an uphill struggle, with negligence, misfortune, and need frequently the winners. The soldiers, poorly paid, exhausted, and crippled by debt, were soon rendered desperate. At Honein, in 1534, for example, it was reported that 'for the last eighteen months they have not been paid with the result that they can't even buy a sardine. The merchants of Malaga and elsewhere in Spain refuse to present themselves, knowing that they won't be paid.' At Bougie in 1535 there were so many desertions that the authorities lost count; men fled back to Spain or enlisted for service in America. Shipowners became people smugglers and conspired with the soldiers to transport them overseas.

The result of all this was that the unhappy soldiers violated the rules whilst their officers increasingly turned on each other, accusing their comrades of incompetence or of collusion with the people smugglers. In Oran, no sooner had a garrison been installed than its commander immediately turned against the officer commanding the fleet. When a royal commissary (*corregidor*) arrived to investigate he wrote a long memorandum on the subject to King Ferdinand. This, it must be said, reflected the desperate state of the garrison: there were too many officers; the artillerymen were worthless and frequently absent; a number of men who were supposed to be present under arms never showed for reviews and inspections; soldiers guilty of misdemeanours sought sanctuary in churches and nobody seemed willing to fetch them out; and many of the soldiers had deserted and had been killed or enslaved by the Moors. The *corregidor* himself had been obliged to purchase food and clothing for the soldiers, who were dying of cold and hunger, and as a result he found himself out of pocket by 4,000 ducats.

At Bougie, in 1529, the commissary Pedro de Amecayan requested that the king despatch somebody who knew how to govern. The present commander was foolishly sending out his garrison in the middle of the night and was running the risk of being ambushed by the Moors. Bougie, it seemed, was in great danger. The curtain wall needed urgent repairs for which 2,000 ducats were required. The town could only be held if sixty cavalry and 600 well-equipped infantry were maintained; and, if the place wasn't to share the fate of the Peñon near Algiers, new cannon were needed. Those which the garrison had 'were found to be of more danger to those firing them'.[67]

Charles V sought to improve matters. Regarding Oran, which, by then, had fallen into anarchy, he split responsibility between the *corregidor* and the general commanding the garrison. In 1534 he made one man responsible for the entire administration of the base. This was Don Martin de Cordoba y Velazos, the Count of Alcaudete. Born in 1498 to one of the older Andalusian families, he married the daughter of Diego Fernandez, the conqueror of Mers-el-Kebir. As *corregidor* at Toledo in 1520 he had overseen the defeat of the Comunidades rebels. He was a remarkable leader and soon shook Oran into a state of order, strengthening its defences and fashioning a reliable garrison out of recruits brought over from Andalusia. Many of these were enlisted by his own relatives or belonged to their households. Soon affairs were sufficiently advanced for the Spanish to launch an offensive against Tlemcen. But Oran remained 'as much isolated as during the early days of the occupation'. Alcaudete found that supplies of arms and munitions were erratic; that pay, as ever, arrived late; and that Bedouins, led by renegades in Turkish service, intercepted the supplies of grain intended for his troops. Still, things were better than at Bône, where, in 1540, the commandant personally stabbed the treasurer Miguel de Penagos, who he blamed for delays and lack of funds.[68] Handgunners in the garrison were claiming that they wanted to become Moors. An inquiry, led by Francisco de Alarcon, established some order and 'those unfortunates who had considered renouncing their faith are now making their confessions and communing'.[69]

Problems such as these, encountered when attempts were made to seize or safeguard power in conquered lands, are the rule rather than the exception. The history of colonialism, from its early days up to more recent times, has been punctuated by conflicts which arise from intrigues at court or from a more localised search for allies and collaborators. But the result has frequently been a bloodbath. Much the same happened after the Columbus brothers and Cortez came to the end of their adventures. Initially idolised as heroes they later had to face a storm of criticism. Their decisions were contested and their achievements defamed, and they were replaced by men of the second hour, appointed by king, court, or minister. In the Indies, however, such infighting had little effect on the peopling of the colonies, the massive extension of empire, and the pacification of vast territories.

Though in Africa the rivalry between captains, governors, and commissaries certainly contributed to such failure, it was not the only reason for it. Contemporary observers, some of whom were royal officials, noted the lethargy and lack of enthusiasm of Spaniards of all ranks to cross over the sea and establish themselves in a land inhabited by hostile people and denuded of its riches. In this respect Africa was very much the poor relation of the Indies, where fortunes could still be made and men were prepared to take risks accordingly. It was an acknowledged fact that attempts to convert the inhabitants had all met with fierce resistance. Earlier missions for the advancement of the Christian faith, such as those of Francis of Assisi to Egypt in 1219 and Raimondo de Penefort, had all failed. Even Ramon Lull's Spiritual Crusade had met with failure in attempts to convert Tunis in 1293 and Bône in 1307. Columbus therefore took great care to stress in his early despatches that the people he encountered in the Americas had no true religion and no clergy, merely a few rituals which he deemed primitive. The Moors, on the other hand, refused to listen to preaching and punished severely any of their number who did decide to convert. They would never be good Christians, nor, indeed, loyal servants of the king.

Without a doubt circumstances and political machinations also formed an obstacle to success. Considerable effort went into the Spanish enterprise in Barbary, and resources of all kinds were mobilised; but despite this their conquests were ephemeral. And here again the comparison to Spanish success in America is odious. In the New World the Spaniards were fortunate enough to encounter tribal leaders engaged in struggles against their peers in which neither side seemed to gain an advantage, and subject peoples chafing against the yoke of tyrannical empires. By contrast, in North Africa the Spaniards found themselves pitted against an empire at the height of its power, still expanding and still victorious on all fronts. How could anyone dream of chasing the Turks from Algiers when even safeguarding Italy from their ravages was proving so difficult? Why else was Lepanto celebrated as a battle which miraculously delivered Europe?

It is true that the Moors themselves had suffered from the imposition of Turkish rule and the Barbarossas' actions. They had lost their own leaders and had submitted to powers which exposed them to all kinds of abuse, even if elements of the native population had found ways to collaborate and ally with the new rulers. Moorish rebellions were always put down with enormous savagery and the Turks made sure that they, and only they, maintained a combat fleet and maintained sufficient men under arms. Nothing could oppose them. Indeed, the Turks could even find allies elsewhere along the Barbary Coast, notably Andalusian emigrants from Spain who were bent on vengeance. No form of Christian domination would be tolerated by such people. Renegades too were unlikely to be anything less than confirmed enemies of the Christian princes. Consequently few Christians were able to impose their rule in Muslim lands, regardless of whose orders they were following or of the zeal with which they carried out their commands.

The Spaniards nevertheless clung to their isolated and besieged conquests, knowing all the while that it was futile to try and do more than maintain a chain of fortified posts. Despite its proximity and despite sharing a common sea, Africa still remained, for the Spanish, enemy territory. And their presence in that territory cost them dear and brought them little profit. Cervantes noted after the fall of La Goulette to Euldj'Ali in 1574 that 'Heaven had done Spain a service in ridding it of this receptacle of perversity, of this insatiable sponge which had sucked in so much money for so little reward'. And he was not alone.[70]

Chapter V

Slavery

Mention of slavery existing in the Middle Ages always seems to elicit surprise. It's still more usual to gloss over this subject or, if it is mentioned at all, to allege that it was a Muslim practice or to suggest that the Christians, having embarked upon the exploitation of conquered lands, were returning to the long-neglected usages of the ancient world. But that is an incorrect assumption, especially for the Mediterranean region. History clearly shows us that throughout these centuries this doleful trade in human beings existed in Christian lands as well as Muslim,[1] in the west as well as the east. Amongst Christians, the practice flourished in Byzantium,[2] the Crusader lands in the Middle East,[3] the Slavonic territories,[4] the Balkan principalities, and those parts of France, Italy, and Spain which lay along the Mediterranean coast.[5]

Northern France had, at the time of Charlemagne, witnessed the sale of Saxon slaves in markets at Verdun and elsewhere. The miserable captives, seized from their homeland, tied, bound and sold by merchants specialising in this inhuman traffic, were sent south to the ports of the Midi and North Africa. Later, when the kingdom of the Franks suffered in turn at the hands of Viking raiders, the prisoners they took were sold at such markets as Rouen. But by the dawn of what we recognise today as the Medieval period the concept of slavery survived only as a distant memory in northern France, England, and the German empire, where it had never become firmly established. True, serfdom is often labelled a form of slavery, but the comparison is inaccurate. The circumstances of feudal serfs, who laboured for their overlords, were not the same as those of individuals seized by force and dragged far away to be sold, with little hope of ever returning to their homes.

Slaves remained relatively common in Roussillon, Catalonia, and Valencia even as late as 1500, although they were much rarer, if not absent altogether, in the heartlands of Castile. Escaped slaves from Barcelona and Perpignan frequently fled northwards, seeking sanctuary in the region around Toulouse. Venice, Genoa, Pisa, and other Italian maritime cities employed a class of servile labourer not to be found in Milan or Lombardy. Even in Provence, numerous slaves could be found in the Mediterranean ports, whereas north of Avignon the practice was virtually non-existent.

One of the few authors to discuss this north/south divide wrote in 1886 that 'slaves could only be found in feudal Europe in those regions close to the Mediterranean, where contact with African races was established'.[6] It's not clear what he meant by 'feudal Europe', nor by 'African races', although the latter probably alluded to all inhabitants of the Muslim lands.

So Africa and Europe, it seemed, were linked in times of war and in times of peace by a chain of contacts and common practices, whereby certain exploitative practices were adopted and became the norm. The fact that such forms of labour persisted can be demonstrated from looking at merchants' reports and the accounts of travellers, and by examining the way in which Mediterranean warfare and raiding was conducted.

The Roman Tradition

Though the quest for cheap forms of labour has persisted throughout history, slavery was not universally adopted. In fact two opposing cultures seem to have developed. On the one hand, in the north, feudal society seems to have largely freed itself from the slave-owning traditions of antiquity. Men were sworn to serve another – be he prince, bishop, or lord – by means of an oath. Feudal warfare was dynastic or was born of family conflict or personal ambition.[7] Once victorious, the host raised by a nobleman returned home but did not drag back with it masses of prisoners intended for penal servitude. Nor were men any longer massacred for the sake of massacre; rather it was deemed more honourable to take prisoners for ransom, and the money raised in this way became a rich source of revenue for the victors. Sophisticated systems governed the transfer of ransom money: advances were paid, loans were raised, guarantees were given and received. Payments for the safe return of Saint Louis, held in Egypt, and Jean le Bon, a captive in England, virtually bankrupted the French royal treasury. Tradition had it that a feudal vassal was obliged to offer up a contribution for the release of his feudal overlord. Thus it was that the daughters of Brittany worked hard at their looms to raise money for the release of Constable du Guesclin when he was held in Castile. The captive, meanwhile, although held far from his homeland, was rarely mistreated or humiliated and was not obliged to work for his keep. His captors were responsible for his welfare, and for clothing and feeding him according to his position. There was no question of abusing the hostage.

In the Mediterranean world, by contrast, such feudal ideas gained little ground. Attitudes and feelings were dictated instead by the extreme practices of the ancient world. Consequently warfare here assumed a different and unique character, one tainted by an undercurrent of malice.[8] Enemies, it seemed, were not just those who fought against you, but could be rivals for political power, relatives intent on seizing your possessions, strangers, latter-day Barbarians; all were prejudged and pre-condemned. With suspicion and mistrust rife warfare was more brutal. Unfortunates vanquished on the field of battle were not simply taken prisoner; their ordeal continued even thereafter. They were held in perpetual captivity or sold for profit, and might suffer persecution on the grounds of ideological or religious convictions. Localised warfare between neighbouring peoples might even take on the character of a holy war, and was frequently preached as such. Enemies were condemned as being enemies of God or, worse, as in Italy, enemies of the people. Such wars were even termed 'good' or 'just', which justified any excess and allowed prisoners to be humiliated and bought and sold.[9]

In 1230 the Florentines attacked Siennese territory, taking more than a thousand prisoners, who were chained up and dragged off to Florence. Even 'the beautiful women of Siena were forced to follow and were abused by those who had seized them'.[10] At the battle of Meloria, in 1284, Pisa lost forty galleys to the Genoese and so many prisoners (9,000 it was said) that 'if you want to see Pisa you must come to Genoa'. The prisoners were at first mistreated, thrown into foul and stinking prisons, but later their captivity became more tolerable. They were allowed to come and go as they pleased and to write, or have letters written, to their families. But as time ticked by there seemed to be no question of liberating them or of asking for a ransom. Genoa wanted to weaken its rival by rendering it incapable of conducting its affairs, depriving it of its leadership and its ability to wage war.[11] Marco Polo, taken prisoner by the Genoese on 7 September 1298 at the battle of Curzola on the Dalmatian coast, was taken to Genoa with 7,000 other prisoners. He recounted in his *Malpaga* that in the debtor's prison he encountered Pisans of good family who had been held by Genoa for fourteen years. Some, it seemed, had been unable to have their ransoms paid and were obliged to work for a living.

Less than a century later the Genoese found the boot on the other foot when thousands of them fell into Aragonese hands at the battle of Alghero in 1353. The captives were dispersed throughout Catalonia, the kingdom of Valencia, and Majorca. They were assigned to live in villages and were kept confined by villagers who, for their pains, were allowed to use them in their fields or hire them out for service elsewhere. A notary at Ampurias, for example, held 'in his power' two Genoese captives. One he hired out to an artisan, receiving in return a part of the profit produced from their labour.[12] Nobles and those of standing tended to be ransomed or exchanged for those of equal rank, something which gave rise to heated negotiations.

In northern and central Italy, amongst those city-states variously termed as free or independent, factions and partisans waged bloody wars to seize and hold power. Ottoman wars and the raids of the Barbary corsairs, during which captives were seized and carried off by hostile parties, were hardly novel experiences. Such internecine strife was augmented by the attempts of each city to claim that it had inherited the glory of Rome. Rome was reflected in the city's functions, feasts, and celebrations and, inevitably, in the way it treated its captives – by humiliating and abusing them. In the 1340s Cola di Rienzo, a restless demagogue, was obsessed with seizing Rome and establishing a new empire. In just one campaign against the Roman barons he seized 2,000 men, chained them together and had them sold off at market.[13] On 24 July 1501, Louis XII and Cesare Borgia finally obtained the capitulation of Capua after a long siege. Twenty years later the fall of the city was still being described as a tragic abomination. Sebastiano di Branca Tedallini, in his *Diario* of 1525, and the more discreet Francesco Guicciardini described the sack of the city, with its churches pillaged, its valuable seized, and its women carried off into slavery, being sold and resold in the soldiers' camp before finally ending up for sale in Rome itself.[14]

Much of this behaviour was deliberately designed to humiliate, to show off the booty of war, or to underline, by means of public spectacle, the trouncing of an enemy. Miserable prisoners were therefore dragged before the public, shuffling in chains and semi-naked, preceded by their humbled chiefs and captains. Emperor Frederick II had ordered just such a triumph in Cremona in 1237 'according to the custom of the ancients', after he had taken prisoners from cities which had backed the papal cause. A Milanese wagon was dragged through the streets by an elephant, whilst the vanquished general, the Venetian Pietro Tiepolo, was exposed on another for public humiliation.[15] Such a gaudy spectacle impressed upon gullible minds the pomp and power of the victor at the expense of the captives. The glorification of the leader was vital. Sigismund, entering Rome in 1433, and Alphonso V of Aragon, entering Naples on 25 June 1421, were celebrated as victors. The latter, in 1443, was met by an even more prestigious show in which chariots carrying allegories of Justice, Might, and Victory accompanied a king seated beneath a richly-ornamented canopy. Two triumphal arches, one wooden and one made of marble, had been erected to greet the victor, each decorated with allegorical scenes flattering the hero. The royal throne had even been draped with the cloak of René of Anjou, the vanquished foe who had fled Naples and left it to the Aragonese.[16]

During the wars against the Moors, and, later, against the Turks, no such victory parade would take place without a show of captives. Cardinal Caraffa had twenty-five marched through the streets of Rome in 1473. The king of Aragon, victorious at Otranto in 1480, had 500 dragged along behind his chariot. In 1487 100 Moors from Granada were exhibited to ambassadors to the Spanish court. These were paraded behind a triumphal chariot bearing effigies of Ferdinand and Isabella poised in triumph with Moorish princes at their feet.[17]

For the Turks, and for the Barbary corsairs, such ancient customs were held just as dear. No crowd would be satisfied unless a vanquished enemy was well and truly humiliated. In 1504 Tunis welcomed the return of the Barbarossas with a tremendous celebration following their triumph over two papal galleys and a Spanish ship. More than 100 captives, all of them gentlemen, were paraded through the streets, whilst the young daughters of the governor of Naples were despatched to Constantinople to serve in the Sultan's harem. Meanwhile the two victors sat back and counted their spoils in the comfort of one of the richest palaces of the town.

In Algiers, as well as in Tunis, victorious captains would swagger through the streets dressed in the richest possible costumes. Booty taken from Christian ships was put on public display. At the gate to Algiers harbour three wooden statues of saints, once the figureheads of Christian ships, were ceremonially hung upside down: the figure of John the Baptist had been taken from the Maltese galley *Santa Anna*, seized off Malta in 1570; that of St Paul came from another Maltese vessel; whilst the *Santange*, a ship captured on 27 April 1578 as it transported the Duke of Terranova from Naples to Sicily, provided the figure of Saint Michael.[18]

Following a victorious campaign against the king of Fez and Morocco in 1550, Hassan Pasha's army was warmly welcomed upon its return to Algiers. The defeated monarch's head was carried aloft on a pike and was later placed in an iron cage and suspended from the Bab Azoub gate. There it hung for twenty years until, in 1573, Arab Ahmed had the gate rebuilt and disposed of the gruesome souvenir.[19]

In 1571 Mustafa Pasha went back on his word after promising to spare the lives of the besieged of Famagusta. Instead he had a good number massacred and others hideously tortured to terrify and cow potential enemies. Marcantonio Bragadin was 'paraded along the city's ramparts carrying a basket of earth on his shoulders and another in his hands. Whenever he passed he had to bow down and grovel on the earth. Then he was taken off to a ship, hauled up to the top of a mast, so that he could be seen by all the other prisoners, and then taken to one of the public squares and burnt alive.' No sooner was he dead than his executioners rescued the body, skinned it, stuffed the skin with straw and had it taken to Syria and exhibited all along the coast.[20]

War, Provider of Slaves

Back in the mists of time, when the Saracens of Mahdia and Bougie raided the villages of Liguria or Provence, it had been the cause of much suffering, fear, and loss. In 934 the 'Africans' surprised Genoa, then without defences, and made off with the city's women and children. They had wanted to pillage the place far more thoroughly but were afraid of the city's soldiery returning unexpectedly from campaign.[21] In the Iberian peninsula armed expeditions set out from Cordoba or came over specially from Africa and penetrated deep into the hinterland, returning laden with booty and slaves. All along the coast pirate fleets, some of them veritable armadas, assaulted Christian towns and provinces. The area around Tarragona suffered greatly from such aggression in 1185. Around the same time the fleet of the Caliph, which had been armed and equipped at Seville, raided Lisbon and took away crowds of captives. Other vessels attacked the Galician coast, prompting the bishop of Santiago to hire Genoese and Pisan craftsmen and sailors to construct and man vessels which might serve to protect the shore from enemy raiders.[22]

The situation in the Iberian peninsula was not, contrary to what some historians might suggest, one of three cultures (Christian, Muslim and Jewish) peacefully coexisting. At that time, living side by side with people of another religion was always fraught with danger. Princes and lords, whether Christian or Muslim, lived in constant fear of raids or attacks. It was inevitable, in such an atmosphere, that alien communities such as the Mudejares or, later, Moriscos (Muslims living in Christian lands) and the Mozarabs (Christians living in Muslim lands), were often suspected of concocting dangerous plots.

Moorish raids and Castilian and Aragonese *chevauchées* were often staged with the specific intention of bringing back captives to sell for profit. At Valencia on 5 June 1276 a Jewish merchant sold 'a Moorish slave, white and very young, who had been taken in the raid of Pedro Fernando, son of our king, against Reballeto'.[23] Things weren't very different in the east. After the conquest of Syria Arab expeditions were sent deep into Anatolia, not, as might be expected, to build colonies or establish Arab rule, but to bring back captives. Such shameless conduct deeply affected Byzantine provinces in Asia Minor and led to considerable shifts in population. Those that dared remain behind shut themselves in fortified villages or sought shelter in the shadow of a castle. Later, in the Balkans, the Turks adopted similar raiding tactics, sweeping through agricultural areas or swooping on unsuspecting towns, all the time making off with prisoners. In 1434 Bertrandon de la Broquière, an envoy of the Duke of Burgundy, was passing through the Balkans on his way back from the east when he noted miserable groups of chained Christian prisoners outside

Adrianopolis: 'They begged for pity at the gates of the city; it was a woeful sight to behold their condition and their suffering.' A little further on towards Serbia he sighted a band of 'fifteen men bound together with chains around their neck; also ten women whom the Turks had seized in a raid into the kingdom of Bosnia and who were now being taken to Adrianopolis for sale.'[24]

In the war between Christians and Muslims the loss of a town or of a province inevitably led to the local population's reduction into a servitude more or less brutal, more or less dire. Following the conquest of Majorca by the king of Aragon's fleet in 1229 numerous bands of Muslim inhabitants attempted to flee southwards; simultaneously a similar number were rounded up and despatched to Italy on Genoese or Pisan ships, or to Catalonia on Barcelonan vessels. It was around this time that the sale of Saracens first occurred before the notaries of Perpignan.[25]

The Norman conquest of Sicily meant that a large number of Muslims were sold into slavery. Those who remained free laboured under the suspicions of their new masters. From 1224 the Emperor Frederick II had some of the more notable Saracens from the island settled around Lucera in Puglia. Such a move was not greeted enthusiastically by the local populace. Charles II, the Angevin king of Naples, was responding to public pressure when he sent a force into this province in 1300 to expel the 'Infidels' and establish a strong Christian presence. More than 400 Muslim notables were arrested and thrown into prison. Only a few, after pleading with the king or having hitherto been agents of the monarchy, were released and allowed to reclaim their goods. One such fortunate was Abd el-Aziz, recorded under his adopted name of Nicolaus de Civitate Sancte Marie, who obtained permission to live in Puglia with his sizeable extended family – forty males and sixty females – and to reclaim his house. He even received a gift of land to cultivate and an annual pension of twelve ounces of gold. But the ordinary Saracens had little choice but to take to the road. Clutching their possessions and accompanied by their livestock, they were taken off under escort to designated areas in Abruzzia and around Bari. Local Christians reacted violently, killing a number of the new arrivals despite the intervention of the royal guards and the penalties imposed for harming them. Most of the rest, more than 6,000 individuals, were seized and sold as slaves by merchants quick to sense a profit. The slaves were taken off to the towns, where demand was higher, and sold to the highest bidder. At

Barletta 2,024 Muslims were sold in 1300 and 1301 with a further 1,634 placed on the market the following year. Some 2,500 were sold in Naples where, chained and humiliated, they were sold after royal officials had set reserve prices of two ounces of gold for males above the age of twelve, three for those artisans who had not already been pressed into royal service, and one for women and children.[26]

Of course an operation on the scale of the reconquest of Granada, an enterprise which took many years, served to feed the demand from Christian slave markets. The fall of Malaga in 1487 was quickly followed by the sale in Seville of more than 3,000 eminent citizens of the town and its environs. Some were taken into Castile or Catalonia whilst others were taken on board ships lying in Barcelona, Valencia, and Seville and shipped off to Italy. The defeat of the Morisco revolt of 1500 in eastern Andalusia led to countless defeated rebels and their families being set to work on royal land or sold off to the public.[27]

For the Christian world the principal source of slaves was war – so much so that words previously used to designate a slave, such as *servus* for a male or *ancilla* for a female, fell into disuse. Instead, in the Iberian peninsula, as well as in Provence and as far afield as Genoa, those taken from the Moors were simply called captives, Moors, or Saracens. Notaries pretty much stuck to this formula, whilst masters tended to refer to their slave as 'my Moor' or 'my Saracen'. In Barcelona in 1404 a shipowner referred to one of his slaves as 'a Moor, that is to say a slave'.[28]

Slavery in Africa and in the East

Despite the constant surge and counter-surge of conquest and reconquest war alone could not satisfy the demand of the labour market. Raids, piracy, and kidnapping in neighbouring countries helped, but once again couldn't meet the demand. Muslims were the first, quickly followed by Christians, to seize slaves from more distant lands. Such a move usually followed a set pattern, the first step being the establishment of merchants or representatives who worked closely with native chiefs and indigenous traders. The slaves, who were treated just like any other commodity, had either been captured from the interior or else purchased from intermediaries.

Even before the birth of Mohammed Arab slave-traders had frequented the eastern coast of Africa. In the 700s – one chronicler gives an exact date of 731 – a number of Muslim Arab notables fled to Pemba, north of Zanzibar, whilst others established themselves on Socotra. They rapidly built up a huge slaving network based around Mombassa, Malinda, and Kilwa which reached far into the interior. Arab merchants accompanied expeditions, and would trade grain, meat, and fish for wood, textiles, iron, gold and, more and more frequently, slaves. Manhunts around the great lakes of East Africa depopulated villages and brought in hordes of captives. These would be crammed aboard Arab merchantmen and, after a voyage of six or seven weeks, would arrive at ports along the Persian Gulf. Such a trade devastated Africa, especially as some tribal leaders initiated wars solely in order to take captives to sell to the merchants.[29]

The trans-Saharan slave-trade was also quite well established before the expansion of Islam. Here the operation was more complicated; the acquisition of slaves took longer, and the merchants were exposed to attack by brigands and had to endure freezing nights and scorching days. But gold and slaves nevertheless flowed along this route in abundance. In 666 Oqbar, the Caliph of Damas, demanded as tribute from Fezzan hundreds of captives; in the following centuries hundreds of thousands of such captives were driven northwards for sale in the ports of the Mediterranean. It was even said that the king of Mali, himself a Muslim and on his way to Mecca, arrived in Cairo accompanied by 500 slaves each one carrying a gold nugget. It has been estimated that this human traffic resulted in thousands of slaves being dragged northwards every year by tribal leaders or slave merchants.[30]

In the Mediterranean region the Christians came to the trade quite late or with limited impact. Italy only really participated after the 1250s, whilst in Provence, Catalonia, and Aragon slave-trading was not particularly widespread – until, that is, the arrival of the Genoese in the Black Sea. The Genoese had been granted trading privileges in this region following the Byzantine emperor's accord with the Latin powers following their seizure of Constantinople in 1204.[31] The Genoese established themselves primarily along the Crimean coast, where they established Kaffa as their main base and colony. They and their Venetian rivals both penetrated much further, of course, reaching as far as the sea of Azov, but the Genoese were the more adventurous, even building fortified strongpoints along the Caucasian coast and at the mouths of great rivers. There they bought not only wood for their ships and bows, but also, more frequently, slaves. Abkhazians, Mingrelians, and Kubans were bought from markets in the interior. The Genoese provided their own products in exchange, preferring to barter rather than pay cash – so much so that cloth became a standard currency in the region, much as it would later do in Africa. Each man and each woman was therefore valued in terms of how much material he or she was worth.[32]

This Italian-dominated trade, run predominantly by the Genoese and Venetians, revolved around selecting slaves, transporting them, and selling them. These were distinct operations. Men and women were usually purchased from markets some distance from the coast and were usually purchased from intermediaries or the soldiers who had actually captured them. There were also cases of merchants buying children off impoverished families, who saw this as a way of alleviating their poverty. When the slaves reached Kaffa, Pera, or Chios the men and women were separated and the men were taken away for sale in Egypt. The Italians crammed a hundred or more into each of their vessels and sold them off in Cairo or Alexandria, where they were employed in the construction industry, shipbuilding or, more frequently, in the Sultan's armies. Warriors from the Black Sea, the Caucasus, or Russia were labelled Mamluks and were housed in vast camps along the banks of the Nile; they later developed into a force which selected its own leaders and, ultimately, into an organisation capable of seizing power.[33] The Mamluks themselves would purchase more slaves to fill their ranks, reinforcing the slave trade in an interminable cycle. So well established was this system that after their conquest of the region the Ottomans would inherit it.

Female slaves were taken further west, usually in smaller batches. Merchants carrying cotton or spices would bring back five or six 'heads' as servants on their ships, frequently knowing who the slaves would be sold to before the ship even docked. For the system was such that orders for slaves of specific ages or skills were often placed beforehand. If no such buyer had been confirmed then the merchant would turn first to a courtier or to a notary in the hope that these might introduce him to a potential buyer. A sales contract would then be drawn up for each particular purchase. No trace remains of a public sale at the harbour or in the city squares. Slavery was more subtle.[34]

Work and Labour

For some time historians have referred to slavery as though it took just the one form. But contemporaries of the wars against the corsairs and the Turks used a variety of terms, knowing full well that there were various shades of bondage. Much depended on the origin of the slave, on the number captured, and on their quality. Men and women captured in the course of a war were evidently not treated in the same manner as those who were purchased in far-off lands. The former could be held for ransom whilst the latter might slowly be integrated into society, adopting its manners, religion, and culture. Their children, indeed, might not even be born slaves. For Christians Moors were more trustworthy than Turks, whilst in Africa, up to 1600, the French were most numerous and more frequently had their liberty bought back than Italians or Spaniards. Slave owners themselves, be they the state, nobles, or merchants, introduced more terms, so that slaves doing different tasks could be differentiated from their fellows. There were domestic servants and artisans at one end and galley slaves and labourers at the other. There were also regional variations, as Muslims were employed differently in Liguria and Provence than they were in Catalonia and Naples. Legal issues further diversified the picture. Laws and ordinances, the musings of town councils, sales contracts, acts of emancipation, and court cases all broadened the definition of what a slave was or might be.

That was the case in Europe, at least. Things were different in Africa, where there are fewer surviving documents, royal or private. Accounts of conditions along the Barbary coast by those who travelled in or escaped from the region are all that remain. Some details can also be found in narratives of those religious entrusted with buying back captives. These spent periods based in towns along the coast, studying life in its ports and harbours. They had time to enquire, investigate, and verify. Some spent longer than intended in Algiers or Tunis as they themselves became hostages held to ransom until money was delivered.[35] Their reports and accounts, by and large, paint a single picture of sale followed by manual labour. But the reports do not give much insight into slaves and their surely complex relationship with the native population. For

here comes

The
MARINE
Quarterly

A JOURNAL OF THE SEA

AUTUMN 2023

www.marinequarterly.com

that we have only such writers' imaginings and conjectures, something we would fain refer to as documentation.

Domestic Slaves and Domestic Disorder

Genoa and Venice only very rarely armed and equipped expeditions directed against Africa. Only small numbers of Muslim captives could therefore drift into these cities, either through the fortunes of war or as a result of chance encounters. It was generally accepted that they would refuse to convert to Christianity and would adhere to their own norms of behaviour; moreover, their penchant for running away was no secret. The best that might be expected was therefore the quick payment of a ransom or an arrangement to exchange such Muslim prisoners for Christians held in North Africa.

Although certain forms of slavery had been established in these Italian states most of the slaves came from the Levant. The majority of these were female and were employed within the house after being baptised and given a Christian name. A few married, thereby emancipating themselves. Most would usually adopt the name of the household which they served, whether it be noble, merchant, or artisan. Their children, born in or out of wedlock, would be freeborn, and the women would themselves be freed upon the death of their owner or his widow. So this form of slavery wasn't hereditary; new slaves could only be supplied by bringing in new captives. When it came to justifying such a system, the most common argument advanced in its defence was that separating Tartars, Circassians, and Mingrelians from their pagan roots and bringing them up in the Roman faith turned them into devout Christians.[36]

Moorish and other slaves from the Barbary coast were less numerous and more difficult to integrate; but those from the Levant caused their fair share of concern and worry. Slaves tended to retain their native customs and traditions whenever they could, holding on to their own language in the hope of meeting others of the same origin. They were frequently blamed for provoking trouble. Family harmony was endangered, morality risked.[37] Local men were drawn to watch young slave girls drawing water from wells or fountains, or chanced upon them doing housework or looking after children. There were furtive love affairs, mentioned in contemporary poems, songs, satirical works and fiction. Moralists pleaded for the isolation of the girls and decried the absence of the restraining influence of parents, whilst statisticians showed that for every 100 females there were 130 men. The men themselves were inclined to see slave girls as easier prey than the dutiful daughters of watchful families.

In the early years of the fifteenth century the city hospice of Lucca received 165 abandoned children; of these fifty-five were born to mothers who were slaves and sixteen to non-slaves. The remainder were of unknown origin, but it can be assumed that many of their mothers were also slaves. The Guinigi family alone sent seven infants, born to slaves working on the family's property, to the hospice.[38] At Florence some 100 children were taken into the Hospital of the Innocents, thirty-four of whom were born to slaves. The scribes who registered these children noted as far as they could the names of the families which had sent them. Fourteen came from artisan families, fifteen from patricians, and three from foreigners. The names of the actual fathers were discreetly omitted.[39] The *Ospitale dei Poveri servi Liberi* and the confraternity known as the *Consortia Liberorum seu Grecorum*, situated in the Santa Maria delle Vigne quarter of Genoa, took in and looked after such abandoned children. The children of all such institutions would, at the appropriate age, be put out as apprentices. In Florence the girls would work in the cloth industry, in Lucca the boys would work in the arsenal. Sometimes children would be put up for adoption by local families. One way or another the children of slaves would be treated as non-slaves.

Around the years 1410 to 1420 the Genoese developed an interesting concept: they took out life insurance on their slaves.[40] The notary would make a record of the girl's name, the name of the owner's family, her ethnic origin and age (which varied from sixteen to thirty-six). The sum assured was usually in round figures of 100, 125, and 150 *livres*, with a premium to be paid every month. The slave was even given a rudimentary medical, to minimise the risk.

Moorish Slaves in Aragon

Throughout the Iberian peninsula the wars waged as a part of the Reconquista rendered slaves from the east of far less importance than in

Italy. However, in the fifteenth century Spanish ships brought in women purchased on Rhodes or at Pera. Frequently such slaves were then taken on to Genoa or Pisa and sold by Catalan merchants, but some made it to the teeming cities of Catalonia, where they were employed in the Italian manner as domestics or household servants. Aragonese lawyers and charitable institutions were therefore faced with much the same problems as experienced by their Italian counterparts. Confraternities of liberated slaves based in Valencia and Barcelona took in and brought up the children of slaves. The hospital of Saint-Jean in Perpiganan was founded in 1456 and housed some fifty 'orphans'. The local municipality worried about the cost, thinking that it was subsidising bastards, and agreed that every time an infant was abandoned on the steps of the hospital at night an inquiry would be started, the father would be traced, and he would be made to contribute to the child's upkeep.[41]

Muslim slaves, however, were much more common. Moorish men were sold off in the port area or in public squares every time a fleet of warships returned to port.[42] Royal officials in Valencia were unsuccessful in keeping a tally of the number of slaves sold off in this manner; Christian corsairs hid their prisoners or sold them on the black market to avoid paying a royal tax on the proceeds. Some were even landed at night on deserted beaches to prevent prying eyes reporting them to customs officials. From the coast the slaves were often marched inland over the mountains and sold off in the remote region around Jativa, Alcoy, and Cocentayna.[43]

The fate of these slaves, usually recorded as being Moors or Saracens, was governed by private agreement and usually wasn't interfered with by local officials or those of the prince. The division of booty taken at sea meant that a captive might end up being owned by two or three different masters. Clerks were kept busy drawing up agreements for the sale of a share of a slave, the recognition of a debt, or the transfer of rights, and were involved in clearing up every kind of dispute arising from co-ownership. A Barcelonan shipowner once wrote that he owed a merchant a sum which was the equivalent to the value of one-fifth of a Saracen and half of another. From 1492 Christian knights and inhabitants of Granada frequently clubbed together to launch an annual raid against the Barbary shore. These expeditions – or *cabalgadas* – were a new development in the old art of cross-border raiding. In 1506 Lorenzo de Zafra brought back thirty-two captives and 300 head of cattle. He then set about giving the shipowner and financiers their due for the latter, some of whom had invested quite modest sums: one slave usually sufficed when shared out between five investors.[44]

Where were such slaves put to work? After the reconquest of the Balearics between 1240–50 prisoners of war were sent to work in Barcelona's arsenal, but this appears to have been a one-off arrangement. Certainly it seems that very few slaves were put to work down mines, and their employment on the region's vast agricultural estates seemed to be getting rarer. Some were used in specialist industries such as the sugar cane plantations around Valencia or the sugar mills owned by the German Ravensburg Company around Gandia.[45] Further afield, in Andalusia, across the Guadalquivir, nobles were turning against the employment of 'those vile slaves who care not nor tend the land'. They were employed for only short periods, the men to drive herds of cattle and the women to gather olives. The salt industry did employ a number of slaves, particularly around Ibiza, but this was such a notorious fate that owners who wished to protect their property included a clause in their purchase contract which stated that the slave should not 'under any circumstances be sent to the Balearics'.[46]

The vast bulk of Turkish or Moorish slaves ended up in the cities, usually attached to some household. The notables of Barcelona, Valencia, the Catalonian ports, and the kingdom of Aragon bought and sold slaves on a whim. A Barcelonan merchant once lent out his Saracen to a master caulker not, as might be thought, for a lump sum but rather for a quarter of the profit the slave's labour produced. The caulker kept the rest. Another lent his Saracen, again for a year, to a company of dyers. These paid fifty *ecus* and, in return, guaranteed to provide the slave with accommodation and to teach him the profession. Two artisans, working as potters, gave another merchant ninety-seven and a half *sous* which they owed him as wages, his slave having 'worked with us and helped us, shaping clay and glazing it'. Such a system also functioned in Seville.[47] There, in the year 1506, Donna Catalina de Ribera had slaves labouring away, one with a carpenter, one with a blacksmith, another with a mason.[48]

Such additions to the labour market must have had an impact, and not a particularly positive one. The arrival of slaves, many of whom were themselves accomplished artisans – potters, for example – made finding employment for local craftsmen that little bit more problematic. In almost all Catalonian towns, and those in Aragon, municipal decrees were proclaimed to limit the number of slaves working in each particular factory or workshop. As early as 1453 the jewellery smiths of Barcelona were restricted to using one male slave and one female slave. The threshold was raised to three slaves in 1481 but, ten years later, reverted to two. No master jeweller could teach his art to a slave without first having attempted to hire a freeman or 'free citizen of the country'. The *barqueros* – dockers who loaded and unloaded ships in the harbour of Barcelona – were, in 1350, restricted to using two slaves to assist them. Few adhered to these rules, however, and it gradually became accepted practice for such workers to be invariably drawn from Saracens.

With slaves and freemen working side by side in the same industry some kind of friction was perhaps inevitable. A process whereby slaves began to dominate one industry whilst being excluded from another was the inevitable result.

And there were trades in which slaves were not put to use. Those involved in producing luxury goods or local specialities did not want outsiders or potential spies prying into their methods. In Catalonia slaves were not permitted to serve goldsmiths, silversmiths, or gilders and, to ensure this, no slave was legally permitted to work with silver, precious stones, or gold. No Saracen could purchase 'any metal object, old or new, whole or broken'. As for bakers, they could employ slaves from other regions, but these had to be paid a daily wage, whilst those from North Africa were banned.[49]

Authorities were very keen to impress upon slave owners the need to be vigilant and to discipline their charges. Slaves would frequently attempt to escape into Granada, a Moorish kingdom until 1492, or would seek asylum amongst communities inhabited primarily by Muslims or those of Muslim sympathies. Many slaves even headed for France, taking refuge in Foix or around Carcassonne, where they were regarded as free men.

Escape was made easier by the fact that slaves carried no special sign and wore no distinctive clothes. In addition some found accomplices or received assistance from unfortunates such as themselves. Some were helped by Christians from abroad, Basques and Gascons who would be paid one way or another to spirit slaves out of the region. In the second decade of the fifteenth century the *Cortés* was so indignant at these goings on that it asked the king himself to intervene on its behalf and have words with the authorities in Carcassonne and Toulouse. It wanted these French authorities to not only agree to stop hiding runaways but also to return them to their rightful owners. Reality for those escaped slaves who made it into Languedoc was sometimes as harsh as the existence they had left behind. Many became serfs for life on the grand estates: 'In the thirteenth and fourteenth century there was no château, no estate which did not have one or more Saracens dependent and labouring upon the land.'[50]

The indignant *Cortés*, meanwhile, had instigated a course of action to prevent escape attempts. In 1413 it announced the organisation of guards to patrol the roads, seeking out fugitives and returning them to their owners. Catalonia was divided into twenty districts, each of which was to be patrolled by a dozen such officers. Owners were obliged to declare their slaves to the authorities and pay a yearly premium. In 1431 1,748 fugitives were caught, 1,225 from Barcelona alone, 186 from Gerona, and 83 from Perpignan. Funds were also raised to hire agents to patrol and to denounce runaways; these would station themselves along the highways, usually at the exits from towns. Rewards were also offered for information. More bizarrely, patrols were sometimes launched across the border to bring back runaways by force from French territory. Sometimes compensation was paid to owners who lost their slaves. Between 1421 and 1430 the loss of some 324 slaves was noted and monies paid accordingly. Some 253 of these had private owners, forty-nine belonged to the crown, and twenty-two came from monastic lands. Those Moors caught were returned to their owners upon payment of a 'navigation tax', a sum which varied according to the number of rivers crossed in the pursuit of the fugitive. Those who were caught and found to belong to no particular owner, or were not claimed, were sold off at a public auction.

In 1430 Juan Arbos, 'a guard of slaves from the diocese of Perpignan', set off for Toulouse and managed, for payment no doubt, to bring back dozens of fugitives. On another level the citizens of Barcelona threatened to bar French merchants from their markets if Charles VII, acting in the name of the people of Toulouse, did not send back escapees. He, or the people of Toulouse, evidently refused, finding, perhaps, that they were better off keeping the fugitives for themselves.[51]

Attempts by slaves to escape across the sea necessitated running a gauntlet fraught with all kinds of additional risks. No sooner had ports such as Granada, Malaga, Almeria, and Vega fallen into Christian hands than these avenues of escape were practically barred. There was little question of successfully stowing away or persuading a fisherman to smuggle them out. Guards were, on the whole, far more vigilant in the ports than they were inland and there were all kinds of other precautions. For example, in 1410 a citizen of Barcelona lent two of his Saracens to Arnoldo Font, a shipowner from Tortosa, for four months so that they might 'serve him aboard ship and learn to master sails and other duties, at his convenience'. Arnoldo took the precautionary measure of having the slaves bound 'with two chains around their shins'.[52]

A number of fugitives attempted to flee to Portugal and, from there, hoped to find passage abroad. Yet again, however, royal commands and police surveillance made such an option increasingly hazardous. Those slaves even suspected of wanting to escape were shackled and were barred from entering taverns or harbours. Lisbon's ferrymen were forbidden to carry slaves across the Tagus without the written permission of their masters. Fishermen took their sails and oars ashore and placed armed guards on their boats at night. Anyone denouncing a slave received 300 pieces of gold as a reward. Christians and Jews found guilty of sheltering runaways were liable to pay the original price of such slaves to their master and, on top of that, pay a stiff fine to the crown. Those who delayed in paying were punished in public or thrown into prison. Anyone who actually aided and abetted a fugitive was sent off to distant Saõ Tome, where they laboured on royal sugar cane plantations. Jews and Moors found guilty of complicity were themselves sold into slavery. Other slaves found guilty had their ears chopped off.[53]

Africa: War and Raiding

During the period when raids were conducted into Andalusia or attempts were made to reconquer Granadan territory it was not uncommon for Christian prisoners to fall into Muslim hands in their hundreds. Jerome Muntzer, a German who visited Spain and Portugal in 1494 and 1495, estimated the number of such captives found in Granada after the liberation of that city to be around 2,000. Tetouan apparently had some 2–3,000, many of them originally from Granada. Peace accords signed in 1410 led to the liberation of 300 Christian slaves, 100 more were released in 1417 and 550 in 1439. In the year 1456 Henry IV of Castile negotiated the immediate release of 1,000 Christians with a further 333 released each year for three years thereafter. The captives were welcomed back by huge celebrations, events which were designed to impress the public and perhaps pave the way for action against the Muslim states.[54]

Documents such as those noticed above are found wanting when it comes to examining the situation along the Barbary coast, as the corsairs were not given to operating similar exchange schemes. The Barbarossas' account books, in which their prizes were noted down, have not survived, even supposing that they recorded such booty methodically. There is evidence to suggest that profits to be had from raiding at sea pale into insignificance when compared to those to be had from trans-border expeditions. Corsairs generally set out with just two or three galleys, making it impossible to come back with anything more than a few dozen prisoners. Usually all they had room for was the crew of a barque or a sloop. Even so, it was a profitable enterprise: the sale of eight or ten men brought in as much money as the sale of an entire cargo of grain, oil, or cheese. Raids carried out against an enemy coastline – which was sometimes guarded – were also hazardous, and there was some doubt as to whether the risks were worthwhile. In the summer of 1550 the corsair captain Ahmed cruised off the coast of Corsica for an entire week but captured just one man, a priest; when he moved on to Sardinia he managed to catch just two young men, found swimming in the sea.[55]

Only large-scale raids offered the prospect of real profit: expeditions which involved a sizeable fleet manned by men-at-arms, and the sack of towns and cities. Then the markets of Constantinople and Africa would be awash with captives. The sack of Mahon, on Minorca, in 1535 brought in 6,000 slaves. Kheir ed-Din seized 1,500 prisoners on Ischia in 1544, and just a few days later had some 12,000 captives crammed aboard his ships following the capture of Lipari, where the entire terrified population was hunted out of its hiding places and dragged away.

A historian needs to ask whether such figures have been exaggerated. Were the Christians over-stressing their loss to make themselves appear more victimised? There is an element of this for sure. But the figures are not pure invention. It is a fact that war between Christendom and the Ottoman Turks, and the raids carried out by the Barbary corsairs, paid for the building of new baths in Algiers, Tunis, and Constantinople, as well as impressive buildings in modest places such as Djerba. We lack accurate statistics and must rely, to an extent, on the word of mouth of travellers and contemporary commentators. But there is an element of concurrence: some talk of 8,000 slaves, others of 18,000 or 20,000, fewer of 25,000.[56] Of course, such figures fluctuated from year to year. Nevertheless, this alien, servile class formed a considerable element of the population of Algiers, which at most numbered 70,000 inhabitants.

Christians for Sale

On Barbary galleys or Ottoman ships there were more Christian slaves than there were volunteers, condemned criminals, or Janissaries. In the centre of Algiers and Tunis and throughout their suburbs, the work-shops, shipyards, and warehouses functioned on the backs of a slave workforce. There was a vast pool of slave labour, constantly renewing itself and being renewed, underpinning the entire economic life of such communities. Whilst the cities of Egypt, hardly very warlike, received shipments of hundreds and thousands of African slaves the cities of the Barbary coast did without this expense. Instead the supply provided by war satisfied their every need.

In contrast to much of what went on in Christian Europe, slave sales, transactions, exchanges, and repatriations were not left in private hands but, rather, became the concern of agents of the pasha – and therefore of the Sultan – who oversaw, and controlled, everything. It was the pasha and his agents who organised the sale of the slaves. Auctions were held in public places or in the courtyards of purpose-built market places. Men, women, and children were led in like lambs to the slaughter:

> There are, in effect, special officials who drive the slaves through the market place, shouting out that they might be purchased . . . The slaves are practically naked, as though this were no matter of shame. Buyers examine the slaves to see that they are strong or weak, healthy or ailing, that they carry not a fateful malady that might prevent them from working. They are made to walk and, by blows of a cudgel, to jump to see that they are not lame. Their teeth are examined, not to learn their age but to see that there are no impediments that might detract from their value. Most attention, however, is devoted to the

slaves' hands, and this is so for two reasons. Firstly, it may be judged whether the slave was a labourer, a thing most sure if his hands were callused and rough; secondly, by looking at the lines on the slaves hands they determined whether he or she might live a long time free from peril or disease. Some, it was said, could even ascertain whether or not a slave would attempt to flee by examining these lines.[57]

A few selected individuals were paraded alone but most were sold as a group in lots. Bids were high for young, fit men, whilst those who were evidently unsuitable for toil or unqualified as artisans or craftsmen, but who might, on the other hand, draw a large ransom, might find themselves fetching ten times the price of a labourer. There were a few Moors and Turks who speculated on the value of slaves, buying them cheap and selling them on. One witness wrote that 'In the towns of the Barbary corsairs, the wealthy invest their money in slaves much as Christians place theirs in a bank'.[58]

Captives who were infirm or wounded in battle might find themselves serving a master as a servant. Jeronimo de Pasamonte survived Lepanto unscathed but was left for dead on the field before Tunis in 1574. He was sold off at market with two other wounded soldiers, fetching fifteen ducats. A Turkish captain bought him, despite the risk of him dying, and took him to Constantinople. He spent some time recuperating at Navarino before finding work in some palatial gardens. The work was not without danger, however, as he was 'loaded with insults, day after day'. Then he had to accompany his master to Tunis along with another 100 slaves. Here they were set to work rebuilding a fort. An attempt to escape failed and he was punished by being sent to the galleys, where he toiled for more than a year. He then rejoined his master and journeyed to Alexandria, Constantinople, Coron, Modon, Rhodes, Chios, and Algiers, until he was finally released following the payment of his ransom.[59]

Most slaves were kept in groups, dressed in rags, watched and guarded. They were held in penal colonies, sleeping in bunks one above the other. They suffered the icy blast of winter and the scorching heat of summer, and endured vermin the whole year round. In addition many were mistreated by their masters and only given rotten biscuits and putrid water. In Granada, when it was still part of the Moorish kingdom, slaves were kept in corals, cellars for the storage of grain. Algiers, at the height of Turkish rule, had six or seven large slave barracks, the principal one of which was on the main souk, in the centre of the city. Here many hundreds were housed, perhaps even a thousand. The front of the building, which was built around a central courtyard, was seventy paces long and forty deep. On the upper level were rooms for the slaves. Under Hassan Pasha, the Venetian renegade, some 2,000 slaves were crammed into quarters much smaller than this and a further 500 were kept in The Bastard, a barrack named after the ship from which the corsairs had captured hundreds of captives in 1558 during the battle of Mostaganem.[60]

Tunis had an active slave market too, particularly after Euldj'Ali came to power in 1574. He oversaw the hasty construction of eight or nine further barracks, all designed according to the same plan – four wings built around a central open space. The slaves were kept ten or fifteen at a time in rooms on the first floor, crammed into the sombre surroundings. The lower floor and cellars served as a prison. The main entrance opened at dawn so that the slaves could be led off in gangs to work; other individuals were accompanied to workshops or houses so that they too could begin their day's work.

Slaves sometimes served in more nefarious trades. Tables would be set up in courtyards so that 'soldiers, sailors and other debauched individuals could eat, drink, sing and smoke, or discuss their business. Some slaves ran such hostelries, paying a sum to the warden for the privilege; he, in turn, protected them and made those unwilling to pay settle their bills.' The warden was master of this underworld, policing his captives, setting sentries, and hiring slaves for dubious errands. Some amassed a fortune by using their slaves as thieves, hiding away the proceeds.[61]

Female Captives

Chroniclers, as well as the writers of cheap novels, have devoted considerable space to the popular theme of captive Christian women. These would 'serve' their Barbary masters, who might own dozens of women, keeping them prisoner and enjoying them in seclusion behind the shuttered windows of the seraglio. Few travellers neglected to eulogise about the palaces of Granada or Constantinople without bringing in imagery of mysterious, but scantily clad, women. Castilians in the fifteenth century knew the names of such slaves, women who had become the wives of sultans and others of the royal household. There was Turayya, who married Emir Abdul-Hassan, and Laila Eohora, a renegade from Vejer de la Frontera, who married Ali ben Rasid, future founder of Xauen in Africa.[62]

In 1471 a pilgrim passing through Tunis noted that the king, although authoritarian and brutal, was, nevertheless, honest in his exercise of justice vis-à-vis the Christians:

> He respected them greatly as his mother was born a Christian in Valencia; taken to Tunis she was purchased by the king's father and became his concubine. He kept some 600 concubines in his palace, the casbah of Tunis. They were guarded by a Christian woman and by numerous eunuchs. Whenever he travelled he took a hundred with him, or, at the very least, sixty. He had numerous sons and daughters from these women.[63]

Half a century later nobody mentioned the Moorish princes, attention being focused instead on the renowned Barbarossas, especially Kheir ed-Din. Many stories, often originating in Italy or Spain, circulated regarding his adventures, his palaces, his harem. He was reputed to have numerous concubines and at least six wives. Among these were Khalidja, a young Moor from Granada, and Aicha, a Moor from Algiers and the mother of Hassan Pasha. Then there were four Christian wives: a Bosnian, selected by his mother, who died before she could give birth; Beatrice of Orea, a Sicilian captured in 1514 on a ship bound for Malaga; Aura, an Italian; and Maria, daughter of Diego Gaetano, governor of Reggio. Barbarossa loved the last so much that he released her father and mother from captivity.[64]

Whilst many accounts gloss over the fate of male captives, they rarely failed, even in early times, to go into considerable detail concerning the women who fell into enemy hands. These were described as being torn from their family, humiliated, kept prisoner for years, abused as servants, and kept as concubines. Later, during the campaigns against the Barbarossas, the same kinds of account dwelt upon how, when towns were devastated, the women were carried off, violated, and subjected to slavery without, it seemed, the slightest chance of escape or of ever seeing their homelands again. The public sale of women, as though they were livestock, was universally condemned, as was their subsequent fate of working as servants for vile owners – prostitutes, to all intents and purposes, for their masters.

For those who did make it back to friendly shores their time at the mercy of the Turks or Moors was a source of painful memories, and as such not something about which they could convey details to their families. The fact that many had doubtless been dishonoured gave rise, in Genoa at least, to malicious rumour-mongering. A few notable houses in that city slandered those bearing the name of Di Mare or Usodimare by suggesting that such people were obviously descended form ancestors who had been bastards of a union between a corsair and a slave. But these stories were pure inventions; the names had much older origins. However, the attitude of such slanderers was symptomatic of a society in which women who had been captives were suspect, and where those associated with the sea had to share in its hazards and fortunes.

Escape

There was a time when a slave revolt might be crowned with success, such as that of the Zanj – black slaves who fought off the Caliph of Baghdad's troops for more than twenty years and set up their own government in Bassorah. But no such thing would have been possible in North Africa under Turkish occupation; the Turks had learnt how to suppress revolt through years of experience in subjugating the Moors and the indigenous tribes. So for those Christians who would not convert to Islam, or who couldn't see themselves being ransomed, the only way to regain their liberty was through flight.

In Christendom, God, his saints and his angels were called upon to look after such fugitives. Throughout Provence, Spain, and Italy prayers were constantly offered up, and processions and acts of grace were undertaken on behalf of the runaways. Braving rough seas, bad weather, and countless risks, successful escapes seemed almost miraculous. Pedro Martin, a monk working in Silos, wrote a long treatise between 1274 and 1287 entitled *How Saint Dominique Liberated Captives from their Prisons*; in all, eighty miraculous deliveries were listed.[65]

There are a number of accounts penned between the Reconquista and the sixteenth century which provide intimate details of such adventurous escapes. Sombre prisons are invoked, chains, plots, dangers, ships stolen from the Moors, dark nights, adventures on the open sea, and divine winds taking the runaways to Spain or Sicily, are all brought before the reader. Desperate prisoners would hear God speaking to them in a compassionate voice before undoing their chains. Guards would then negligently let them pass, and they would flee almost instantaneously across the sea. Few such tales were more fantastic than the story of an escaped slave from Algiers, a certain Alvarez, who was dying of thirst on the road to Oran, his feet bloody, when a lion came to him and carried him to his destination.[66]

If a slave did escape or was bought back by his prince, his church, or his family, he was sure to be greeted enthusiastically and made a Christian hero, like a pilgrim who had ventured to Compostella or the Holy Land. He would become a local celebrity. Antonio Veneziano, a Sicilian poet, was thirty-five when he was captured aboard a galley carrying the household of the Duke of Terranova. Along with thirty gentlemen and seventy servants he was taken to Algiers. Two years later his ransom was paid by the Senate of Palermo and, upon his return to Sicily, he was met by feasting and celebration the like of which had rarely been seen.[67]

Years spent in captivity certainly form a very interesting part of the reminiscences penned by soldiers, clerics, and sailors. Many are rich in detail, while others evoke hopes and aspirations. Some are fine pieces of work in their own right, gripping the reader and thrilling him with every twist of fortune. Their writers were sure to find a large audience in their native lands, where there was a constant clamour for such depressing tales.[68]

The most woeful fate was that which befell galley slaves. In 1544 Barbarossa's fleet, heading for Constantinople, was hit by a storm as it traversed the Gulf of Salerno. A galley loaded with captured slaves went down. Many of the passengers got away by swimming, but the galley slaves, chained to their oars, went down with the ship.[69] It was said that corsair captains preferred to see their slaves drown rather than let them swim off and, potentially, reach a Christian shore. If they did that they might give the authorities vital information about the corsairs' ships, their complements and handling, and where the corsairs sheltered or anchored. Using slaves at the oars also meant that corsair captains could expect their Christian enemies not to make full use of their guns for fear that they might kill their co-religionists.

Nevertheless, despite the risks and the danger nothing could stop the galley slaves praying for deliverance. A storm might provide a fleeting chance for escape, as might collision with rocks on a Christian coast or, better still, an encounter with a Spanish ship or one belonging to the Knights of Malta. When eleven Ottoman galleys were wrecked on the coast of Sardinia in 1534 many Turks got ashore, dragging with them 800 slaves. When they came under attack the Turks fled on board three undamaged galleys, abandoning their captives.[70]

Combat also renewed hope in the heart of a galley slave by providing a chance for escape. Confusion in the heat of battle might enable him to work free from his chains and swim to a friendly ship, or the ship itself might be captured by friendly forces. Cervantes described how, in 1572, the galley *La Loba*, captained by Alvaro de Bazan, Marquis of Santa Cruz, captured the *Presa*, a galley belonging to Barbarossa's son: 'The galley slaves onboard were so badly and cruelly treated that no sooner had they caught sight of us than they jumped up, seized their captain and dragged him along the full length of the ship, administering so many blows to him that his soul departed for hell; so much hatred had he inspired among them.'[71]

By contrast the conditions in which slaves were held on land offered few opportunities for possible escape. Corsairs and Janissaries kept a watchful eye on the comings and goings of prisoners, as well as those of Christian merchants, shipowners, and clerics. Spies were ever active, many of them renegades, some of them even slaves prepared to inform on their fellows. Prisoners caught even planning an escape were subjected to dire punishment, torture even. Hassan Pasha, the renegade Venetian, earned himself a terrible reputation for cruelty in his zeal to hunt down and punish fugitives: 'No sooner was a Christian retaken than he was dragged before the slaves and burnt alive in their view; he beat others to death with his own hand or cut off noses and ears or had others tortured before him.'[72] Ahmed Pasha was a man who was 'naturally cruel and so accustomed to guarding slaves that he strolled up and down holding a cudgel with which he lashed out at slaves as he came across them. Should any attempt to get out of the way he turned into an executioner, beating his victim to death with his own hand.'[73]

Those slaves sent to toil in workshops or those allowed the freedom to circulate in the streets – perhaps on an errand for some merchant or other – hoped that they might receive help from the local Moors, a people who had suffered from the arrogance of the Turks. But no records have survived to suggest that this ever happened. All we have are accounts by those who did manage to effect an escape through their own courage, determination, or good fortune.

A handful clandestinely built their own vessels in which to escape, day after day secreting wood and other materials to this end. Others managed to hijack a barque or sloop, overpowering the crew. On occasion men – and it was usually men, as women had less chance of overpowering their guards – invented complicated ruses, trusting some individuals, lying to others.

Cervantes was kept as a slave in Algiers for five years. His first attempt at escape was an outright failure. Accompanied by a few companions, he overcame a guard detailed to escort them, but the fugitives didn't get far before they were recaptured. As punishment the Spaniard was sentenced to working in a quarry, crushing stones and transporting them to where the port's fortifications were being rebuilt. His next escape involved liaising with a mysterious intermediary who arranged for a brigantine to arrive off a certain part of the coast. But the brigantine was ambushed and Cervantes and his fellows were captured hiding in a cave. After this attempt he spent five months chained in a dungeon before being bought, in 1577, by Hassan, Pasha of Algiers. His fellow fugitives were not so fortunate, being hanged or impaled, whilst the Janissaries who had negligently allowed them to escape were also executed. Two years later, in the fourth year of his captivity, he managed to escape once again, this time accompanied by a renegade known by the name of Abderramann or, in a previous life, Giron, a native of Granada. This Giron persuaded Cervantes that he wanted to get back to Spain. They negotiated with a Valencian merchant to get on board his frigate but a defrocked priest, Blanco de Paz, betrayed them and, using another renegade, this one a Florentine, alerted Hassan that one of his slaves was attempting to escape. Cervantes spent the next five months in another slimy dungeon.[74]

Jeronimo de Pasamonte spent eighteen years accompanying his master throughout the Islamic world. As a result they became quite familiar with one another. The slave had so much contact with Turks, Moors, Jews, renegades, and foreign merchants that, inevitably, opportunities for escape presented themselves. Indeed, he did attempt five or six times to get away, but failure dogged him at every turn. When he was working at Bizerte, he noticed that the slaves working on the walls of the port were so numerous that their guards were unable to keep a close eye on all of them. He became the leader of a small band of desperate men who, swearing allegiance to one another, secreted arms, observed the movements of their guards, and chose their moment to escape. Attempting to steal a boat they were discovered and many were killed or wounded in the ensuing skirmish.

Later, in Egypt, he entered into an agreement with the Christian owner of a boat and set about planning how to evade his guards. Doing this would be difficult as, in addition to the irons which were round his legs, more irons had been added to his wrists. His movements were also restricted by his being 'master of the bank' (*cabode casa*) on a galley, seated at the worst place (at the foot of the mast, to the right) on the ship, where the heaviest oar was located. Later still a Catalan goldsmith took the money of he and his fellow conspirators and promised to come to their assistance but instead abandoned them to their fate. In Alexandria a short Franciscan monk, preaching in the Venetian *fondouk*, gathered a group of slaves around him and told them he would lead them in an attempt to capture a boat. But they had neither weapons nor the means to cast off their chains, and were, anyway, denounced before they even took action. There followed another attempt, this time on Rhodes, when the galley slaves called out to those working in the harbour to come on board and overpower their guards; they would then sail off together, but this unrealistic plan was no more than a dream. So Pasamonte gave up trying to escape and submitted to his fate. The only hope left to him was of finding enough money to obtain his release. But his master, who had bought him wounded and sick for fifteen ducats, told him that he would not let him go for a thousand.[75]

Exchanges, Buy-backs and Ransoms

Before 1492 and the fall of Granada to the Christians the border between Christendom and Muslim territory was a notorious despoiled wasteland marked by burnt houses, where kidnapping and the selling of goods to raise ransoms for loved ones were equally widespread. In the 1400s

Castile could boast of a number of organisations dedicated to raising funds for the liberation of slaves. These were aided by sponsors from Christian society as well as by Jews and Mudejares. Indeed, pious donations by Mudejares were often used to liberate Christians.

A breed of royal officers, the so-called *Alcades entre los Cristianos y los Moros*, assisted by mounted soldiers (*caballeros de la sierra*) and infantrymen (*ballesteros de monte* and *fieles ad rastro*) were responsible for attempting to impede the kidnapping of individuals, the pursuit of raiders, and intervention in disputes between various communities. The actual buying-back of slaves necessitated lengthy negotiations and endless comings and goings between Jaen and the Granadan territories.

These arrangements were either carried out in broad daylight or in secret, initially through intermediaries such as the *alfaqueques*. Many of these go-betweens traded on their contacts and made a profit out of their role. Some were paid up front whilst others sought long-term gains. But not all were respected; some were accused of fraud, extorting money from prisoners' families or cheating on the Muslims by promising them funds which never actually materialised. In order to stamp out such misdeeds the king created the post of *Alfaqueque real en la frontera de Moros de Lorca a Tarifa* and designated the Arias de Saavedra to run the institution as hereditary beneficiaries. But these worthies fell under suspicion in turn and were even accused of serving as Muslim spies. The *Alfaquequerya mayor* of Castile was suspended just after the fall of Granada, but was quickly reinstated when the authorities realised that such an institution was still necessary for the liberation of prisoners transported overseas. It was expected to 'buy back and carry back from all ports and harbours those Christians held in far-off lands'.[76]

Agreements and Money

War and piracy brought poverty but also provided opportunities, not always honest ones, for profit. Such opportunities could present themselves quite quickly after the capture of a prisoner. Many families, upon learning that a relative had been taken, rushed to the scene of the event and offered the corsairs money on the spot: 'It was common for pirates of all kinds and from all countries, Christian as well as Muslim, to attempt to sell off their slaves in the same region they had been kidnapped from. That way they might quickly receive money and avoid the trouble of transporting the human cargo.'[77] The corsair captains of Algiers and Tunis had precious little room on board their galleys for anything more than a small number of captives, and lacked the resources to feed them. Selling the captive back to his or her family brought in a guaranteed sum quickly, which allowed them, perhaps, to prolong their expedition.

After sacking the town of Castellmare, close to Naples, Dragut established a slave market on the island of Procida and sent out word that the slaves would be sold back to those coming to claim them – for the right price. On 26 June 1544 'the Turks held a market of Christian slaves below the walls of the castle of Baies; there they sold those they had taken from Ischia, to the number of 2,400 of both sexes'. A few days later another such auction was held at Catona, in Calabria, for those captives taken from Lipari. The people of Messina, acting collectively, offered 15,000 ducats for the release of all the captives. Barbarossa, whose food supplies were beginning to run out, asked for and obtained 8,000 quintals of biscuit in addition to the money. The deal went through.[78]

Christian shipowners and pirates were similarly inclined to dispose of their captives in or close to their native land. In part this was to avoid onerous fiscal duties levied on profits from such activities. Captives were sold back to relatives or to slave-dealers and the money was divided up between members of the crew. Two Majorcan ships seized a Muslim galley off Almeria; without wasting any time the vessel was taken into Malaga and the officers of the king of Granada were informed that they could buy back the captives. On 23 September 1462 the Egyptian, Abdalbarit Ben Ali, spied two Frankish vessels in the roads of Tunis. These were offering to sell Moorish slaves back to the populace. He purchased a Turk for forty dinars and, in gratitude, the man served him faithfully for more than a decade.[79]

Of course, the fate of those seized and carried away to distant shores was particularly gloomy. Hopes of recovering their liberty rapidly diminished as time wore on. Isolated, surrounded by an alien culture, loaded with work by demanding masters, many nevertheless fought for an opportunity to alert their loved ones of their plight or to organise a ransom. But it took patience, extraordinary patience.

Muslims held captive in Spain depended, to a large extent, on the generosity of the Muslim community in the Iberian peninsula to open doors.

A few, with the king's consent, were granted permission by their masters to go among the Muslim villages and beg to raise a ransom. Their owners weren't always being altruistic – many expected to make more from such a ransom than from the labour of the slave. The license to beg (*licencia por acaptar*) bore the slave's name, his origin and, sometimes, a physical description. In addition there were details of the slave's owner and a stipulation as to the amount he could receive by begging. Such a system, which developed into something of an institution, allowed Moorish captives to wander relatively freely among villages inhabited by fellow Muslims. There were abuses of the system, just as there was talk of espionage and the plotting of revolts. Royal agents were quick to proclaim that certain specific regions, those suspected of being rebellious, were out of bounds. In April 1496 any beggar found plying his trade in the regions of Manessa, Paterna, and Benaguacil was declared a state prisoner.[80] Others, who had strayed from the areas designated for them, were pursued by cavalry. A certain Pere de Besalu, a lieutenant from the kingdom of Naples, was expressly summoned over in 1441 'to capture the so-called Moors or Barbary men'; those who denounced such itinerants were promised large rewards. De Besalu enrolled a body of men-at-arms, both mounted and foot, and set out into the mountainous districts around Gandia, Alcoy, and Oliva. His mobile column spent several months in the field but returned comparatively empty-handed. It did seize some slaves, selling them off at Jativa, Majorca, and Valencia, but for the most part these were older males, sold off as a group of 'elderly' for little money.[81]

At around the same time the process of selling back captive Moors to their families was developing into a sophisticated trade for numerous sailors, financiers, and merchants. Registers of the levies exacted by the crown on such transactions (known as *leyda* in Catalonia, *delma* in Valencia) are testament to this activity, much of which was conducted through the hands of slave merchants (for want of a better term). On Majorca, between 1395 and 1497, the tax for at least 500 Moorish captives was paid and the carefully kept accounts give us an insight into the procedure. Gabriel Benvire took custody of some fifteen slaves on a single day. Luis Benvire, a relative, took charge of twenty-two. Foreigners, many of them sailors passing through, also participated in the enterprise. Three Venetian galley owners paid dues of thirty *livres* to obtain twenty captives and take them back to Africa for sale.[82]

Further to the east, in Genoa, two Moors from Barbey – Ahmet Mazus, who said that he understood the 'Genoese language', and Mohammed Zamai – were brought before one of the city's notaries. They confessed that they were owned (*sub dominio et servitudine*) by one Giovanni Raibaldi, a merchant, who had purchased them from their enemies. They swore to pay Giovanni's brother Marino 161 golden doubloons within twenty days of reaching Tunis. Three Genoese, of good family, acted as guarantors for them.[83]

In the struggle between Christian and Muslim both sides took similar numbers of prisoners. But during the wars against the Turks in the 1520s the Italians and Spanish lost far more to the Ottomans than they took. Exchanges consequently became more difficult and the cost of paying ransoms very burdensome. In 1531 Genoese revenue officials, charged with drawing up a description of the resources of Andora on the Ponante coast, noted that the town had 500 chimneys and 2,500 souls, of whom 550 were men between the ages of fourteen and sixty-five capable of bearing arms, but that 130 men were missing, 'prisoners of the Moors or Turks' – which means that a staggering one man in five had been abducted and carried off.[84]

No sooner had corsair captains seized a Christian ship than they set about interrogating the crew to determine the possible size of the ransom or to find out what services the captives could render their new masters. Each of the captives, on the other hand, sought to persuade the corsairs of their infirmities and illnesses, bewailing the fact that they were better suited to a hospital bed than sale in chains in some distant market-place. Corsairs and Janissaries examined their clothes and hands, promising a quick release to those who seemed to be of some social standing and, until then, decent treatment. 'They invested considerable trouble in identifying the captain, scribe, pilot, caulker, carpenter and all who might be valued greater than just simple mariners.'[85] Then, upon reaching Algiers or another Barbary port, the prisoners were paraded in front of merchants, some of whom were Christian and some of whom had no scruple in denouncing a captive if they recognised which family he came from.

It was something of a rule, amongst those taken captive by the pirates, that they would not reveal their identities, nor would those around them do so; for it was through such knowledge that the masters regulated the ransom. They used spies to discover such information from newcomers but these were advised to say that they had no hope of a ransom, that their parents were too poor, that they had only lived from the fruit of the labour of their own hands and that they were indifferent when it came to living in one country or another in conditions that fate decreed.[86]

For those held in Algiers, Tunis, or the Levant it was almost impossible to know whether or not they would be ransomed. For one thing news travelled incredibly slowly, and it was entirely possible for hope to die completely before a captive heard that money had been forwarded for his release. Pere Bele, a sailor on a Catalan ship captured by a Saracen galley off Aguablava, was dragged off to Constantinople but, along with a dozen other prisoners, managed to escape and make his way back to Barcelona. His wife didn't even know that he'd been taken.[87]

When most families did hear about the capture of their nearest and dearest they acted promptly, designating an agent to manage the prisoner's estate and working on ways to collect and gather money for his or her release. Sometimes it was necessary to sell land or a house, a barn, or tools. Wives, mothers, and sisters frequently strained every muscle to gather in revenue, calling on past favours, accepting hardship, keeping creditors at bay. A few took to begging. In 1488 the council of the city of Jaen was issuing licenses for this very purpose. Others bought Moorish slaves in the hope that they could organise an exchange. A few shipowners and fishermen from Malaga even dared sail to North Africa, seizing captives with the sole aim of exchanging them for men of their own kind held prisoner there.[88]

Dealing with the corsairs on their home ground was an adventure all by itself. Some, be they simple sailors or men come purposely to free their immediate family, were content to negotiate a release and not make a profit; but others negotiated with financial gain in mind.

Records show that a good number of people elected to hazard their chances by crossing to Africa. Many of these were sailors or merchants familiar with the Barbary coast. The notaries of Marseilles oversaw a good number of contracts between the families or friends of a captive and an intermediary, whether Catalan or Provencal, willing to go to Africa. In the 1390s one family hired Thomas Colomier, a Catalan based at Marseilles but trading with Bône. He received a sum of money, representing the ransom, and undertook to find, purchase, and bring back the prisoner. Hedged in with terms and conditions, these contracts neverthe-less ran to an established form. It sometimes happened that a captive had died before the ransom could be paid, or that he had escaped or been sold on to another master; under which circumstances the intermediary returned empty-handed and was obliged to pay back the ransom. In May 1427 Bertrand Forbin equipped the *Sainte Marie* and on behalf of the families of Marseilles, taking their money in return, he set out to buy back Provencal prisoners. He returned two months later having established a rate for ransoms of eighty florins for an elderly man and 200 for a youth, valid in Bougie and other Barbary ports.[89]

The king of Aragon had frequent recourse to a certain Anselm Turmeda, a renegade who had carved quite a reputation for himself in this form of negotiation. He had been born in Majorca in 1350, converted to Islam when he was thirty-five – although exact details of this are somewhat vague to say the least – and took the name Abdallah. Five months later he married and was promoted to chief customs officer in Tunis. He had an excellent understanding of trade and was a gifted inter-preter, having served the Genoese when they besieged Mahdia in 1390. He acted as treasurer to King Abu'l Abbas and intendant to his succes-sor. He won renown as a scholar and even refused a pardon granted by Pope Benedict XIII, who, having been deposed by the Council of Constance, had fled to Aragon. Indeed, he went so far as to publish a trea-tise on Islamic theology, refuting Christianity. Nevertheless he was a fre-quent visitor to Aragon, negotiating the release or re-purchase of slaves, and the king duly issued him with certificates of safe conduct as he passed through with his 'wives, sons and daughters, servants and valets, all as many Christians as Muslims'.[90]

In Andalusia the key players in the trade were inevitably those Moors from Granada who had established themselves in North Africa. There were men such as Almandair and Mohammed Abdali, from Baza, and Ali Barrax, or ben Rasid, who arrived in Africa in 1471 and founded the city of Xauen. Although he was theoretically a vassal of the king of Fez he was effectively monarch of his own enclave. Such individuals maintained links with Spain, to which they sent their agents, many of whom were received as ambassadors and, indeed, were authorised to act as ambassa-dors, signing agreements and negotiating conditions for the release or exchange of captives. Abraham Zerchiel (Ezechiel) was Ali Barrax's prin-cipal agent. At one point he fell foul of the authorities and ended up in prison, from where he wrote a message to his master listing those Christian families from Velez Malaga and Puerto de Santa Maria who had offered money for the release of their relatives – twenty-nine names providing 740,000 *maravedis*.[91]

Andalusians in Tunis also maintained links with their native land and many of them also acted as mediators in the exchange or ransoming of prisoners. Often fluent in the languages of Christendom, they advanced money or purchased slaves themselves, and housed and fed them until their families managed to provide the necessary ransom. It was a trade like any other but could be quite a lucrative one; a deal might bring in a profit of more than a quarter of the original investment.[92]

Risks

Anyone writing from Algiers asking for assistance exposed himself to immense risk. Cervantes, who knew that his own ransom would weigh too heavily on the finances of his relatives, instead wrote to Martin de Cordoba, the governor of Oran, for assistance. But the letter was intercepted en route and the Moor who was carrying it was strung up on the spot. Cervantes himself was sentenced to 200 blows of a baton.

Generally it was common knowledge that if ransom money was slow in coming Turkish or Moorish masters would make the slave work harder or find them unacceptably demanding labour. Some were made to carry timber 'which was not the lightest of work'. Those sent over with ransom money were, however, themselves subject to the whims of misfortune; indeed, some paid with their lives. Of the Cervantes brothers, Miguel and Rodrigo, only the younger could be released by Brother Jorge de Olivares, as he was 'less important' and consequently less expensive. Miguel had to remain in Algiers until the ransom could be paid in full, for even though Rodrigo had been released his mother had only been able to gather 250 ducats of the 750 due; Juan Gil, in Algiers, had been able to supplement this with 300 more, mostly raised from charitable donations. So 200 were owing and Miguel acted as surety. He was eventually released after the money was collected in Spain, and on 24 October 1580 he found himself and eight fellow slaves on board a Spanish ship bound for Denia. Reaching Christian lands they 'jumped ashore and kissed the soil'. It was many, many years before he could repay his debts, calling on favours from many quarters. Fortunately he was left 1,000 ducats in the will of Diego de Bernui, governor of Burgos, but disaster struck when his widow challenged the bequest, won the case, and had the will annulled.[93]

Father Jerónimo Gracian (1545–1614), son of Diego Gracian de Alderete, the secretary of Charles V, and later, Philip II, had an interesting life. A pupil of Saint Teresa of Avila, he was disgraced upon her death in 1582 and expelled from the order in 1592. Condemned to wander alone, he was captured by corsairs on the Neapolitan coast two leagues from Gaeta. They seized his clothes and the manuscript of a work entitled *Armonia Mistica*, which he had hoped to get published in Rome. At Bizerte the corsairs tried to pass him off as an archbishop seized whilst on his way to Rome to meet the cardinals. Others swore that he had been responsible for executing renegades in Spain and Italy and he was sentenced to be burnt alive for his crimes. But the pasha intervened and saved his life. However, he preached, said mass, and attempted to convert the renegade who gave him Arabic lessons. For this he was arrested and placed in chains so heavy that he could barely move. His ransom was set at 1,300 *ecus*. Fifteen of twenty brothers were still alive and his family came to his rescue. They liberated a rich Jew from Tunis (a certain Simon Escanasi, captured whilst in Naples), gave him 600 *ecus* and despatched him to Tabarca, a Genoese post on the coast of Africa. The director of the Genoese company there advanced 700 *ecus* more, and Gracian was allowed to leave Tunis and make his way to Tabarca. There the Genoese held him until they received the money due to them.[94]

Not all merchants and bankers caught up in the trade escaped with their reputations intact. A merchant from Chios, Pedro de Crassi, received numerous instalments towards the ransom of Jeronimo de Pasamonte. But the merchant allowed the captive to rot, refusing to release him. Complaints were followed by a more dramatic form of persuasion – a relative of the prisoner brandished a huge knife under Crassi's nose as he was attending mass in Rhodes. Letters were sent off to the Venetian consul in Constantinople but he showed little interest. Finally, however, Pasamonte was released, but he was destitute and could not afford to pay for his passage home. The owner of a Greek ship took pity on him and his twenty-seven companions and allowed them to come on board after Pasamonte pledged to give the owner his wife's ring. Setting foot ashore at Otranto the unfortunate then had to borrow a further six

ducats in order to get to Naples, where he arrived 'famished and destitute'.[95] A tale, indeed, of misfortune, anguish, and ruin.

Charity

Numerous religious and charitable institutions pledged their assistance
in the resolving and payment of ransoms. They raised money and awareness, and called upon lords, bishops, and sovereigns for assistance, com-
passion, and solidarity.

Ever since the days of the Reconquista in the Iberian peninsula communal charters had been drawn up in towns and villages along the border
to press the authorities for the exchange of captives. This system continued to an extent even after the capture of Malaga and Granada. In Aragon
– especially in Barcelona and Valencia, but also as far afield as Saragossa
– select confraternities had a system for organising the collection of
donations and for making some of their own funds available. The confraternity of fishermen of Barcelona, and that for the rope-makers of
Valencia, had their members swear that 'if one of our brethren, for sins
and misfortune, is captured and has not the means to pay his ransom then
each of us, for the pity and love of God, must contribute two *sous*.'[96]

But it was the Church, above all, which became involved. Simple
parish priests from Marseilles were known to risk life and limb in efforts
to liberate parishioners captured by the corsairs. Bishops customarily
distributed alms to the poor, the starving, and the ill, but in the
Mediterranean world a large part of their charitable work was directed
towards the buying back of captives.

Throughout the Turkish wars the Popes were actively involved in
attempting to intervene on behalf of captives, donating money and
offering up prayers. Between 1566 and 1592 the Papacy sent out 6,000
letters (*litterae hertatoriae*) requesting donations for the release of
Hungarians, Austrians, Poles, Croats, and Transylvanians taken prisoner
by the Turks in the Balkans, and for the release of Spanish and Italian
prisoners captured on the high seas or taken from coastal villages.
Cypriots, taken from their native land after it fell to the Turks in 1571,
were also assisted. It was nevertheless hard to trace captives who were
sent to the galleys as oarsmen, or dragged off to distant lands and sold in

obscure provincial markets. Slaves employed in Cyprus or kept in the Balkans had a better chance of benefiting from such charitable work. They might also be bought back by merchants passing through these lands, or be freed as a result of requests made by the Venetian consul in Constantinople.

Occasionally exchanges of prisoners took place. Giacomo Malatesta, liberated in January 1573, was sent back home carrying a letter from Sultan Mehmet Pasha which proposed a large-scale exchange of captives. Two years later a party of prisoners held in Tunis and their commander, Gabriele Serbollini, were exchanged for Turkish prisoners. A French knight, a relative of the Grand Master of Naples, was exchanged for Amar Mustapha. More complicated was the case of two Cypriot noble-women who, in 1574, attempted to organise the release of their children held by the Turks. Viena Palol had four and Beatrice Flatre five sons in Turkish hands.

Papal letters urging succour for the captured often stressed the Christian duty of charity and the need to relieve the suffering of the cap-tives' families. They detailed the woes of the prisoners, their torment and humiliation, and also dwelt upon the dangers of a captive losing faith and even turning to Islam. This latter showed that nobody could ignore the fact that the number of renegades was growing.[97]

Throughout the countries directly threatened by Barbary raiding, men of the church, whether members of religious or military orders, col-lected money and set out to buy back or release captives. In the Iberian peninsula military orders founded during the Reconquista played an important role. The orders of Calatrava (founded in 1158), Alcantara (1166), Santiago (1170), and Montjoye (1174) had hospices built for captive fugitives and used donations and the profits from the sale of goods pro-duced on their own lands for the payment of ransoms.[98] In addition to these important institutions there were also a number of smaller soci-eties, often founded by soldiers, dedicated to the same purpose. These included the orders of the Holy Cross (founded in 1163 in Catalonia), Santa Maria de Merida (c.1200), the Holy Trinity (founded in Marseilles in 1198 by Jean de Matha), and Our Lady of Mercy (founded in Barcelona in 1218 by Pedro Nolasco).

Houses of Trinitarians and Mercedarians were scattered throughout the western world, with some fifty monasteries based as far apart as the Mediterranean, Saint Quentin, and Scotland.[99] Captives liberated by an order would often give themselves to it for a year, working as servants in the cloisters. They would roam the streets dressed in white robes, showing their chains and evoking their suffering. Through acts such as this, and through the preaching of the order's brethren, the general public were made aware of its valuable work.[100]

In an Italy menaced by Turkish fleets, the last two decades of the sixteenth century saw the flourishing of institutions dedicated to the release of captives. Charles V himself had established the *Real Casa Santa delle Redentione dell'Cattivi* in Naples in 1548. A number of the kingdom's key nobles took an active part in the organisation and missions were sent to Tunis to liberate (in order of preference) children, youths, women, men, elderly men, and men without family. In 1581, in Rome, Pope Gregory XIII made the Confraternity of Gonfalaon responsible for organising the buying back of slaves who came originally from Rome. A chest was placed at the door of the church of Santa Lucia and the commissioners began collecting information on the identity and whereabouts of such prisoners. Those who were eventually sent off to Tunis to track them down were given detailed instructions:

> Make it clear that you have come for the purchase of poor slaves but show to the Turks and Moors that you have little money. Pay careful attention towards the settling of taxes and duties; buy first those slaves who are named on your list, and pay the indicated sum, but be sure not to leave unfortunates in servitude when they could be released for just ten or fifteen sous more.

In 1583 the guardians of the Confraternity of Gonfalaon opened negotiations with a Turkish merchant called Haggi Mohammed who had proposed exchanging Christian prisoners for those Turks serving as slaves on the papal galleys.

Two years later two Capuchin monks obtained the release of seventy-one Roman, Neapolitan, Calabrian, and Genoese captives after lengthy discussions in Algiers. Paraded through Rome, the liberated slaves were solemnly blessed by the Pope. The list of those released was printed and nailed to the doors of churches. Meanwhile the two monks who remained in Algiers, working on the release of other unfortunates, caught the plague and died.

Cities outside of Rome had similar institutions which acted like the

Confraternity of Gonfalaon. Bologna had the *Opera de Santa Maria delle Neve*; Palermo had the *Opera della Redenzione*, founded in 1596 by the Marquis of Geraci; Venice had the *Ospitali e Luoghi Pii*, established by a decree of the Senate; Genoa had the *Magistrato del Riscatto*; and Ferrara had the *Opera Pia del Riscatto de'Schiavi*, based at the church of San Leonardo. Such organisations were commonplace in the Mediterranean world, but both Hamburg and Lübeck also had a *Sklavenkasse*, founded in 1614 and 1619 respectively.[101]

Chapter VI

War and Propaganda

That part of North Africa known as the Barbary Coast or Barbarie in contemporary literature was a place beheld in horror and fear. The corsairs themselves, whether Turks or natives of the northern coast, were so successful that not only did they raid at sea but also, increasingly, swept down on coastal villages in Spain and Italy. They sowed terror, ruin, and desolation among rich and poor alike. It wasn't inconvenient and sporadic brigandage – it was open war. Armed galleys, carrying armed men, on the warpath.

Reality: Fear

For many centuries Corsica, Sardinia, and the coast of Catalonia had been on the alert for Saracen pirates. Watchtowers perched on promontories kept ships under surveillance. Warnings would be sent, beacon fires lit, and messengers despatched.

Following the conquest of Granada the kings of Spain actively set about finding ways of preventing raids by corsairs based in Tlemcen or Fez. Muslims living in the kingdom were barred from living within a league of the coast. However, it proved impossible to transplant entire communities of coastal villages; these, it was decided, would instead pay a tribute which would be used to maintain coastguards. In addition Muslims were forbidden from moving between towns without official authorisation; nor were they allowed to fish in coastal waters unless employed under a Christian captain. Official *visitaciones*, or inspectors, were sent along the coasts, initially around Malaga but later along the entire Andalusian coast, to check that guards were in place and sufficiently organised. In support of these personnel the authorities also established a chain of fortified posts up and down the coast, each commanded by a military officer. These proved to be insufficient and, later, more such posts were established around Marbella, Vellez, Fuengirola and, just to make sure, even inland.[1]

Despite a brief lull in piratical activity, the arrival of the Barbarossas and the Turks soon dispelled hopes of progress. The Andalous – Muslims from the Iberian peninsula who had fled to Africa – were given new hope and began not only to raid but also to plan a possible reconquest of Granada. Arms and supplies were sent over and the revolt of 1526, although brutally suppressed, gave rise to all kinds of fears. Officials in Valencia complained that the city walls were too thin and too weak to withstand an attack by the corsairs. In 1529 the Archbishop of Saragossa issued a long memorandum on how the population of Spain might be defended from the Muslims and Turks. In the Balearics a civil guard, basing itself on the *Santa Hermandad* of Toledo, was established to protect the population from the ravages of these seaborne bandits, but with what success is not clear; a petition to the *Cortés* in 1560 declared that the peasants were too scared to venture within four or five leagues of the coast.[2]

In Italy, especially around Rome and in Sicily, princes and civic authorities were aware of the suffering brought about by corsair raids, and spent considerable sums attempting to prevent them. After all, it was no longer a question of scattering a few bandits; the corsairs could land hundreds, even thousands, of troops equipped with artillery as well as hand-weapons. To meet and defeat such an enemy the Italians would have to establish an entirely new system of defence. The Ottoman threat was everywhere.

In 1534 Pope Paul III decreed that the defences of the city of Rome needed to be overhauled. But the financial investment necessary for such a project was sadly lacking and the work was only imperfectly carried out. When real or imagined dangers raised their heads the labourers were kept busy; when the danger passed the repairs were halted. In 1565 Pope Pius V had two large towers erected near Anzio and, two years later, issued the Bull *De aedificandis turribus in littere maris*, which established fortified posts along the coast of the Papal States. Militia and cavalry – known as *battitori* – patrolled the region, forever vigilant.[3]

In the kingdom of Naples and in Sicily horsemen were stationed along the coast to raise the alarm if suspicious vessels were spotted. Viceroys, such as Pedro de Toledo in Naples, and Ferrante Gonzaga in Sicily, had a vast number of watchtowers built. Not all were welcomed by the populace; land was requisitioned, the garrisons of the towers had to be fed at local expense and, increasingly, the soldiers took up criminal activities (especially smuggling) to supplement their meagre wages. Some even made out that they controlled fishing rights and levied dues on boats and catches. The royal council in Naples was so surprised when informed of the abuse that, in 1566, it banned the guards from owning boats or from becoming involved, at any level, in trade or enterprise.[4]

It isn't clear whether such measures were effective; but it can be seen that concern about the corsairs led to a dramatic overhaul of Italian defences and, indeed, had a significant impact on the Italian way of life.

Reality: Danger at Sea

Seamen, threatened as they were with countless dangers on a daily basis, were inclined to be religious and superstitious. Italian ships bore the name of their owner, protector, or some mythological figure representing bravery: *Leone*, *Falcone*, *Guadabene*, or *Allegrancia*, for example. From the thirteenth century onwards more and more ships took the name of a saint. Thus we have *Giorgio*, *Benedetto*, *Giuliano*, and even *Nazario*. A *Santa Maria* appeared in 1270, and from then on the Virgin's name was used again and again. This is perhaps a sign that fear was on the increase; fear, not of shipwreck, which was a constant, unchanging problem, but of a potentially fatal encounter with a corsair. In the 1450s some Genoese ships were named after two or three saints with the Virgin's name thrown in for good measure.[5] In 1449, at Chios, a shipowner from Savona chartered a huge ship baptised *Santa Maria*, *San Giuliano*, *Sant'Agostino*, *Sant'Antonio*.[6] A little later vessels armed by Florentine merchants, men from a city wallowing in humanism and fixated with antiquity, were still being named after holy persons, sites of pilgrimages, or simple churches: *Santa Julia di Livorno*, *Santa Maria delle Grazie di Monte Nero di Livorno*,

Santa Maria del Ponte Nuovo di Pisa, and *San Piero di Grado di Pisa*. If anyone catalogued such names they might conclude that they bear testament 'to the spiritual life of Italy, Provence and Spain'.[7]

Princes and civic authorities were also more watchful. From the thirteenth century on more and more regulations were issued designed to promote the security of vessels setting out across the sea. In many of the maritime states, from Barcelona to Genoa, from Pisa to Venice, such rules were among the first ever issued on behalf of civic authorities. Many of them went into considerable detail, from specifying how many men should be employed to crew a vessel, to how many weapons should be carried on board a specific kind of ship.[8] In Genoa the *Officium Maris*, an official initially entrusted with regulating conflict and noting down the consequence of delays at sea, shipwreck, loss of goods and so on, began to take on a wider role. His agents took to inspecting boats before departure (a process known as the *cerca*) and levying hefty taxes for the equipping of armed escort vessels. They made it clear that vessels should sail together, two or three at a time, a system known as the *conserva*, in order to come to each other's assistance. In addition to the usual ship's complement, many were to carry a dozen crossbowmen for fear of pirates 'who come and go across the seas, causing grievous harm'. The agents also attempted to control the timing of voyages, ordering vessels to remain in port during particular crises or asking them to await the arrival of other vessels so that they might venture out together.[9] Such agents and officials were subsequently imitated by other states across the Mediterranean world.

The nascent strictures they imposed gradually evolved until, in Venice and Florence at least, they resulted in a systematic approach to the protection of ships – the use of merchant convoys. Venice, that great builder of galleys, equipped, armed, and crewed its ships according to regulations, and its vessels usually sailed in a convoy (*mude*) which operated according to complex rules that seemed to continually adjust themselves to suit political circumstances.[10]

Captains operating within a convoy adhered to instructions issued on the day of departure and were made aware of which ports they should use. Instructions were also given regarding which signals the ships should use whilst on convoy. An inventory of a Genoese vessel, dating from the fifteenth century, noted that it carried fifteen beacons, a large lamp, seven lanterns, and three torches for use in making signals.[11]

In addition to looking after their ships, Italian states also paid more attention to punishing those in breach of the law. The *Officium Robarie* of Genoa routinely compensated merchants, whether Christian or not, who had suffered loss at the hands of *Genoese* pirates. Victims had to place a confidential letter denouncing the guilty in a strongbox placed in the communal palace. Captured pirates were tortured and their goods, and those of their families, associates, and accomplices, were seized or destroyed.[12] The seignory of Venice kept two records, the *Libero delle prede* (Book of Goods Seized) and the *Libero dei pirati* (Book of Pirates), in which the value of goods lost and the possible identity of the thieves were recorded. Any pirate taken prisoner at sea was instantly put to death and his ship burnt or sold. Any profit from the sale was divided and given to merchants who had been his victims, and to the state so that it could build more galleys to guard the seaways. In 1360 a list was drawn up at Coron and despatched to Venice containing the names and origins of those pirates seized and executed. It included men from Zara, Marseilles, Trapani, Valencia, Barcelona, Majorca, and Lisbon.[13]

Another development brought about by the increase of dangers at sea was maritime insurance. Many people wished to insure themselves against the usual hazards of a sea voyage – storm and shipwreck – as well as against pirates and corsairs. It is an interesting fact that maritime insurance developed well before it became customary to seek similar financial security against the risk of fire, theft, and natural disasters on land. In the 1450s Genoa, Barcelona, and Valencia had scores of insurance agents, positioned along the quays, well versed in assessing risks and devising premiums. These premiums were usually higher in the summer, when there was a greater chance of running into corsairs, than in the winter, when storms were the chief hazard.[14]

It can truly be said that the advent of the corsairs had an impact on the science of seamanship. The organisation and conduct of a convoy was no simple matter, and the state was obliged to become involved. Seaborne trade consequently lost much of the independence it had previously enjoyed, and seamen and merchants found their activities increasingly governed by official intervention and regulation. Some, of course, benefited nevertheless, and many made their fortunes – especially the insurance brokers.

Propaganda and Legend

As early as the tenth century the Christians saw themselves as players in an all-out war against the pirates of North Africa. Italian soldiers and sailors were at the forefront of this holy war. Troubadours sang the praises of such heroes whilst lamenting the devastation caused by Barbary pirates – the burning of towns and the abduction of women and children.

History and legend began to blend. The infidels would attack, the sky would be shrouded in smoke, and the streets would run with blood. But then the manhood of Genoa would ride in beneath their banner of the Virgin Mary, sweep the infidels from the shore, and, pursuing them across the sea, would force them to hand back their captives. Such richly-embroidered episodes inspired countless oral traditions and legends; they also raised awareness of North Africa as a base for pirates.

Later other traditions supplemented the stories of Christian and Muslim conflict. Caffaro, a distinguished Genoan and one-time ambassador to the Lateran Council (1123) and to Emperor Frederick I (1154), wrote a detailed study of the siege of Antioch. In 1098 the Franks had besieged this city during the First Crusade. Cafarro focuses on the Genoese contribution – soldiers, engineers, and carpenters – to both this siege and that of Jerusalem. It's a glorious tale of derring-do, a veritable anthem of holy war which calls to mind some of the earlier legends. His history of the expeditions into the Holy land between 1098 and 1109 is of the same genre and his *De capitone Almerie et Tortuose*, telling of the Christian conquest of Almeria and Tortosa, revels in the triumph of the Christians.[15]

In Iberia, where knights charged Muslims with lances and towns were liberated by assault, works such as the *Roman Fronterizo* gained considerable popularity.[16] Even though it was published under Juan II (1406–54), it drew on earlier texts such as the Song of Roland. These tales not only idealised chivalry but also served to inspire young men to seek adventure by transforming Spain from a land lost to a land liberated and complete.[17]

War in Africa and against the Ottomans produced its own body of literature. Some of these works were rather ordinary but others worked their way into the collective consciousness. Fernando de Herrera (1534–87) was a humanist scholar of repute whose sonnets and poems dwelt on love, gallantry, and the divine. But he was also the author of the *Cancion per la Victoria di Lepanto* and the *Cancion a don Juan de Austria*. He wrote the *Cancion per la perdida del Rey don Sebastian* too, an elegy in which he mourns the woes of Christendom following King Sebastian of Portugal's death at Kar el-Kebir.[18]

The Barbarossa brothers gave rise to legends all of their own. Kheir ed-Din was often shown sporting his red beard, in part so that he could be differentiated from his elder brother. In 1520, just four years after the capture of Algiers, an inscription appeared in a mosque claiming that he was the son of the Turkish emir Abou Youssef Yacoub. This was quickly picked up by Christian and Muslim authors alike. One of the greatest of the Arabic chronicles, the *Gazaouet*, was rediscovered in Algiers by Ventre de Paradis in 1788; although it was the Arab translation of a Turkish text it seemed to be by Siman Chaouch. It sang the praises of Kheir ed-Din and diplomatically neglected to tell of his setbacks or defeats. For example, nothing was said about the assassination of Selim Eutemi, king of Algiers, in 1516. Nor did it hesitate to assign the Barbarossas illustrious parentage, no doubt taking advantage of the obscurity of their true origins. Jacob, their father, was transformed overnight from being a Christian convert to Islam and a simple labourer into a Muslim admiral.[19] The Turks deliberately glossed over the Barbarossas' Christian origins and treated them as their own, even after death. A rumour persisted that Kheir ed-Din refused to be buried: 'Five or six times he emerged from his tomb, to general astonishment. Finally a Greek magician declared that the only way to keep him in his tomb was to bury a black dog with him; this was done and the body never appeared again.'[20]

Seid Mouradi, a sailor and companion to Dragut, was the author of a number of works of poetry. When he evoked Kheir ed-Din he didn't hesitate to declare that the corsair was a man without fear and without reproach.[21]

Christendom both feared and respected its redoubtable enemy. In France, at least, such admiration went hand-in-hand with sympathy for a useful ally. When the narration of even a simple corsair's exploits spread like wildfire and grew with their retelling in every Mediterranean port, it is hardly surprising that the Barbarossas attained legendary status. One of the more curious tales is told by Brantôme. This recorded that the Barbarossas were not Turks at all but were adventurers converted to Islam; indeed, the brothers were noblemen from Authon and Montsoreau in France who had enlisted to take part in a Venetian expedition against the Turks. They deserted and became pirates, and, converting to Islam, pretended to be from Lesbos and called themselves Aroudj and Kheir ed-Din. Brantôme rounds off his account with the incredible statement that 'if they were French they rendered honour to the French name; if they weren't they have leant honour to it'. An interesting historical footnote to this tale is the fact that when, in 1543, Kheir ed-Din was in France, baron d'Authon, believing himself to be the corsair's nephew, asked him why he did not reveal his true origins as a Frenchman.[22] Such tales got repeated down the years, and in 1786 the *Vie des plus célèbres marins* revived the claim that Barbarossa was originally French. Of course, making him out to be French made being allied with the king of the corsairs somewhat more palatable.

In Italy the legend was somewhat different, but essentially revolved around Barbarossa being the terror of the sea and a brave warrior. On 28 January 1530 Rabelais, then in Rome, sent Geoffroy d'Estissac, Bishop of Maillezais, a present: 'I send you his portrait, drawn from life.' It was the work of Agostino Musi and the engraving was later published in Basle in 1577.[23]

Giovanni Diongi Galena was the son of a simple fisherman from Squillice in Calabria. In 1536 he was captured by Kheir ed-Din and sold in the markets of Constantinople; he took the name of Euldj'Ali, married the daughter of his owner, and set out on career of piracy. He raided Sardinia in 1554, oversaw the disembarkation of the Turks at Villefranche in 1560, became pasha of Algiers in 1568, and died in 1587 in obscure circumstances. Such a death inevitably led to many stories. Was he poisoned by a Christian slave? Did he have his throat cut by his barber? Or did he succumb whilst in the embrace of a ravishingly beautiful Greek slave? We shall never know; what is more certain is his audacity. In 1569 Charles V offered him the title Marquis of Calabria if only he would convert back to Christianity; he refused but, in 1572, asked to be made prince of Calabria. In the popular imagination it was pretended that he secretly never renounced his true faith, being a Muslim on the surface only through necessity. After all, hadn't he been just and merciful to captured priests? Hadn't he always maintained a longing to return to Italy? He certainly had a liking for Italian women. In 1560 he was very desirous to meet the duchess of Savoy, wife of the captured duke. Fearing for her safety the duke and his suite had Maria de Gondi, one of her ladies in waiting, dress up in the duchess' clothes.

Euldj'Ali certainly had an impact on contemporary imagination, which attributed to him a number of exploits, some of which were invented, while others should really have been attributed to other corsair captains. During one expedition off Calabria in 1562 he is rumoured to have anchored off his native village and called out to the villagers promising to spare them if they would let him see his mother:

> He offered her great treasure, superb clothes, and told her that it was not fitting for the mother of a Turkish Pasha to live in such miserable condition. She, an old woman of much courage, kicked the gifts away and told him that a faith in Christ our Lord was worth more than even the richest of gifts . . . and that whilst he was an infidel she would not be his mother.[24]

Whilst such a tale might be true we do know for a fact that in 1600 Scipione Cigala, a renegade corsair from Messina, actually applied to the Viceroy of Sicily for permission to see his mother. It therefore seems that the legend of Euldj'Ali has become mixed up with extraordinary fact.

Returning briefly to France, it should be made clear that anyone who aided the Spanish or the Pope was suspected of supporting the enemy. There was a real desire to fight the king of Spain, something looked upon as a crusade; there was no question of delivering Jerusalem, rather it was a case of helping the Turks against Spanish power. But not everyone was convinced that such a course of action was correct, and a group of individuals sought to oppose the king's wishes in this respect. Perhaps they were loyal to their Catholic faith or perhaps they were goaded by tales of Turkish atrocities or the Sultan's scarcely secret plan to conquer Rome. However, such people were persecuted and sent into exile, where they gathered around them other devout Catholics. These formed societies such as that which went to the aid of the Knights of Malta in 1565.[25] The following year the Confraternity of the Holy Spirit called for those prepared to follow the Pope to gather in Burgundy. A few, and not only monks, were present at Lepanto, fighting side-by-side with the Spanish and against the express wishes of the king of France.[26] Many of the French at Lepanto had fled Languedoc to escape the Wars of Religion, and enlisted aboard Spanish ships anchored in Alicante. In 1572 2,000 Frenchmen were serving in the Venetian armed forces, all of them fugitives and exiles, and none of them operating with the accord of his majesty.[27]

On the other hand there were those who strove to justify the actions of the king of France, making him out to be a man devoted to peace, as were his loyal followers. One such follower was Le Paulin, Baron of La Garde, commander of the French fleet which accompanied Kheir ed-Din from Toulon to Calabria. It was Guillaume du Bellay, the king's lieutenant in Piedmont, who first suggested that Le Paulin should take the place of the deceased Ricon as the king's ambassador 'as he knows your majesty's wishes'. Du Bellay had been taken prisoner with King Francis at the battle of Pavia and had served his majesty loyally following his release. He had acted as ambassador to the Protestant princes of Germany but showed most zeal in singing the praises of the Turks' conduct in Toulon. Doubtless he exaggerated the size of their forces there to impress his readers and, perhaps, to bring them over to the king's point of view. That he was not adverse to manipulating figures, or creating false ones, is quite apparent; he also 'habitually changed dates to make one believe that one thing occurred as a consequence of the other'.

Pierre de Bourdeilles, Lord of Brantôme (1537–1614), was a faithful servant of kings Henri II, Charles IX, and Henri III, and was very careful to promote other royal cronies. His *Vie des homes illustres et des grands capitaines* devotes four pages to singing the praises of Le Paulin, 'a man of spirit, valour, vigorous in manner and appearance for he was handsome and tall'. This was the man who, on behalf of the king, negotiated with the Sultan 'and presented to him several large warships to make war at sea and against the coasts of the Emperor'. In so doing he had to resolutely overcome the intrigues of the pasha, the resistance of the Venetians, and the indecision of the Sultan: 'He came, he went, he asked, he bribed, and did so well as to win over the Captain of Janissaries that he said unto the Sultan whatever Paulin wished and made him agreeable to his venture; so it was that Barbarossa was given the fleet which none in Provence or Nice had seen the like of.'[28] The Ottomans set out across the sea 'and none could be found who might complain of their conduct; they showed every courtesy, allowing free passage to any ship they encountered and paying for everything they took – a thing most unheard of. This was due to the presence of Captain Paulin who saw to it that Turk and Christian behaved with modesty.'[29]

Le Paulin, who died when he was eighty, was still much praised in his old age 'for his handsome appearance and good grace; he was much admired for his accounts of times past, of his voyages and his combats.

His name was renowned from France, Spain, Italy to Barbary, Constantinople and the Levant'.[30] He was certainly an energetic ambassador, but we are more in the dark when it comes to his actual battles. Were there any? We know that the brave 'Captain' had a fleet accompany Barbarossa and he followed in their wake, anchoring wherever they wanted to so that they could rob and kill or carry off captives. Did he and his men lend a hand in this form of warfare? Probably not. At Policastro the Turks captured an Italian nobleman who offered the French admiral a present. But Barbarossa had the man enslaved and, says Jean Morand, 'my illustrious master [Le Paulin] was a wise man and acted as though he never heard of this prisoner'. He sailed across the Mediterranean after his mission had been completed without encountering any resistance. He was present throughout the Turkish occupation of Toulon, giving in to their caprice and demands and resolving arguments and recriminations, but he managed to retain only a superficial memory of those days: 'None behave better nor maintained such order as they did.'[31]

Le Paulin's exploits were minor and sordid but his propagandists turned such seedy episodes into great feats of arms. Such methods elevated men who would otherwise have long been forgotten. Leone Strozzi, a Knight of Malta, was so taken with Le Paulin that he thought 'all the ports, coasts, and seas of the Levant resonate with his name; sailors, pilots, patrons, slaves, and soldiers know him as none other than the greatest captain of his time.'[32]

After Lepanto the Franco-Turkish alliance continued but was rendered irrelevant. The time when a Turkish fleet could anchor in Toulon, or when Le Paulin could flatter the Sultan, were long gone. Barbary Corsairs would just as happily raid the French coast as the Spanish or Italian; Marseilles suffered at their hands and French citizens filled the slave quarters of Tunis and Algiers. Nevertheless, the French continued to respect the Turks; it was good politics. It was the troops of Charles of Lorraine and Jan Sobieski of Poland, not those of Louis XIV, which delivered Vienna from the Turks in 1683.

In addition French propaganda kept trying to justify the kingdom's alliance with the Ottomans, seeking to convince or seduce doubters and the public at large. Turkomania, a love of all things Turkish, was born during the reign of Francis I and significantly influenced French cultural life.

The French differed from the Spanish and Italians by not seeing the Barbary corsairs as cruel and bloody robbers. The king's circle and his ambassadors even went as far as to accuse those who had escaped from captivity of exaggerating their sufferings and presenting their captors in the worst possible light. They claimed that the clerics charged with buying back such prisoners made the same mistake or deliberately made the most of their hardships in order to accumulate more money and enrich their orders.

Paris published very little by way of narratives by escaped slaves or Spanish soldiers fighting the corsairs. Durand de Villegagnon's *Discours de la guerre de Malte* was published in Lyon, as was Thomas de Carrelieres' *L'Histoire de l'enterprise de Tripoli* of 1561. Lepanto brought about a brief flurry of interest and four works were published in 1573: *La Conquete de Tunes*, *La Nouvelle Conquete des villes de Tunis*, the *Chronique des plus notables guerres advenues entre les Turcs et les princes chretiens*, and *La Prise de Bizerte*. Rather than publish accounts like those of Cervantes or Gracian, dealing with the conditions of slaves in the Barbary ports, accounts by royal agents were preferred. These were exactly what one might expect.

After all, hadn't Rabelais said that a slave in Algiers was happier than a student at Montaigu college? Was it a witticism or an irresponsible provocation? The Chevalier d'Arvieux visited Palestine when he was just eighteen and later served as French consul at Aleppo between 1679 and 1686. He gave Molière the idea of including a Turkish theme in the *Bourgeois gentilhomme*. His memoirs, published after his death, did much to introduce Arabic themes and Orientalism into western culture. There one might find the description of an Arab as being tall and majestic, draped in fine cloth; he would be brave, generous, and disinterested, and whilst he might occasionally take from a caravan 'he would do so with such nobility'. Arvieux went so far as to suggest that the fate of slaves was not as dark as had previously been suggested: 'One imagines that the Christian slaves unfortunate enough to be taken to Barbary were tortured in a most cruel and inhuman way. There are people who excite one's charity by repeating these pious lies.' He insisted that the Turks dealt with their slaves much as they would with any other merchandise and that they would lose money if they mistreated their captives, made them ill, or killed them. In any case, many of them got what they deserved: 'They were robbers of the first degree; if they found houses unlocked they entered and made off with everything. They broke into shops and emptied them in a moment.'[33]

Laugier de Tracy spent many years as a resident of the Barbary states, not as a captive, chained and incarcerated, but as a public figure on royal duty. He too criticised the narratives of escaped slaves and those who sought to criticise their masters, often in an acerbic tone: 'The slaves of Algiers are not forced to do the things that they pretend they are made to do; they have their reasons for saying these things but, in their quarters, they want for nothing. They are given three loaves a day, a sheet and a blanket.' Christian slaves aboard Algerine pirate ships 'serve as officers or as simple sailors'. True, those belonging to the Algerian state were branded on the sole of one of their feet but 'such an order is not universally carried out'. 'Some slaves', attested Tracy, 'have good masters and are well fed and clothed. Some have as much influence over a family as their master and are treated as children of the house'. He suggested that slaves in Algiers were more respected than free Christians living in the city and that 'some live so well off the fruits of their labours or loves that they purchase the right to remain as slaves for a period or even seek to be so for the rest of their lives.'[34]

Not all such works were as outrageous. Interest in the Sultans of Turkey and the admirals and captains of Barbary gave rise to works of a higher standard. Accounts by ambassadors and explorers brought 'exotic scents of the east' back to the court of Louis XIV.[35] Jean Baptiste Tavernier was an indefatigable traveller who made his way through Hungary, Poland, Turkey and the Middle East and, in 1675, wrote the *Relation du sérail du Grand Seigneur* about the Sultan's harem. Only then, in the years which followed, did he publish a complete account of his travels.

There were some discordant notes from some authors who spoke plainly and were not afraid to tell the simple truth; some suggested that the corsairs were not men of honour worthy of praise. Voltaire, for one, thought them 'shameless, carrying off our vessels from the Mediterranean', and that their armies were 'composed of the scum of nations – Mauritanians, Nubians, Arabs, Turks – infesting the seas and hovering, like vultures, for the appearance of their prey'. He knew that 'if our friends or relatives become slaves then we must need beg of these barbarians to accept our money and send them back'. Cunegonde, a young princess captured by corsairs and dragged from Algiers to Tunis, Tripoli, Alexandria, and Smyrna before finishing up in the harem in Constantinople, certainly didn't enjoy her tribulations. Voltaire certainly didn't dwell on the splendour of the palace she found herself in, nor on the generosity of the Sultan.[36] But Voltaire was, it's true, a rebel.

The Romance of the Pirate

There were certain universal themes common to all weavers of legends and tales of stirring adventure: fascination with the sea, with its secrets and dangers, and with exotic distant shores. Add to this a taste for adventure and brave and honourable men (pirates, rebels, and warriors) and you have a powerful mix. This was just as true during the age of the Barbarossas. In fact, many of these storytellers were drawing on well established clichés and weren't contributing anything new. There was the captive woman who fell in love with the man who captured her; there was the valiant pirate who fought against the greedy merchants (frequently fat, old, and reprehensible); there were the kings of Tunis and Algiers who took pity on lovelorn slaves and sent them back to their native lands; and so on.

Boccaccio wrote his *Decameron* more than 100 years before the advent of the Barbarossas. In it Ricciardo di Chiuzica, an old man, marries Bartolomea, a young and attractive woman, but she is captured at sea. Paganino, a pirate, treats her so well that she refuses to leave his side. Alatielle, daughter of the Sultan of Babylonia, is engaged to the king of Algarve and heads off to Alexandria to take ship. But she is captured by brigands. In the four years which follow she takes eight chiefs as lovers. Returning to her father, she convinces him that she has retained her virtue because all the men were men of honour; so he again has her engaged to be married. Another tale features Martruccio and Constanza on Lipari; they are in love and wish to be married but they are too poor. So he becomes a pirate and amasses vast wealth before being captured by the Saracens and taken to Tunis. Hearing this, Constanza wants to put an end to her life so she throws herself into a boat and abandons her fate to the mercy of the wind and the waves. Amazingly, despite dangers along the way, she eventually finds herself floating off Tunis and is taken in by a rich and generous lady. The two lovers meet again and the king of Tunis, unwilling to oppose such good fortune, liberates them and returns them to Lipari. Finally there is the story of Saladin; he disguises himself as a Cypriot merchant and is received warmly by Torello di Stria in Pavia. Shortly afterwards Torello sets off on the crusades and asks his wife not to marry. Captured in the east, Torello is recognised by Saladin, who arranges for a magician to transport him back to Pavia overnight. He arrives back just in time to prevent his wife remarrying in the church of San Pietro in Ciel d'Oro.

The *Decameron* was all the rage for nearly a century and gave rise to numerous imitations, including the *Cent Nouvelles* of 1458 and Philippe de Vigneulles' *Cent Nouvelles* of 1505–15. Nicolas de Troyes finished his *Grand Paragon des Cent Nouvelles* in 1536; there were in fact 180 tales, but 57 were copied from Boccaccio.

Other tales which found popular favour revolved about men who, having been taken prisoner by corsairs, fell in love with beautiful, mysterious Moorish women; these would help the captive to escape and accompany him back to his native land. Such tales weren't necessarily pure invention. For example, Pedro de Almanc, taken prisoner in 1486 whilst campaigning against Granada, was sold into slavery at Fez. He was kept there for three years but eventually fell in love with the daughter of his owner; they met secretly at the port and took ship to Castile, where they married. Their story, richly embroidered, was a great success. More followed. Captives wooed daughters of Moors, corsairs, and even pashas. The prisoner would tell her tales of his native land and sing its charms, and then, without too much trouble, convince her to accompany him as he escaped. After clandestine planning the couple would flee by night and succeed in escaping.[37]

More fanciful tales involved magicians, sorcerers' castles, elixirs, trips to the moon or, just as exotic, to the West or East Indies. *Orlando Amoroso* was begun by Matteo Mario Boiardo, a protégé of the Duke of Ferrara, in 1476 but was interrupted by the French invasion of Italy. Its style is very gallant and it draws heavily on stories of the Round Table. The story, in which Roland and Renaud de Montauban are rivals in love for the beautiful Angelique, takes place against the backdrop of a holy war between Christians and Muslims. This Orlando theme was taken up again by Ariosto who wrote his *Orlando Furioso* between 1516 and 1532. In this Bradamante, Montauban's sister, falls for Roger, a prisoner of the Christians and commander of the Moorish king's armies. She releases him, converts him and, the day after his baptism, marries him.

Even Cervantes, whose experience at the hands of the corsairs was brutal, was not above employing such storylines and plots; many of his heroes, however, were brave men captured by corsairs. His *Vie d'Algiers*, published in Madrid in 1583, heaps blame and anger on his own native land for failing to do anything about the terrible fate awaiting its loyal subjects, prisoners of the Barbary states. Later, however, he adjusted his tone, perhaps by popular demand or perhaps in search of literary success. In the tale of the captive, found in Don Quixote, he ably pens a story as gallant as any of the populist storytellers. The captive, a Spanish gentleman, spies a lady at the window of a Moorish merchant; she throws down a packet containing ten gold pieces. The following day she throws forty, accompanied by a note written in Arabic which a renegade from Murcia helpfully translates: 'When I was a child my father had a slave who taught me the language and faith of the Christians and told me of the glories of the Virgin Mary; she told me I must travel to the Christian lands in order to see her.' There follow secret meetings, long conversations, escape, and the despair of a father.

Ariosto's heroine, Bradamante, reappeared in France as part of a tragicomedy written by Robert Garnier, an advocate and member of the Parisian *parlement*. She was back in 1637 in other works, which testified to the enduring power of the exotic and fascination with sultans and distant lands. Jean Mouret's *Illustrious Corsair* is another example, as are tales spun around the life of Polexandre, king of the Canaries. But for the French at least even the Great Turk was someone exotic and neither particularly cruel nor dangerous. It followed logically that his viziers, admirals, and corsairs fell into the same category. Whilst Venice might celebrate to the music of *Judith Triumphant* (Vivaldi, 1717), which gloried in the victory of the Christian faith over the infidel, Louis XIV's court was entertained by Turkish themes. Jean-Philippe Rameau produced the *Indes galantes*, in which Turkish morality was praised. In this, Sultan Oman holds Emilie prisoner when her fiancé, Valere, is shipwrecked on the Turkish coast and also falls into his hands. He gallantly liberates them and provides one of his squadrons for the happy couple to be married on.

It might be said that a great many of these fables lack any of the qualities of great literature, and are devoid of talent or invention. But they hold in common a theme of a Sultan or a corsair, or both together, who acted honourably. Women did not suffer at their hands and came through the experience with their honour intact. Molière's work *L'Avare* of 1688 tells the story of Marianne who is captured by corsairs and only returns after ten years; but she returns with her reputation intact and is allowed to marry Harpagon without anyone raising an eyebrow. A little adventure at sea didn't seem to have done her any harm.

One work which was a little different was Jean-François Regnard's *La Provencale*, published in 1731. This was perhaps because the author had himself been captured by corsairs in 1678 and liberated in 1681. His novel tells the story of a beautiful girl who is making her way to Genoa on board an English ship. The voyage is dangerous – 'nowhere else in the world is life so at risk as on the sea' – but becomes even more so when the ship is boarded by corsairs. His description of the attack does not spare us from the horror or the cruelty. The girl is then taken before the king of Algiers, Baba Hassan, before being sold to Achmet Talim. But the ending is happy and, after numerous gallant adventures, finishes well.

And, when all is said and done, the public accepted these works – suffused as they were with their authors' admiration for the Barbary sea-rovers – rather well. Indeed, the public seemed to be fascinated by such generous, gallant enemies.[38]

Of course, positive comments on the Turks and their system of government had a deeper purpose – they allowed an author to criticise his own land's government, manners, or religion under the guise of writing a novel. Such tactics produced some quite revolutionary works which, however, restricted themselves to abusing the vices of western society when compared to those of the east. Giovanni Paolo Marana's *Esploratore turco e le di lui relazioni secreti alla Porta Ottomana* was published in 1684 and was so popular that more than thirty editions were printed. In a sense it was a forerunner of Montesquieu's more famous *Persian Letters* of 1721. He, of course, ventured into the imperial palace and harem but did not devote much space to such facile clichés; nor was he unhesitatingly flattering. He described the way women were imprisoned in 'terrible places' and how they might be executed if they were found straying outside the apartments set aside for them. But his French imitators wove quite another tale, often contradicting him and providing for the French a far more positive picture of Ottoman rule.

We might close by considering Germain de Saint-Foix's *Lettres d'un Turque à Paris* of 1730. Here a Christian slave named Hussem marries Rosalinde, a vizier's favourite. They set off to live in Paris and Rosalinde writes letters to her sister Fatima in Constantinople. She describes French life, comparing French culture with that of the Turks; the Christian faith suffers a scathing attack, whilst Muslims are painted as being the only true and faithful believers. A sequel published in 1732 describes the life of Nedim Coggia, a secretary to Mehemet Effendi, the

Porte's ambassador to the court of France. His letters would doubtless kill the modern reader with boredom but they are of interest in as much as Nedim is allowed to paint a glowing picture of life in the east and in Constantinople. He describes splendid palaces, the harems, and such beauties as the galley of Captain Bassa: 'The satin sails were purple in colour; rich odours of perfume pervaded the air. Ten or twelve young slaves were sat on the deck dressed in natural nudity.'[39] Such works were written to edify and convince but what they actually did was to project an image of the marvellous east, more virtuous than the corrupt west. In doing so they were far more than mere entertainment or fantastic tales.

Conclusion

In the last hundred years or so studies of the corsairs have moved on from merely echoing with the glorious exploits of the Barbarossa brothers or their gallant captains. Some authors have attempted to analyse the corsairs themselves, presenting them not as simple adventurers but rather as victims of circumstances struggling against a political or social order. But few have managed to connect the Barbarossas with the fact that they were officers of the Ottoman sultan, dedicated to his will, acting at his behest and with his support. Their lives were replete with exploits worth telling, adventures on the high seas and all, but it should also be stressed that they were political men, admirals, governors of provinces, and capable of holding their own through the intrigues of court and palace.

Sometimes attempts have been made to study pirates and corsairs together as a group whether they be Barbary or Buccaneer. But this is rather at odds with the historian's methods as he attempts to analyse context, geography, and fluctuating systems. The corsair sailing out of Algiers has almost nothing in common with the dashing villain of some adventure film. The Mediterranean was not the Caribbean, and raiding in one region was very different from the tactics employed in the other. The Barbary corsairs, for instance, would not, with just one ship, attempt to take on and overpower a vessel, boarding it or surprising it at night; rather they would venture forth in a swarm, making liberal use of their artillery. Few merchantmen could resist. In addition the corsairs mounted full-blown assaults on the coasts and cities of Italy and Catalonia; they had no qualms about laying siege to a place and bombarding it into submission.

Buccaneers did not operate like this. They used stealth and relied on clandestine methods. Barbary corsairs, on the other hand, operated overtly, for all to see. Buccaneers would sneak off with a couple of boats loaded with booty, sheltering at their base camp or in a secret cove. The Barbary corsairs operated out of great ports such as Tunis, Algiers, Constantinople, or Tripoli. They sold their booty as legitimately acquired gains in some of the Mediterranean's most flourishing markets. The ships of the corsairs, moreover, were supported and operated almost like state run enterprises; booty was carefully noted on detailed inventories and the pasha made sure he received his share.

Really the Barbary corsair was a man who might have come to Algiers from any part of the Mediterranean region and who had earned his place through adventure. Moors were almost strangely absent from their ranks, while tracing the input of Turks hailing from Anatolia is extremely difficult. Certainly Christian accounts hardly mention them or, at most, merely cite their names. Those termed renegades, however, received far more attention. Such Christian converts to Islam were notorious and were either hostile to the king of Spain and the Pope, and all they stood for, or were determined to appear so to their new protectors. Their history is certainly fascinating and in many cases their origins are easier to determine.

Diego de Haedo was in agreement with royal spies when he declared that of those galleys harboured in Algiers the majority were captained by renegades and that these men outnumbered Turks or Moors. Contemporaries were certainly keen to find out why such men ended up in Africa as Muslims. Had they come of their own free will? In the almost complete absence of statistics we can only presume that a good number of renegades were captured whilst still young and renounced the faith of their fathers at some point thereafter. Perhaps they did this to avoid an unpleasant captivity or to advance their careers. Despite the temptation to draw parallels, this isn't the same as someone who betrays his cause in order to receive a handsome reward.

Were the renegades drawn to becoming corsairs by the lure of easy booty or by a spirit of adventure? Pierre de Brantôme thought that 'nothing on land or at sea can compare to the wealth which might be taken'. His enthusiasm was greater when he spoke of the corsairs' spirit of enterprise and of their valiant wish to venture across the seas rather than take up 'a base and vile trade' or 'dying of hunger in one's native land'. Wouldn't it be natural to fight for a cause which had benefited you rather than one which had not? There were corsairs who had been Christian in their youth and had become officers or had reached quite high social standing before fate had dealt them a blow; perhaps they had to flee after a tragic duel, or were exiled for clinging faithfully to a lost political cause, or perhaps they were military men rendered unemployed by the end of a campaign or the signing of peace. Brantôme mentions the story of his young brother, Captain Bourdeille, who served in the army under Marshal de Saxe but who was almost tempted into being recruited into the Ottoman army by Robert de Valzergues, one of the Sultan's agents. Just as there were Frenchmen who rushed to aid the Knights of Malta there were those who sought employment in the Ottoman forces.[1] Many doubtless believed that they were merely continuing the Renaissance *condottieri* tradition. Few mention the possibility that those who became corsairs were merely seeking the means to make a profit by exercising their natural talents abroad.

There were historians who insisted that the renegade was motivated by a greater moral cause – the desire to escape an affront to his dignity, or oppression from feudal masters, or religious persecution. Maybe he was a free-thinking man who could not abide injustice or the kind of intolerance prevalent in western society at that time. But others saw the corsairs as being an element in a continual war of the classes. Were not the poor *servi di feudo* of Naples so down-trodden by the exactions of Spanish rule or that imposed by their own rulers that it was inevitable many had no other option but to flee? Riggio, author of *Les Etats barbaresques et la Calabre*, even suggested that many of the locals actually awaited the arrival of the corsairs so that they could go aboard their vessels to Africa, and that the coastguards were employed to prevent this migration. It's open to debate whether such unfortunates would have found the well-being and contentment they ardently sought on the far side of the Mediterranean. Would working as a slave be better than cultivating the land of one's master? Perhaps for the most intelligent, or the most enterprising, captivity in Africa could bring opportunities. No doubt there were some who seized such opportunities, converted to Islam, and revenged themselves for past injustice.[2]

There are studies which just repeat the clichés of the past, some, for example, attempting to justify the policies of the French king. Some historians content themselves with reading and copying but neglect analysis altogether. Some repeat the myth of Francis I, prince of chivalry, and don't question his misguided obsession with Italy. Was France really menaced by Charles V, was it facing encirclement by his possessions? Many have insisted that Europe had to have an equilibrium restored that had been upset by Charles V's election as Holy Roman Emperor in 1519. But they then ignore the fact that Francis too had been a candidate, and that perhaps he took the rejection badly. Was restoring the equilibrium really more important than allowing Asian domination of a large part of Europe?

Jean Monod's *Politique orientale de François I* of 1908 is one such book which doesn't question why Francis lusted after Genoa and Milan. He doesn't ask whether this was an act which would benefit the people of France. Nor does he blink when he compares Charles V's employment of Doria with Francis I's use of Barbarossa. Indeed, he excuses the king by saying that Francis had to continually 'balance Christian sentiments with political reasoning'. He even accuses Montmorency and his followers of seeking to foist 'political Christianity' upon the king. Such brutes.

A huge Turkish squadron spent an entire winter in Toulon, ruining the city as a consequence. Why do they not mention this? Why is Lepanto so quickly glossed over? Or, if it is mentioned, it's as though the battle was fought and won against the wind.[3] It's almost as though they take more delight in the defeat of the Armada, ridiculing Medina Sidonia in the process, and noting that the weather favoured the cause of the Just against that of the Intolerant, champions in the cause of bigotry. Voltaire, more honest than his predecessors, cites Lepanto in his *Encyclopedie* of 1780 as being an illustrious battle and one which does the men of Italy and Spain great merit: 'Not since the battle of Actium have the seas of Greece seen such vast fleets and so memorable an encounter.' He also recalled that 'the victory liberated more than 5,000 Christian slaves' and that Constantinople was thrown into consternation. And all for what particular gain on the part of the League's members? The Venetians, for example, did not take any territory as a result. Hubac's book of 1949 is one which lavishes much praise on the adventurous corsairs yet devotes but four lines to Toulon and just one page to Lepanto (in which he remarks that 'the Turks were defeated'). He insists that the 'victory so much celebrated gained nothing' and that the League's master, Philip II, sacrificed thousands for his own ends: 'The dead of Lepanto truly died for nothing'. Of Cervantes he even noted that 'he, just one among a thousand, enlisted to save civilisation from a great danger. Good propaganda had enflamed his soul.' A mere victim of his own gullibility, then. Faith, fidelity, and the desire to serve were in reality nothing more than an orchestrated scheme spun by the Church. Hubac might have mentioned that Cervantes, when a captive in Algiers, truly had his eyes opened and saw that the way in which prisoners were treated was certainly not propaganda.

Those who wished to nurture hostility towards the house of Austria or of Spain weren't slow to make out that the Barbarossas weren't only skilled in the arts of war but were also men of letters.[4] Everything was possible if one considered Charles V, adversary of the great Renaissance king of France, to be evil personified.

It has taken some time, but now we can look at the works of Jean-Pierre Soisson, Pierre Chaunu, and Michele Escamilla to see something other than old clichés. It would be worth noting, as Pierre Chaunu puts it, that, far from threatening France, controlling lands as far apart as Flanders, Italy, Germany, and Spain was a severe strain on the resources of Charles V.

Notes

Introduction

1. Turbet-Delof, *L'Afrique Barbaresque*.
2. Musset, *Les Invasions* (Paris, 1971).
3. Jehel, *Les Genois en Méditerranée occidentale*.
4. See McJoynt's *The Art of War in Spain* (London, 1995) for the military history of the reconquest of the Iberian peninsula.
5. Braudel, *The Mediterranean*.
6. Carrelieres, *Histoire de l'enterprise de Tripoli*.
7. Braudel, *Les Espagnols en Afrique du Nord*.
8. Zakythinos, 'Corsairs et pirates dans les mers grecques au temps de la domination turque', *Hellenisme contemporain*, 1939.
9. Boccaccio's *Decameron*.
10. State Archives of Genoa, Notai, Antonio di Fazio, 1, no.142; Tomaso di Recco, 2, no.95.99; Risso Baromeo, 5, no.159.
11. Jacoby, 'La compagnie catalan et l'Etat catalan en Grèce', *Journal des savants*, 1966, pp.78–103. See also Kenneth M. Setton, *Catalan Domination of Athens 1311–1388* (Cambridge, 1948).
12. Tenenti, 'I corsari nel Mediterraneo all'inizio del Cinquecento', *Rivista Storica Italiana*, 1960, pp.234–87.
13. Paviot, *La politique navale des ducs de Bourgogne* (Lille, 1955), pp.113–23.
14. Brun, *Annales avignonnaises*, p.162.
15. They did continue to be a menace. Between 1677 and 1680 160 British ships were captured by Algerine pirates. In 1794 the master of the

American ship *George Barclay* was paying a premium of $100 to insure himself 'against capture by Algerines and other Barbary Corsairs'. Only after the French invasion of North Africa in the 1830s did the corsairs vanish from the international stage.

Chapter I

1. Guiraud, *Recherches et conclusions niouvelles sur le pretendu rôle de Jacques Coeur* (Paris, 1900), p.2.
2. Adorno, *Itineraire*, pp.56–7.
3. Archives of the State of Genoa, Notai, no.25.76.83–13, no.101; 16, no.52.336.
4. N. Coll Julia, 'Aspectos del corso catalan', *Estudios de Historia Moderna*, 1954; and Heers, *L'Esilio la Vita politica e la Societa del Medioevo* (Naples, 1997), p.189.
5. Baratier and Reynaud, *Histoire du commerce*, p.260.
6. Telling the time in the early modern period is fraught with difficulties. Naval galleys often noted down the hour according to which of the ship's crew were at watch. For example, the first guardia began at noon and worked for four hours. The sixth guardia therefore worked from 0800 to noon the following day.
7. Brun, *Annales avignonnaises*, pp.69–74.
8. Giustiniani, *Annali della Repubblica di Genova* (Genoa, 1935), pp.441–52. See also the Archives of the State of Genoa, Diversorum Registri, no.77-572, an entry for 16 June 1462: 'The Council heard the complaint of Giuliano Gattilusio and his associates whose ship was impounded by the archbishop for they knew not what cause. Awarded damages of 25,000 ducats.'
9. Unali, *Il Libro de acordament: Arruolamento di equipaggi per la Guerra di corsa nel'Quattrocentro* (Cagliari), pp.83–102.
10. State Archives of Florence, Signori Missive Estere, reg.39, fol.56r.
11. *Ibid*, fol.155v.
12. State Archives of Genoa, Diversorum Filze, no.17, 24 September 1457.
13. State Archives of Florence, Signori Missive Estere, reg.42, fol.174.
14. *Ibid*, fol.190v.
15. State Archives of Genoa, Notai, Tomaso Duracino, 7, no.72.
16. *Ibid*, Benedetto Pilosio, 10 February 1457.
17. Adorno, *Itineraire*, p.144.

18. Gourdin, 'Emigrer au XVe siècle: la communiauté des pêcheurs ligures de corail à Marsacares', *Mélanges de l'Ecole Française de Rome*, 1986, pp.543–605.

19. See H. Garrot, *La pêche du corail sur les cotes de l'Algérie* (Algiers, 1900).

20. J. Heers, 'Le royaume de Grenade et la politique marchande des Gênes en Occident', *Le Moyen Age*, 1957.

21. J. Heers, 'Les Génois et l'Afrique du Nord vers 1450', *Anuario de Estudios medievales*, 1991, pp.233–45.

22. C. Dufourcq, *Catalogue chronologique et analytique du register intitulé Guerre Sarracenorum, 1367–1386* (Barcelona, 1974).

23. C. Dufourcq, 'Commerce du Maghreb médiéval avec l'Europe chrétienne', *Histoire* (Tunis), 1979.

24. J. Guiral Hadzhossie, *Valence, port méditerranéen*, pp.124.

25. State Archives of Genoa, Notai, Tomaso Duracino 2, no.117.118.

26. Adorno, *Itinéraire*, p.141.

27. C. Dufourcq, *Catalogue chronologique et analytique*.

28. E. Barratier and F. Reynaud, *Histoire du commerce*, p.405.

29. L. de Mas-Latrie, *Traités de paix et de commerce*.

30. R. Brunschvig, *La Berbérie orientale* (Paris, 1947), pp.124–5.

31. R. Brunschvig, *Deux récits de voyage en Afrique du Nord au XVe siècle* (Paris, 1936).

32. Adorno, *Itinéraire*, p.147.

33. M. del Treppo, *I mercanti catalane e l'espanzione della Corona d'Aragon* (Naples, 1971).

34. E. Barratier and F. Reynaud, *Histoire du commerce*, p.412.

35. L. de Fonesca, 'As relacoes comerciais entre Portugal e os reinos peninsulares nos seculos XIV e XV', *Actas de II Jornados Luso-Espanholas de Historia Medieval*, 1987, pp.1–23.

36. See the *Cronica de los Reyes Catolicos*, edited by J. Carriazo (Madrid, 1943), p.243.

37. E. Aznar, 'Course et piraterie dans les relations entre la Castile et le maroc au bas Moyen Age', *Publications de la Faculté des Lettres et Sciences humaines* 48, Rabat.

38. C. Dufourcq, *Catalogue chronologique et analytique*.

39. C. Carrere, *Barcelone*, p.624.

40. R. Brun, *Annales Avignonnaises*, p.35.

41. E. Barratier and F. Reynaud, *Histoire du commerce*, p.105.

42. M. del Treppo, *I mercanti catalane e l'espanzione*, p.624.

43. Dufourcq, 'Commerce du Maghreb médiéval'.

44. J. Guiral-Hadzhossie, *Valence*, p.100.

45. *Ibid*, p.109.

46. H. Noiret, *Documents inédits pour servir à l'histoire de la domination vénitienne en Crete* (Paris, 1892), p.520.

47. I. Melikoff-Sayar, *Le Destan*.

48. J. Gay, *Le Pape Clément VI et les affaires d'Orient, 1342–1352* (Paris, 1904), p.32.

49. J. Delaville le Roulx, *Les Hospitaliers à Rhodes* (Paris, 1913), pp.98–107.

50. See Melikoff-Sayar's *Le Destan* for the background to these events.

51. L. de Mas-Latrie, *Histoire de l'île de Chypre sous le regne des princes de la maison de Lusignan* (Paris, 1852), vol.III, p.238.

52. C.W. Bracewell's *The Uskoks of Senj* is useful here.

53. S. Karpov, *La navigazione veneziano nel Mar Nero* (Ravenna, 2000), pp.48–59.

54. F. Thiriet, *Regestes des deliberations du sénat vénitien concernant la Romanie* (2 vols, Paris, 1966–71), vol.I, p.121.

55. *Ibid*, vol.II, p.41.

56. C. Manfroni, 'La disciplina dei marinai veneziani nel secolo XIV', *Atti e memorie della Reale Accademia Pataonia di Scienze, Lettere ed Arti*, 1901, pp.109–29.

57. N. Jorga, 'Notes et extraits pour servir à l'histoire des Croisades au XV siècle', *Revue de l'Orient latin*, 1896.

58. C. Kowarch, *Venise et la piraterie en Orient, 1204–1479*, dissertation, University of Paris, 1990.

59. Adorno, *op. cit.*, p.361.

60. *Ibid*, p.362.

61. *Ibid*, p.343.

62. *Ibid*, p.367. This event took place on 14 November 1471.

63. J. Delaville le Roulx's work *Les Hospitaliers à Rhodes* (Paris, 1913) is essential reading for details of the siege.

64. Adorno, *op. cit.*, p.305.

65. E. Asthor, 'Una Guerra fra Genova e i Mamelucchi negli anni 1380', *Archivo Storico Italiano*, 1975, pp.3–44.

66. E. Barratier and F. Reynaud, *Histoire du commerce*, p.339.

67. A. Germain, *Histoire du commerce de Montpellier* (Montpellier, 1851), vol.II, p.261.

68. Adorno, *op. cit.*, p.173.

69. G. Wiet, *Histoire de l'Egypte*, p.375.

70. *Ibid*, pp.552–4.

71. Adorno, *op. cit.*, p.180.

72. One of the best studies of the fall of Egypt to the Ottomans is A. Clot's *L'Egypte des Mameloukes: L'empire des esclaves* (Paris, 1996).

Chapter II

1. D. de Haedo, *Histoire des rois*, p.20.

2. *Ibid*, p.26.

3. J. Belachemi, *Nous les frères Barberouuse*, p.221.

4. Haedo, *op. cit.*, p.24.

5. C. Julien, *Histoire de l'Afrique du Nord*, p.231.

6. *Ibid*, p.242.

7. J. Belachemi, *op. cit.*, p.310

8. F. Reynaud, *Expéditions et etablissements des Espagnols en Barbarie* (Paris, 1845).

9. Haedo, *op. cit.*, p.55.

10. Andrea Doria's galleys were certainly present in Tunis in 1535, and also took part in the Algiers expedition of 1541. Doria also personally supervised operations against Djerba in 1560. For details of Doria's life see Petit's biography published in Paris in 1887.

11. The *buonavoglia* was actually paid one ducat a month, while a galley slave cost 100 ducats.

12. E. Jurien, *Doria et Barberousse*, p.96.

13. P. Hubac, *Les Barberesques*, p.47.

14. In 1527 the fourteen-year-old Giulia Gonzaga had married Vespasiano Colonna; she was widowed the following year.

15. But Moulay Hassan would not rule for long. He was deposed by his son, who blinded him for good measure, and went into exile and lived off a miserable pension in Augsburg, and then in Italy.

16. Hubac, *op. cit.*, p.58.

17. See, for example, Dumont's *Lépante*, p.164.

18. See the first volume of E. Charrière's *Négociations de la France*.

19. J. Perez, *La Révolution des Communidades* (Bordeaux, 1970).

20. Ferdinand's letter to his brother is dated 14 March 1525 and was written at Innsbruck. It appears in Ursu's *La politique orientale*, p.29.

21. Our source for this is Pietro Bragadin, Venetian envoy in Constantinople, who wrote to his political masters about the letters on 6 December 1525. See Ursu, p.29.

22. P. Heinrich, *L'Alliance Franco-algérienne au XVIe siècle* (Paris, 1898).

23. Andrea Gritti spent a long time in Constantinople. He was a friend of the Vizier Ibrahim Pasha and was hostile to imperial power. In 1529 he secured assistance for John Zapolya in his war against Ferdinand and was even present at the siege of Buda.

24. Paris, Bibliothèque nationale, manuscripts, Fr.20977, f.8.

25. Ursu, *op. cit.*, p.175.

26. P. Cenival, 'Relations commerciales de la France avec le maroc au XVe siècle', *Revue d'Histoire des Colonies*, 1932.

27. Charrière, *op. cit.*, pp.340–6.

28. See *Comptes de l'Ambassade de France en Turquie*, pp.474–6.

29. Nicolas Durand de Villegagnon was born in 1510 and was a nephew of the Grand Master of the Order of St John. He became a Knight of Malta in 1531 and took part in the expedition against Algiers in 1541. His book (*L'expedition et voyage de l'empereur Charles V en Afrique contre Alger*) was published in Lyon the following year and charts the disaster which befell the expedition.

30. P. Ruff, *La Domination Espagnole*.

31. See *Mémoires de Vieilleville*, pp.36–7.

32. Haedo, *op. cit.*, p.71.

33. Ursu, *op. cit.*, p.144.

34. A letter from the Venetian ambassador, written on 23 November 1539, cited in Ursu, p.145.

35. See the important article by J. Deny in *Turcica*, 1969, entitled 'L'éxpedition en Provence de l'armée de mer du sultan Suleyman sous le commandement de l'admiral Hayreddin Pasha, dit Barberousse'.

36. See Belachemi, *Nous les frères Barberousse*, p.376. This cites Toulon's *Inventaire des Titres et Privileges*, which gives an indication of the city's position around the time of the Turkish arrival.

37. Leone Strozzi was Filippo Strozzi's son. Leone had fought in Doria's fleet against Suleiman, being present at the victory of 22 July 1537. The Pope made him Prior of the Order of St John at Capua. Later he pledged his service to Francis I and, along with his brother Piero, served at the siege of Nice in 1543. A prominent exile, he was later

captured and executed by the Medicis despite the intervention of both Francis and the Pope.

38. Vieilleville, *op. cit.*, pp.40–2.

39. Charrière, *op. cit.*, vol.I, p.570.

40. A royal ordonnance cited by Charrière, vol.I, p.571.

41. This appears in Ursu, p.149, who has taken it from *The Calendar of State Papers* (London, 1873).

42. J. Maurand, *Itinéraire*, p.315.

43. See Belachemi, *Nous les frères Barberousse*, p.376.

44. J. Maurand, *Itinéraire*, p.xxiii.

45. Charrière, *op. cit.*, vol.I, p.570.

46. A quote by Cervantes in Belachemi, *Nous les frères Barberousse*, p.427.

47. For details of Le Paulin's voyage see the map in Maurand's *Itinéraire*.

48. B. de Montluc, *Commentaires*, p.417.

49. Haedo, *op. cit.*, p.74.

50. Euldj'Ali is one of the most interesting figures. Born Giovanni Diongi Galeni in 1520, he was variously known in the west as Uciali, Ochiali, or Aluchali. Pasha of Algiers, he took Tunis in 1574 and died in 1587.

51. Charrière, *op. cit.*, vol.II, p.181.

52. Haedo, *op. cit.*, p.90.

53. C. Julien, *Histoire de l'Afrique du Nord*, p.649.

54. Haedo, *op. cit.*, p.104.

55. J. Dumont, *Lépante*, pp.38–9.

56. C. Monchicourt, 'Episodes de la carrière tunisienne de Dragut', *Revue Tunisienne*, 1917, pp.317–24, and 1918, pp.263–73.

57. P. Courteault, *Blaise de Monluc, historien* (Paris, 1907).

Chapter III

1. Haedo, *op. cit.*, p.106.

2. P. Varillon, *L'épopée des chevaliers de Malte* (Paris, 1957).

3. Brantôme, *Oeuvres*, vol.IV.

4. The Dorias were an important naval family. Giovanni Andrea Doria (1540–1606) was the illustrious Andrea Doria's nephew. Giovanni had a brother, Pagano, who also fought at Lepanto but was killed by corsairs three years later.

5. Labat Saint-Vincent, 'Malte', *Ulysée* 14.

6. Brantôme, *Oeuvres*, vol.IV.

7. The Knights of the Order of Saint-Etienne, a military order founded by the Medicis in March 1562, went much the same way. They assisted the Knights of Malta and were present at Lepanto, fighting with the Venetians. In fact they struggled on, attacking Collo, opposite Cape Bon, in 1586, and Monastir.

8. J. Dumont, *Lépante*, pp.48–50.

9. Haedo, *op. cit.*, p.311.

10. F. Braudel, *The Mediterranean* (French edition), pp.302–6

11. Dumont, *op. cit.*, pp.222–3.

12. Ursu, *op. cit.*, p.166.

13. Dumont, *op. cit.*, pp.175–7.

14. Haedo quotes a letter about these schemes by M. de Fourquevaux, written at the end of March 1568.

15. L. del Marmol-Carvajal, *L'Afrique*, vol.I, p.520.

16. Exhaustive details are available in Marosini's *La perdita di Famagosta e la Gloriosa morte di Marcantonio Bragadin* (Venice, 1893).

17. See C. Himber's 'The Navy of Suleyman the Magnificent', *Archivium Ottomanium*, 1980.

18. See Lupo Gentile's 'La battaglia di Lepanto', *Studi storici in onore G. Volpe*, 1958, pp.543–55.

19. Colonna (1535–84) was Captain-General of the Pope's fleet. He fell foul of the Inquisition in 1584 and died under suspicious circumstances.

20. See the seven-voulme study of Cervantes by Astrana Martin, published in Madrid in 1949.

21. Don Juan wrote to Philip II that he had 208 galleys with 26,000 soldiers.

22. One of Don Juan's key lieutenants, he became governor of Milan in 1572 and was later sent to Flanders to put down the rebellion there. He failed.

23. Alexander Farnese, Prince of Parma (1545–92), was the son of Margaret of Austria, daughter of Charles V. He too would later fight in Flanders.

24. Orsini came from a powerful Italian family and married into the Medici clan of Florence. He was rumoured to have strangled his wife.

25. Biographies of these key figures can be found in Dumont, pp.67–78.

26. Giovanni Negroni was a Genoese shipowner of repute. He rented four galleys for service with the king of Spain.

27. Marmol-Carvajal, *op. cit.*, p.522.

28. Scetti was due to be executed in Arezzo, but his death sentence was commuted to life on the galleys. With a 'chain around his neck like a dog' the galley captains drew lots for him. He ended up on the *Pisana*, belonging to the Knights of St Stephen, and served in Appiani's Tuscan squadron.

29. A. Scetti, *Journal du galerien florentin*.

30. R. Main, *Nouvelle Histoire de la Marine* (Paris, 1977), vol.I, p.73.

31. P. Molmenti, *Sebastiano Veniero e la battaglia di Lepanto* (Florence, 1899).

32. Scetti, *op. cit.*, note 21.

33. Manfroni, *Storia della Marina italiana della caduta di Constantonopoli alla battaglia di Lepanto* (Rome, 1897).

34. On 22 October the Venetian Veniero wrote to the Doge of Venice complaining that the booty had been unfairly divided and that Don Juan and the Spaniards had seized the best part for themselves.

35. Fr. Garnier, *Le Journal de Lépante*.

36. M. Lescure, 'Les vaincus de la bataiile de Lépante', *L'Histoire*, 1981.

37. Garnier, *op. cit.*

38. Dumont, *op. cit.*, p.92.

39. Cervantes remembers it thus in *Don Quixote*.

40. For Charles V's expedition to Tunis we have *La grande armée de l'empereur lequel s'en va combattre contre le Turc Barberousse* and *La Copie d'une letter datée de Tunis de la prise de La Goulette*. Jan Cornelisz Vermeyen, a portrait painter in the service of Charles's sister Mary of Hungary, also took part in the expedition. He brought back a number of sketches and drawings and later published a portrait of Moulay Ahmad. Between 1546 and 1554 he worked on a series of tapestries representing the chief episodes of the expedition. These now hang in Seville. Between 1554 and 1559 he worked on a further series of more modest dimensions. For more details see H. Horn, *Jan Cornelisz Vermeyen: Painter of Charles V and his Conquest of Tunis* (Doornspijk, 1989).

41. Marco Antonio Barbaro was a diplomat who had been sent to Constantinople in 1568. He had been imprisoned and badly mistreated, and was only set free in 1573. He spent his time in prison well, gathering as much material on the Turkish armed forces as he

possibly could. He later released this work of espionage as the *Ritratti delle forze turchese*.

42. A. Morel Fatio, *L'Hymne à Lépante* (Paris, 1893).
43. Quarti's book is *La battaglia di Lepanto nei canti popolari dell'epoca* (Milan, 1930).
44. Haedo, *op. cit.*, p.164.
45. M. Mantran, 'L'echo de la bataille de Lépante à Constantinople', *Annales*, 1973, pp.396–405.
46. Dumont, *op. cit.*, p.102.
47. E. Charrière, *Négociations de la France dans le Levant*, vol.IV, p.124.
48. In Hubac, *Les Barbaresques*, p.185.
49. *Ibid*, p.47.
50. Dumont, *op. cit.*, p.104.

Chapter IV

1. M. Ladero Quesada, *Granada*, p.209.
2. E. Rossi, 'La Lingua Franca in Berberia' in *Rivista delle colonie italiane*, 1928, pp.143–50.
3. See Haedo's *Topographie* for a discussion of these issues.
4. L. del Marmol-Carvajal, *L'Afrique*, pp.434, 470, and 538.
5. These details are from Villegagnon's *Le discours de la guerre de Malte* published in Lyon in 1553.
6. Translations into the French can be found in the *Revue africaine* of 1970.
7. S. Bono, *I Corsari*, p.387.
8. Haedo, *Histoire*, p.29.
9. Adorno, *Itinéraire*, p.101.
10. P. Hubac, *Les Barbaresques*, p.93.
11. G. Marcais, 'Recherches d'archeologie musulmane Honein' in *Revue africaine*, 1928, pp.333–50.
12. R. Lespes, 'Oran, ville et port avant l'occupation française' in *Revue africaine*, 1934, pp.287–95.
13. Leon the African, *Description of Africa* (London, 1898).
14. F. Cresti's 'Description d'Alger au XVIe siècle' in *Revue de l'Occident musulman*, 1982, is invaluable.
15. H. de Grammont, *Histoire d'Alger sous la domination turque* (Paris, 1887).

16. Marmol-Carvajal, *L'Afrique*, vol.III, p.407.
17. See Cresti, who compares and contrasts descriptions of the city.
18. Haedo's *Topographie*, vol.XIV, pp.364–74.
19. Marmol-Carvajal, *op. cit.*, vol.III, p.402.
20. Cresti is again invaluable here.
21. Haedo's *Topographie*, vol.XIV, pp.414–33.
22. Haedo and Dan are the principal sources for details of the ethnic composition of Algiers.
23. See the *Mémoires du chevalier d'Arvieux*, p.45.
24. Haedo details the conditions of the city's Jews at length in his *Topographie*.
25. *Ibid*, p.52.
26. *Ibid*, p.71.
27. Quesada, *op. cit.*
28. All these details are to be found in Turbet-Delof, *L'Afrique barbaresque*, p.135.
29. Haedo, *op. cit.*, p.82.
30. Cervantes, *Le Captif*, p.400.
31. N. Weissmann, *Les Janissaires* (Paris, 1964).
32. J. Deny, 'Chansons de janissaires' in *Mémoires de René Basset* (Paris, 1923), p.82.
33. *Ibid*, p.84.
34. Haedo, *op. cit.*, p.79.
35. Deny, *op. cit.*, p.81.
36. Daedo has much to say about these two groups, *op. cit.*, p.41.
37. C. Monchicourt, *Insécurité*, pp.318–19.
38. This famous officer was the inspiration behind Lope de Vega, a character in Cervantes' *Alcalde de Zalamea*.
39. See *El trato de Argel*, a French translation of which appears on pp.143–5 of the 1891 edition of the *Revue africaine*.
40. Monchicourt, *op. cit.*, p.320.
41. *Ibid*, p.322.
42. Haedo, *op. cit.*, p.66.
43. J. Belachemi, *Nous les frères Barberousses*.
44. This is from Haedo's *Histoire*.
45. Marmol-Carvajal, *op. cit.*, vol.I, p.522.
46. G. Diedo, *La battaglia di Lepanto*, p.42.
47. Haedo's *Histoire*, pp.122, 135, 143, and 177.

48. J. Belachemi, *Nous les frères Barberousses*, p.418.

49. See Dan's *Histoire de la Barbarie*.

50. See the song cited on p.84 of Deny's *Chansons de Janissaries*.

51. Haedo, *op. cit.*, p.160.

52. J. Hammer, *Histoire de l'Empire Ottoman*, vol.III, p.156.

53. The entire episode is detailed in A. Devaulx, 'La premiere révolte des janissaries à Alger', *Revue africaine*, 1871, pp.1–6.

54. E. Watbled, *Négociations entre Charles V et Kheir ed-Din* (Paris, 1881).

55. See the Introduction to Deny's *Chansons de Janissaries*.

56. Haedo, *op. cit.*, pp.132–3.

57. C. Monchicourt, 'Episodes de la carrière tunisienne de Dragut', *Revue tunisienne*, 1917, pp.317–24.

58. These documents are to be found in E. Primaudaie, *Documents inédits*, and R. Ricard, 'Ibero-Africana: Textes espagnols sur la Berberie', *Revue africaine*, 1945.

59. F. Braudel, *Les Espagnols et l'Afrique du Nord*, p.421.

60. E. Primaudaie, *Documents inédits*, documents IV, XXXIII, and XXXIV.

61. *Ibid*, documents XXV and LXVIII.

62. *Ibid*, document XXIX.

63. Marmol-Carvajal, *op. cit.*, vol.III, p.539.

64. Primaudaie, *op. cit.*, document XXXVI.

65. *Ibid*, document II.

66. Ribera's words cited in Braudel, *op. cit.*

67. Primaudaie, *op. cit.*, documents XXX, XL, VII, and XII.

68. P. Ruff, *La domination espagnole*, p.23.

69. See Braudel, *op.cit.*

70. Cervantes, *Don Quixote*.

Chapter V

1. M. Ladero Quesada, *La esclavitud por Guerra*.

2. E. Bousquet, *Les conditions des serfs et des esclaves à Byzance et dans l'Orient latin* (Lausanne, 1962).

3. C. Verlinden, 'Aspects de l'esclavaga dans les colonies médiévales italiennes', in *Hommage à Lucien Febvre* (Paris, 1953), vol.II, pp.91–103.

4. B. Krekic, *Dubrovnik et le Levant au Moyen Age* (Paris, 1961). Also A. Teja, 'La schiavitu domestica e il traffico degli schiavi', *Rivista Dalmatica*, 1940–2.

5. J. Heers, *Esclaves et domestiques au Moyen Age dans le monde méditerranéen* (Paris, 1981).

6. A. Brutails, 'Etudes sur l'esclavage en Roussillon', *Nouvelle Revue d'Histoire du Droit*, 1886, pp.5–44.

7. *Recueil de la Societé Jean Bodin pour l'Histoire comparative des institutions* (Brussels, 1962), vol.XIV, pp.397–545.

8. J. Heers, *Les parties et la vie politique dans l'Occident médiéval* (Paris, 1981).

9. J. Madriel Marimon, 'Ventas de esclavos sardes de Guerra a Barcelona en 1374' in *IV Congresso de Historia de la Corona de Aragon* (1959), pp.285–9.

10. A. Schiaffini, 'Testi fiorentini del Duecento e dei primi del Trecento', in *Cronica fiorentina del secolo XIV, anno 1230* (Florence, 1926).

11. E. Cristiani, *Nobilita e Popolo nel Comune di Pisa* (Naples, 1962).

12. G. Meloni, *Genova e Aragona all'epoca di Piero il Ceremonio* (Padua 1976). Vol.II covers the period 1335–60.

13. See Bracciano's *Vita di Cola di Rienzo* (1924), p.259.

14. Guicciardini's *Storia d'Italia*, vol.II, book V, p.24.

15. G. Caradente, *I trifoni nel primo Rinascimento* (Turin, 1963).

16. G. Hersey, *The Aragonese Arch, 1443–75* (London, 1973).

17. Antonio de Vascho's *Diario della citta di Roma dall'anno 1480 all'anno 1492*, reprinted in *Rerum Italicarum Scriptores*, vol.XXIII, p.541.

18. Haedo, *op. cit.*, p.36.

19. *Ibid*, p.9.

20. L. del Marmol-Carvajal, *L'Afrique*, vol.I, p.521.

21. G. Jehel, *Les Génois en méditerranée*, p.12.

22. E. Mitre Fernandez, 'La frontière de Grenade aux environs de 1400', *Le Moyen Age*, 1972, pp.489–522.

23. J. Miret y Sans, 'La esclavitud'.

24. B. de la Broquière, *Le Voyage en terre d'outre-Mer*, edited by H.A. Scheffer (Paris, 1892).

25. Brutails, *op. cit.*

26. The full story is in P. Egidi 'La colonia sarracena di Lucera e la sua distruzione', *Archivo storico per le provincie napoletane*, XXXVI, 1911, pp.597–694; XXXVII, 1912, pp.71–89, 664–96; XXXVIII, 1913, pp.681–707; and XXXIX, 1914, pp.132–71.

27. M. Ladero Quesada, *Granada*, p.522.

28. Miret y Sans, *op. cit.*
29. Ladero Quesada, *op. cit.*
30. J. Heers, *Esclaves et domestiques au Moyen Age dans le monde méditerranéen.*
31. M. Balard's book on the Genoese in the Black Sea is essential for an understanding of the Italian traders in the Levant.
32. See Verlinden, *op. cit.*
33. A. Clot, *L'Egypte des Mamelouks: L'empire des esclaves* (Paris, 1996).
34. L. Cibrario, 'Note sul commercio degli schiavi a Genova nel secolo XIV', *Opere varie*, 1960.
35. Haedo's *Topographie* and Dan's *Histoire de barbarie et de ses corsairs* are invaluable.
36. L. Tria, *La Schiavitu in Liguria* (Genoa, 1947).
37. I. Orgio, 'The Domestic Enemy: Eastern Slaves in Tuscany in the Fourteenth and Fifteenth Century', *Speculum*, 1955.
38. R. Livi, *La Schiavitu domestica nei tempi di mezzo e nei moderni* (Padua, 1928).
39. R. Texler, 'The Foundlings of Florence', *History of Childhood Quarterly*, 1973, pp.259–84.
40. Heers, *op. cit.*, pp.217–21.
41. Brutails, *op. cit.*
42. Miret y Sans, *op. cit.*
43. V. Cortes, *La Esclavitud en Valencia.*
44. T. Garcia Figueras, 'Cabalgados, correrias y entradas de los Andaluces en el littoral africano', *Revista de Historia militar*, 1957, pp.51–79.
45. Cortes, *op. cit.*
46. Tria, *op. cit.*
47. Moret y Sans, *op. cit.*, p.7.
48. A. Franco, *La Esclavitud in Sevilla y su tierra a fine de la Edad Media* (Seville, 1979).
49. P. Bonnasie, 'La organisacion del Trabajo en Barcelona a fines del siglo XV' (Barcelona, 1975).
50. Miret y Sans, *op. cit.*, p.60.
51. Marimon, *op. cit.*
52. Brutails, *op. cit.*
53. A. Rodrigues, 'Les Esclaves dans la societé portugaise au Moyen Age', University of Paris dissertation, 1979.

54. Quesada, *op. cit.*

55. A. Devoulx, *Le registre des prises maritimes, traduction d'un document inédit concernant le partage des captures* (Algiers, 1873); E. Friedman, *Spanish Captives in North Africa in the Early Modern Age* (Wisconsin, 1983).

56. Haedo, *op. cit.*

57. P. Dan, *Histoire*.

58. *Ibid*, p.378.

59. Cervantes, 'Et trato de Argel', *Revue africaine*, 1891, pp.109–60.

60. Cervantes, as quoted in Babelon's *L'esclavage de Cervantes*, p.88.

61. See the *Voyage du chevalier d'Avrieux*.

62. Quesada, *op. cit.*, p.203.

63. A. Adorno, *Itinéraire*, p.127.

64. J. Belachemi, *Nous, les frères Barberousse*, p.214.

65. Quesada, *op. cit.*, p.201.

66. *Ibid*, p.203.

67. S. Bono, *I corsari barbareschi*, pp.140–1.

68. *Ibid*, p.338.

69. J. Morand, *Itinéraire d'Antibes*.

70. S. Bono, *op. cit.*, p.340.

71. Babelon's *L'esclavage de Cervantes*, p.51.

72. Haedo, *op. cit.*, p.182.

73. *Ibid*, pp.165–6.

74. Cervantes, *Le Captif*.

75. J. de Pasamonte, *Vida y Trabajos*.

76. E. Mitre Fernandez, *op. cit.*

77. C. Monchicourt, *L'insécurité*, pp.319–20.

78. Maurand, *op. cit.*, p.91.

79. P. Macaire, 'Majorque et le Maghreb au XVe siècle', University of Paris dissertation, 1977.

80. P. Lopez Elum, 'Apresamento y Ventas de Moros cautivos en 1441 por acceptar sin licencia', *Al Andalus*, 1969, pp.329–56.

81. Cortes, *op. cit.*, p.46.

82. Macaire, *op. cit.*

83. Heers, *op. cit.*, p.238.

84. *Ibid*, p.227.

85. T. Vinyoles, 'La vita quotidiana della gente di mare', *Medioevo, Saggi e Rassegni*, 1996, pp.9–36.

86. See the *Voyage du chevalier d'Avrieux*.

87. M. de Espalza, 'Moriscos y Andalusiez en Tunez durante el siglo XVII', *Al Andalus*, 1969, pp.248–327.

88. Quesada, *op. cit.*

89. Monchicourt, *op. cit.*, p.20.

90. C. Carrère, *Barcelone, centre économique à l'époque*, pp.624–5.

91. E. Lopez de Cosat Castanar, *Esclavos*, pp.293–300.

92. Espalza, *op. cit.*

93. Babelon's *L'esclavage de Cervantes*, pp.58–73.

94. Gracian, *Tractado de la redempcion de captives* (Rome, 1597).

95. Pasamonte, *op. cit.*

96. J.W. Brodman, *The Trinitarian Order*.

97. W. Rudt de Collenberg, *Les Litterae*.

98. J. Delaville le Roux, 'L'Ordre de Montjoye', *Revue de l'Orient latin*, 1893, pp.39–50.

99. J. Gari y Siumell, *La Orden redentora de la Merced o sea Historia de las redenciones de cautivos cristianos* (Barcelona, 1873).

100. Brodman, *op. cit.*

101. Bono, *op. cit.*, p.330

Chapter VI

1. A. Garcia Sandoval, *Organizacion de la defensa de la costa del regno de Granada desde su reconquista hasta finales del siglo XVI* (Granada, 1947).

2. F. Braudel, *The Mediterranean* (French-language edition), p.211.

3. In 1569 the Pope also arranged for four of the Duke of Tuscany's galleys to cruise off shore. In return he provided the Duke with all of his condemned prisoners for service on board the vessels.

4. S. Bono, *I corsari barbareschi*, pp.193–7.

5. G. Petti Balbi, 'I nomi di navi a Genova nei secoli XII e XIII', *Miscellanea Falco*, vol.II, pp.65–86.

6. State Archives of Genoa, Notai, Tommaso di Recco, f.1, n.45 for 24 May 1449.

7. V. Borghesi, *Il Mediterraneo tra due rivoluzioni nautiche* (Florence, 1980).

8. M. Pardessus, *Collection de droit maritime*, vol.IV (Paris, 1937).

9. M. Ferrer I Mallol, 'Dos registros de l'Officium Maris de Genova', *Congresso Storico Liguria*, 1974, pp.248–348.

10. F.C. Lane, 'Fleet and Fairs: the Function of the Venetian Muda' in

Studi in onore di A. Sapori (Milan, 1937). M. Mallett, *The Florentine Galleys in the XVth Century* (Oxford, 1967).

11. A. Unali, 'Il Libro de acordament di equipaggi per la Guerra di corsa nel'400', *Collana di Studi Italo-Iberici*, 1982, pp.83–102.

12. G. Jehel, *Les Génois en Méditerranée occidentale*, p.15.

13. See I. Parlos, *Les Pirates en Méditerranée*, chapter I.

14. J. Heers, 'Le prix de l'assurance maritime à la fin du Moyen Age', *Revue d'Histoire économique et sociale*, 1952, pp.7–19.

15. G. Petti Balbi, *Caffaro e la chronachistica* (Genoa, 1982).

16. A. Mackay, 'The Ballad and the Frontier in Late Medieval Spain', *Bulletin of Hispanic Studies*, 1976, pp.15–33.

17. Quesada, *op. cit.*, pp.226–30.

18. A. Coster, *Fernando de Herrera*.

19. H. Grammont, *Le R'azaouat, est-il l'oeuvre de Kheir ed-Din?* (Villeneuve-sur-Lot, 1873).

20. Haedo, *Histoire*, p.74.

21. J. Belachemi, *Nous, les frères Barberousse*, p.429.

22. *Ibid*, p.430.

23. G. Esquer, *Iconographie historique de l'Algérie*, vol.I, plate II.

24. G. Valente, *Vita di Occhiali* (Milan, 1960). See also G. Quarti, 'Notizie intorno al corsaro Luca Galeni-Occhiali, cristiano renegato', *Rivista di cultura marinara*, 1931, pp.241–2.

25. P. Champion, *Dictionnaire des lettres françaises*, p.130.

26. J. Dumont, *L'Eglise au risque de l'Histoire* (Paris, 1984), p.177.

27. J. Dumont, *Lépante*, pp.233–5.

28. Brantôme, *Ouevres*, vol.IV, p.140.

29. *Ibid*, p.142.

30. *Ibid*, p.149.

31. Belachemi, *op. cit.*, p.426.

32. Brantôme, *Vie des hommes illustres*.

33. *Mémoires du chevalier d'Arvieux*.

34. Cited in Hubac's *Les Barbaresques*, p.214.

35. M. Dufresnoy, *L'Orient Romanesque en France*, p.18.

36. Cited in Hubac's *Les Barbaresques*, p.230.

37. Quesada, *op. cit.*, p.200.

38. See Boyer, *La Vie quotidienne à Alger à la veille de l'intervention française* (Paris, 1963), p.76.

39. Dufresnoy, *op. cit.*, p.10.

Conclusion

1. Brantôme, *Vie des hommes illustres*, cited in Turbet-Delof's *L'Afrique Romanesque*, p.138.
2. S. Bono, *I Corsari barbareschi*, pp.253–5, discusses the work of Riggio and examines his conclusions.
3. J. Dumont, *Lépante*, p.90.
4. G. Fisher, *Barbary Legend*.

Bibliography

Books

Achard, P., *Histoire de la Méditerranée: la vie extraordinaire des frères Barberousse* (Paris, 1939)

Adorno, A., *Itinéraire d'Anselme Adorno en Terre Sainte (1470–1471)* (edited by J. Heers, Paris, 1978)

Anon, *Discours du rachat de cent quatre-vingt-six chrétiens que chrétiennes captifs d'entre les Maures* (Paris, 1582)

Anon, *Voyage du chevalier d'Avrieux à Tunis* (edited by M. de Favieres, Paris, 1994)

d'Aranda, E., *Relation de la captivité et la liberté du sieur Emmanule d'Aranda* (Paris, 1656)

Babelon, J., *Cervantes* (Paris, 1939)

Balard, M., *La Romanie génoise* (2 vols, Rome, 1978)

Baratier, E., and Reynaud, F., *Histoire du commerce de Marseille* (Paris, 1951)

Belachemi, J., *Nous, les frères Barberousse* (Paris, 1984)

Bono, S., *I corsari, barbareschi* (Turin, 1964)

Bracewell, C.W., *The Uskoks of Senj* (Ithaca, 1992)

Brantôme, Seigneur de, *Oeuvres complètes* (edited by L. Lalanne, 12 vols, Paris, 1864–93)

Braudel, F., *The Mediterranean* (French edition, Paris, 1949)

Braun, G., and Hogenberg, F., *Theatre des cités du monde* (Cologne, 1579)

Bridge, A., *Suleiman the Magnificent: Scourge of Heaven* (London, 1983)

Brodman, J., *The Trinitarian and Mercedarian Orders: A Study of Religious*

Redemptions in the Thirteenth Century (PhD dissertation, University of Virginia, 1974.)

Brun, R., *Annales avignonnaises de Datiini* (1935)

Brunschvig, R., *La Berbérie orientale sous les Hafsides des origins au XVe siècle* (2 vols, Paris, 1940–7)

Capelloni, L., *Vita del Principe Andrea Doria* (Genoa, 1863)

Carrelières, T., *Histoire de l'enterprise de Tripoli* (Lyon, 1560)

Carrère, C., *Barcelone, centre économique à l'époque des difficultés, 1380–1462* (Paris, 1967)

Cervantes, M., *Don Quixote* (London, 1889)

Charrière, E., *Négociations de la France dans le Levant* (4 vols, Paris, 1848–60)

Chaunu, P., and Escamilla, M., *Charles Quint* (Paris, 2000)

Christian, P., *Histoire des corsaires et des pirates* (Paris, 1846–50)

Comande, G., *La Sicilia contro il corsaro Dragut* (Palermo, 1956)

Cook, W., *The Hundred Years War for Morocco* (Boulder, 1994)

Cortes, V. *La Esclavitud en Valencia durante el reinado de los reyes catolicos* (Valencia, 1964)

Coster, A., *Fernando de Herrera* (Paris, 1908)

Cour, A., *L'éstablissement des dynasties des chérifs au maroc et leur rivalité avec les Turcs d'Alger* (Paris, 1904)

Crooks, E., *The Influence of Cervantes in the 17th Century* (Baltimore, 1931)

Dan, P., *Histoire de la Barbarie et de ses corsiares* (Paris, 1637)

Davis, Robert, *Christian Slaves, Muslim Masters* (London, 2003)

Deny, J., *Chansons de janissaries d'Alger* (Paris, 1923)

Deslandres, P., *L'ordre des Trinitaires pour le rachat des captifs* (Paris, 1903)

Diedo, G., *Battaglia di Lepante* (Milan, 1863)

Dufresnoy, M., *L'Orient Romanesque en France* (Montreal, 1946)

Dumont, J., *Lépante: l'Histoire étouffé* (Paris, 1997)

Earle, P., *Corsairs of Malta and Barbary* (London, 1970)

El Bekri, *Description de l'Afrique septentrionale* (edited by Slane, Paris, 1859)

Elie de la Primaudaie, F., *Documents inédits sur l'Histoire de l'occupation espagnole en Afrique* (1875)

Engel, C., *L'ordre de Malte en Méditerranée* (Monaco, 1957)

Espinchard, J., *Histoire des Ottomans* (Paris, 1600)

Esquer, G., *Iconographie historique de l'Algerie* (Paris, 1929)

Farine, C., *Deux pirates du XVe siècle* (Paris, 1869)

Fisher, G., *Barbary Legend: War, Trade and Piracy in North Africa* (Oxford, 1957)

Fontenay, M., and Tenenti, A., *Course et piraterie en Méditerranée de la fin du Moyen Age au debut du XIXe siècle* (Paris, 1975)

Fresne-Canay, Comte de, *Voyage du Levant* (Paris, 1897)

Friedman, E., *Spanish Captives in North Africa in the Early Modern Age* (Wisconsin, 1983)

Garnier, Fr., *Le Journal de Lépante* (Paris, 1956)

Georis, M., *Charles Quint, un césar catholique* (Paris, 1999)

Gracian, J., *Tractado de la redempcion de captivos* (Rome, 1597)

Gramaye, J.B., *Les cruautés exercées sur les chrétiens dans la ville d'Alger* (Paris, 1620)

Grammont, H., *Histoire d'Alger sous la domination turque* (Paris, 1887)

Guilmartin, J., *Gunpowder and Galleys* (Cambridge, 1974)

Guiral, J., *Valence: port Méditerranéen au XVe siècle* (Paris, 1985)

Haedo, Diego de, *Histoire des rois d'Algers* and *Topographia e historia general de Argel* (Valladolid, 1612)

Hammer, J., *Histoire de l'Empire ottoman* (Paris, 1833–48)

Hubac, P., *Les Barbaresques et la course en Méditerranée* (Paris, 1959)

Inalick, H., *The Ottoman Empire* (London, 1973)

Jaeger, G., *Bibliographie thématique des aventuriers de la mer* (Lausanne, 1983)

— *Pirates, flibustiers et corsaires* (Paris, 1987)

Jehel, G., *Les Génois en Méditerranée occidentale* (Amiens, 1993)

Julien, C., *Histoire de l'Afrique du Nord* (2 vols, Paris, 1978)

Jurien de la Gravière, E., *Doria et Barberousse* (Paris, 1886)

– *Les Corsaires barbaresques et la marine de Soliman* (Paris, 1887)

Ladero Quesada, M., *Granada historia de ma ciudad* (Madrid, 1970)

Lami, M., *La confession d'un corsaire inconnu* (Paris, 1911)

Lamouche, L., *Histoire de la Turquie* (Paris, 1953)

Laugier de Tracy, *Histoire du royaume d'Alger* (Amsterdam, 1725)

Leon the African, *Description of Africa* (London, 1898)

Marmol, Caravajal del, *Description general de Africa* (3 vols, Granada, 1573–9)

Mas-Latrie, L. de, *Traités de paix et documents divers concernant les relations des Chrétiens avec les Arabes* (2 vols, Paris, 1866–72)

Maurand, J., *Itinéraire d'Antibes à Constantinople* (Paris, 1901)

McJoynt, A., *The Art of War in Spain: The Conquest of Granada, 1481–1492* (based on the work of W. Prescott, London, 1995)

Melikoff-Sayar, I., *Le Destan d'Umur Pasha* (Paris, 1954)

Monlau, J., *Les Etats barbaresques* (Paris, 1973)

Montluc, B. de, *Commentaires* (3 vols, Paris, 1821)

Nicolay, Nicolas de, *Les quatres premiers livres de navigations orientales* (Lyon, 1568)

Oman, C., *The Art of War in the Sixteenth Century* (Oxford, 1937, reprinted London, 1999)

Pasamonte, J. de, *Vida y Trabajos* (Madrid, 1956)

Picard, C., *La mer et les Musulmans d'Occident* (Paris, 1997)

Pipes, D., *Slave Soldiers and Islam* (New Haven, 1981)

Quarti, G., *La battaglia di Lepante nei canti popolari dell'epoca* (Milan, 1930)

Ruff, P., *La Domination Espagnole à Oran sous le gouvernement de comte d'Alcaudete* (Paris, 1900)

Soisson, J., *Charles Quint* (Paris, 2000)

Tailliart, C., *L'Algerie dans la literature française* (Paris, 1925)

Turbet-Delof, G., *L'Afrique barbaresque dans la literature française* (Geneva, 1973)

Ursu, J., *La Politique orientale de François Ier* (Paris, 1908)

Weismann, N., *Les Janissaires* (Paris, 1964)

Wiet, G., *Histoire de l'Egypte arabe* (Paris, 1957)

Articles

Bourilly, V., 'Les diplomates de François I: Antonio Ricon', *Revue historique*, 1913

Cazenave, J., 'L'esclavage de Cervantes à Alger', *Bulletin de la Societe de geographie d'Alger*, 1924

Cresti, P., 'Description d'Alger au XVIe siècle', *Revue de l'Occident musulmann et de la Méditerranée*, 1982

Devoulx, A., 'Alger: Etude archaéologique et topographique', *Revue africaine*, 1875

Guiral, J., 'Commerce et piraterie à Valence de 1410 à 1430', *Annuario de Estudios Medievales*, 1980

Hess, A., 'The Evolution of the Ottoman Seaborne Empire', *American Historical Review* 75, 1970

Imber, C., 'The Navy of Suleyman the Magnificent', *Archivum Ottomanicum*, 1980

Katele, Irene B., 'Piracy and the Venetian State: The Dilemma of Maritime Defense in the Fourteenth Century', *Speculum* 63, 1988

Ladero Quesada, M., 'La esclavitud por Guerra a fines del siglo XV: el caso de Malaga', *Hispania*, 1967

Lanfredducci, Fr., 'Costa e Discursi di Barberia', translated by Granchamp, *Revue Africaine*, 1925

Lespès, R., 'Oran: Ville et port avant l'occupation française', *Revue africaine*, 1934

Lopez de Coca Castañar, J., 'Esclavos, alfuqueques y mercaderes en la frontera del mar de Alboran', *Hispania*, 1978

Miret y Sans, J., 'La esclavitud en Cataluna en los ultimos tiempos de la Edad media', *Revue hispanique*, 1917

Monchicourt, C., 'L'insecurité en Méditerranée Durant l'été 1550', *Revue tunisienne*, 1917

– 'Episodes de la carrière tunisienne de Dragut', *Revue tunisienne*, 1917–18

Ricard, R., 'Ibero-Africana: Textes espagnoles sur la Berbérie', *Revue africaine*, 1945

Rudt de Collenberg, W., 'Les Litterae Hortatoriae accordés par les papes en faveur de la redemption des Chypriotes captifs des Turcs', *Epetheris*, 1981

Tenenti, A., 'I corsari nel Mediterraneo all'inizio del Cinquecento', *Rivista storica Italiana*, 1960

Voyard, A., 'Chez les pirates barbaresques', *Bulletin de la Section de Geographie du Comité du Travaux historiques*, 1949

Index

Boccaccio, 26, 232
Boiardo, Matteo, 233
Boniface IX, Pope, 23
Bonivet, Admiral, 74
Borgne, Simon le, 160
Bosio, Gion Ottone, 120, 170
Bou Sian, 64
Bragadin, Marcantonio, 103, 182
Brantôme, Pierre de, 99, 225, 228,
238–9
Braudel, Fernand, 73
Broquière, Betrandon de, 183–4

Caïd Saffa, 91
Cano, Thome, 113
Cara Mustafa, 158
Carbó, Jaime, 44
Cardona, Diego Fernandez de, 25
Carraciolo, Nicolo, 121
Carrelieres, Thomas de, 230
Cavaretto, Simone de, 83
Celi, Medina, 95
Cervantes, Miguel de, 104, 154,
156, 175, 203–4, 211, 230,
233–4, 240–1
Cervantes, Rodrigo de, 154, 212
Chamite, 154
Charles of Anjou, 28–9, 95
Charles V, 66, 69–71, 73–4, 76,
79–81, 90, 95–6, 105, 122, 128,
163, 166, 168, 173, 213, 216,
226, 240–1
Charles IX of France, 102, 114,
228
Charles VII of France, 58, 74, 78,
194
Chaunu, Pierre, 73, 241
Cisneros, Cardinal, 44

Ciudad real, Alvaro Gomez de,
105
Clement IV, Pope, 23, 50
Clement VII, Pope, 105
Cochon, Louis, 86
Coeur, Jacques, 33, 58, 78
Colomier, Thomas, 210
Colonna, Marco Antonio, 104–5,
109–10
Comares, Marquis of, 65, 166
Cordoba, Cabrera de, 115
Cordoba, Martin de, 212
Cornaro, Francesco, 111
Cornia, Ascania de la, 100

d'Abusson, Pierre, 55, 61
d'Amalfi, Landolfo, 26
Damergi, 156
Dan, Father Pierre, 122, 148, 157
d'Aramon, 91
d'Authon, Baron, 226
de l'Isle-Adam, Philippe de
Villiers, 56
d'Evreux, Philippe, 24
Diaz, Pedro, 154
Diedo, Girolamo, 111, 158
Djanbirdi, 60
Don Juan of Austria, 103–9, 111,
114, 123, 158, 225
Donato, Giovanni Battista, 112
Doria, Andrea, 68–9, 83, 159
Doria, Antonio, 28
Doria, Giovanni Andrea, 100, 102,
104–7
Dragut, 90–92, 98–9, 121–23,
159–60, 165, 207, 225
Dumont, Jean, 73, 115
Duprat, Chancellor, 77